JUNGLE OF SNAKES

JUNGLE OF SNAKES

A CENTURY OF COUNTERINSURGENCY WARFARE FROM THE PHILIPPINES TO IRAQ

JAMES R. ARNOLD

BLOOMSBURY PRESS

NEW YORK   BERLIN   LONDON

Published by Bloomsbury Press, New York

All papers used by Bloomsbury Press are natural, recyclable products made from wood grown in well-managed forests. The manufacturing processes conform to the environmental regulations of the country of origin.

LIBRARY OF CONGRESS CATALOGING-IN-PUBLICATION DATA HAS BEEN APPLIED FOR.

Arnold, James R.
Jungle of snakes : a century of counterinsurgency warfare from the Philippines to Iraq / James R. Arnold.—1st U.S. ed.
p. cm.
Includes bibliographical references and index.
ISBN-13: 978-1-59691-503-9 (alk. paper)
ISBN-10: 1-59691-503-x (alk. paper)
1. Counterinsurgency—History—20th century. 2. Military history, Modern—20th century. 3. Counterinsurgency—United States—History—20th century.
4. Counterinsurgency—Great Britain—History—20th century.
5. Counterinsurgency—France—History—20th century. 6. United States—History, Military—20th century. 7. Great Britain—History, Military—20th century. 8. France—History, Military—20th century. I. Title.

U241.A765 2009
355.02'180904—dc22
2008054018

First U.S. Edition 2009

1 3 5 7 9 10 8 6 4 2

Typeset by Westchester Book Group
Printed in the United States of America by Quebecor World Fairfield

To the American soldier

Contents

Maps

Introduction

THE FALL OF THE BERLIN WALL IN 1989 and subsequent collapse of the Soviet Union signaled the end of the Cold War. A new dawn gave promise that a more peaceful era was at hand. Citizens of the United States anticipated that for them at least, the scourge of war was no more. The emergence of a fresh set of conflicts dashed this promise. In the words of a former director of the Central Intelligence Agency, James Woolsey, "It is as if we were struggling with a large dragon for 45 years, killed it, and then found ourselves in a jungle full of poisonous snakes."[1] The snakes he referred to are insurgents, guerrillas, and terrorists.

Insurgents are people who forcibly strive to overthrow constituted authority. One's view of them depends on where one's loyalties lie. America proudly celebrates its patriots of 1776. By any definition, from George Washington down to the humblest Continental private shivering in his camp at Valley Forge, they were insurgents. They rebelled against established British authority and unlawfully formed fighting units to violently resist British government controls. The British were, conversely, the counterinsurgents, fighting to restore order.

While some of the fighting in the War of Independence was a formal clash of armies on recognizable battlefields, the American rebels were opposing the full might of a great empire and often avoided conventional warfare. It was what would today be called an "asymmetric conflict," where the weaker force resorts to whatever tactics work, including many that appall the counterinsurgents. American leaders included men such as Francis Marion, the Swamp Fox, whose guerrilla approach to war helped defeat the British invasion of the southern colonies. And the American rebels freely employed terror—whether the tarring and

1

feathering of a British tax collector or the hanging of a backwoods loyalist leader—to advance their cause. In the end, because their victory gave birth to our nation, they are remembered as Founding Fathers rather than treasonous insurgents.

While insurgents and counterinsurgents look at the same set of facts differently, there is general agreement that today, as in the past, Woolsey's "jungle full of poisonous snakes" can present a lethal threat to established order. September 11, 2001, brought that threat into shocking public view.

The attacks on the World Trade Center and Pentagon caused American political leaders to commit the nation's armed forces to a global war on terror. Pursuing terrorists in Afghanistan and Iraq, the United States invaded, displaced the existing regimes, and took on the job of stabilizing the newly occupied territory. What had begun as a hunt for small bands of violent, ruthless men became a counterinsurgency, seeking to impose order in places most U.S. citizens had never heard of. Concerned citizens learned a new vocabulary. In place of intercontinental ballistic missiles, mutually assured destruction, and the Fulda Gap, they heard about roadside bombs, jihad, and a Baghdad slum called Sadr City.

Like the American public, the U.S. military had to learn, or in some cases relearn, what appeared to be a new way of war. When deliberating about how to defeat the Taliban in Afghanistan, insurgents in Iraq, or a seemingly omnipresent Al Qaeda wherever it can be found, some military thinkers returned to the lessons of history. From the campaigns of Spanish insurgents against Napoleon—the era that gave the world the term *guerrilla*, or "small war"—to the Communist insurgencies in Vietnam and the triumph of Afghan rebels against the Soviets, they found numerous well-known examples of skillfully waged insurgencies. These conflicts along with a host of less well-remembered episodes demonstrate that insurgents, guerrillas, and terrorists enjoy many advantages in their struggles to overthrow a government or evict foreign occupiers. However, they are not predestined to win.

A successful counterinsurgency requires a deft blend of military and political policies. Formulating this blend is a supremely daunting challenge. Both the insurgents and the counterinsurgents compete for the support of the civilian population. Mao Tse-tung's classic formulation, that to survive guerrillas must be like fish swimming in a sheltering sea of popular support, appropriately focuses attention on the salient importance of this competition. Likewise, the classic counterinsurgency formulation describes this competition as the battle for "hearts and minds."

History shows that if insurgents build, maintain, and eventually expand a network of support within the general population, they will triumph. For a counterinsurgency to win, it must also gain civilian support. Such support is critical in order to obtain timely intelligence that allows the counterinsurgency power to separate the insurgents from the general population. It may seem simplistic to say that government forces cannot defeat guerrillas unless they can find them, except that history records that this task is painfully difficult.

Given that civilian support is critical to ultimate victory, insurgents work to prevent civilians from assisting the government by employing intimidation tactics ranging from threats and extortion to kidnappings and assassinations. Insurgent terror eliminates government supporters and silences the mass of neutrals.

A government will not receive civilian support against the insurgents unless it can provide physical security for the population. However, a government seldom has enough military strength to garrison every vulnerable place. It must therefore enlist local self-defense forces in the form of police and militia. Able recruits for those forces will not be forthcoming if the recruits perceive that government service puts their lives and their families at excessive risk.

The conundrum for a counterinsurgency power is as follows: it will not obtain civilian support unless it can provide physical security; it is very hard to provide that security without civilian support. This conundrum brings politics to the forefront in two arenas: the internal politics of the government that the insurgents are seeking to topple and the home politics of the counterinsurgent power.

A government confronting an internal insurgency is usually a weak government in crisis. To undermine popular support for the insurgents, the government must address civil grievances and make meaningful reforms. However, weak governments by definition have a precarious hold on power. They usually depend on support from the internal security forces, the military, government bureaucrats, and perhaps a business elite. If such a government responds to civil grievances by offering to share power with the disenfranchised, it risks losing the support of its core backers. Reform measures are equally fraught with peril for a weak government. Weak governments provide supporters with rewards to ensure their continuing support. These rewards are often official licenses to exploit the unrest by some form of corruption. Reform, on the other hand, requires an elimination of corruption and an emphasis on efficient performance. Changes in the social, political, and economic status quo will always be resisted, which is a large part of the reason that few tasks are as difficult as nation building in the midst of a violent insurgency.

Meanwhile, the home government of the counterinsurgent power that is trying to prop up a foreign government under attack has to address its own set of political issues. The people ask their leaders—with public voice in a democracy, with muted tones elsewhere—why sacrifice on foreign soil is necessary. How those leaders answer is as important as how well their soldiers conduct the fight.

JUNGLE OF SNAKES describes four counterinsurgency wars. In two cases, the United States in the Philippines and Great Britain in Malaya, a major power defeated an insurgency. In the other two cases, France in Algeria and the United States in Vietnam, the insurgents won.

In 1898 the United States declared war on Spain. The ensuing "Splendid Little War" brought the Philippines under American control by right of conquest. However, when President William McKinley decided to retain control of the islands for the indefinite future, Filipino nationalists violently resisted.

McKinley had little understanding of the country to where he was committing U.S. troops. His administration and its military advisers grossly underestimated the number of troops required to achieve the objective. Thereafter, they underestimated the depth of Filipino resistance to the American occupation. To undermine that resistance, administration policy tried simultaneously to impose a civil government and defeat an insurgency. At first, the American policy relied upon a variety of social and economic measures designed to persuade would-be insurgents that they could enjoy a better life if they laid down their weapons and accepted the American version of civil government. When these policies failed, the United States adopted sterner measures.

Thereafter, several times senior military men claimed the war all but won, only to reverse course when a new round of violence exploded. Meanwhile, an influential chorus of American intellectuals including Samuel Clemens (Mark Twain), William James, Samuel Gompers, and

Andrew Carnegie formed a movement to oppose the war. As time passed with inconclusive military results and as reports of military misconduct, abuse, and torture gained currency, the American public began to turn against the war. The *New York Times* pronounced:

> The American people are plainly tired of the Philippine War. The administration must be aware that the case of its enemies is not weakened nor the confidence of its friends augmented by the daily reading about all this cost and killing. To kill rebellion by inches and trust to patience and slow time to bring back peace and contentment is not a humane or wise policy.[2]

Yet in spite of fighting in an alien environment far from home against an insurgency partially fueled by nationalist sentiment and hatred of foreigners, the United States did win.

In 1948 Great Britain faced a Communist insurgency in Malaya. The insurgents depended on terrorism to cow the civilian population and to drive out the British. London insurance firms would not cover British-owned Malayan businesses against losses incurred during a civil war. Accordingly, British authorities proclaimed the insurrection an "Emergency" instead of a rebellion or war, and set in train a counterinsurgency. As was the case with the United States' response to guerrilla warfare in the Philippines, the British initial reaction was sluggish and off target. Yet, like the United States, Great Britain managed to recover and defeat the insurgents. The victory is recognized as the outstanding example of a successful counterinsurgency campaign. The British stressed the importance of operating within the rule of law. They emphasized that a successful counterinsurgency had to rely on an honest and competent civil service. Above all, the British recognized the centrality of gaining the loyalty and commitment of the civilian population.

The 1954 war in Algeria pitted France against Muslim nationalists directed by the Front of National Liberation (FLN). The FLN objective was the restoration of a sovereign Algerian state. It advocated social democracy within an Islamic framework. To accomplish its goals, the FLN promoted armed struggle against France's colonial occupation. A majority of French politicians of all stripes believed that Algeria was a fundamental part of France. They committed France's armed might to retaining possession. After much trial and error, the French military developed a successful strategy. A combination of fortified barriers and population regrouping shifted the war's military momentum decisively in favor of the French. The senior French general in Algeria proclaimed, "The military phrase of the rebellion is terminated in the interior." For one last agonizing time, French military leaders believed that the army's blood sacrifices had brought victory. This belief would heighten their sense of betrayal when Charles de Gaulle concluded that France had to abandon Algeria because the war was being irretrievably lost politically both on the international front and within France itself.

When American ground forces entered Vietnam in 1965 they confronted a nationalist-inspired Communist insurgency. Whereas the Communists understood local needs and attitudes, the South Vietnamese government did not. It was weak, disorganized, corrupt, aloof from its own people, and unable to perform the routine tasks of governing. The American commander, General William C. Westmoreland, described the formidable challenge: "Vietnam is involved in two simultaneous and very difficult tasks, nation building and fighting a vicious and well-organized enemy." He ruefully added that if South Vietnam could do either alone, the task would be simplified, but instead "it's got to do both at once."[3]

As was the case in the Philippines, Malaya, and Algeria, in Vietnam trial and error led to a counterinsurgency approach that might have led to victory. But it came too late. The American public demanded an end, even if it meant something far short of victory. In spite of heroic sacrifice, victory in Vietnam had proved beyond American capacity.

THE LESSONS OF Vietnam and the merits of various counterinsurgency approaches elsewhere continue to be debated furiously among those who believe that historical experience can provide signposts for future conduct. Simultaneously, the first decade of the twenty-first century witnesses active counterinsurgency operations on every populated continent except North America and Australia. The battle rages across what American military thinkers call the zone of instability—an arc stretching from northwest Africa across the Middle East and through Central Asia to the Islamic frontiers in Indonesia and the Philippines.

Today, the American architects of the global war on terrorism—or the "Long War," as it may become known—describe the fighting as asymmetric conflict. The paradox is stark. An ostensibly superior military power confronts an inferior foe. The superior power has unlimited means but only limited goals. Compared to their superior opponent, the insurgents have limited means and inferior armaments. But the insurgents have a high tolerance for casualties while the stronger power does not. More important, the insurgents know that their enemy's unwillingness to suffer casualties stems from his uncertain will. The insurgents do not have to defeat their enemy; they merely must outlast him.

The battle is fought on many fronts but none surpasses the importance of the information front. In the Philippines in 1900 the insurgents crafted their strategy to influence the American presidential election. Poor communications and hardworking U.S. Army censors helped thwart this strategy. When Communist insurgents in Vietnam employed the same strategy in the 1960s, advances in communications technology enabled them to broadcast their messages. Today's globalized information environment gives insurgents an even more powerful tool. Whether from hideouts on the Pakistan border or from bases deep in the Colombian jungle, insurgent leaders often wield this tool with great skill.

David Kilcullen, an Australian expert whose advice has influenced General David Petraeus among others, observes that contemporary counterinsurgencies are "fundamentally an information fight. The enemy gets that, and we don't yet."[4] *Jungle of Snakes* seeks to contribute to that information fight. The author fully understands that any historical example involves a set of influences of which some are unique to a certain place and time. But the reader will see common themes emerge. One inescapable conclusion is that a counterinsurgency is a long fight. *Jungle of Snakes* provides readers with a historical foundation so that informed citizens can assess how the fight is going.

PART ONE
The Philippine Insurrection

ONE

An American Victory Yields a Guerrilla War

Finally, it should be the earnest and paramount aim of the military administration to win the confidence, respect, and affection of the inhabitants of the Philippines . . . by proving to them that the mission of the United States is one of benevolent assimilation.

—President William McKinley, December 21, 1898[1]

An American Challenge

THE AMERICANS HAD COME TO FIGHT and now, on the morning of August 13, 1898, they were finally getting their chance. For the veterans among them, the Spanish line of trenches and blockhouses defending Manila appeared formidable. Civil War experience had taught that determined infantry dug in up to their eyebrows behind log and dirt breastworks could hold their position even if outnumbered four or five to one. On this field the sides were roughly equal, with each having about 13,000 men. Furthermore, the attackers would have to make a frontal assault on a narrow strip of land hemmed in on one side by Manila Bay and on the inland side by a flooded swamp.

The soldiers expected little assistance from their informal allies, a ragtag force of Filipino revolutionaries who followed the banner of twenty-nine-year-old Emilio Aguinaldo. Indeed, the senior American leadership had planned carefully to prevent the Filipinos from participating in the assault. When the Americans claimed they needed the position to establish an artillery battery, the revolutionaries had reluctantly ceded the trenches facing this section of Spanish works back on July 29. Since that time, the Americans had endured a life in the trenches made miserable by either a baking tropical sun or, as was the case on this morning, a pelting rain. Their shoes and uniforms had quickly rotted on their bodies, while Spanish snipers shot at anyone who unwisely revealed himself. Now, finally, with their contemptible allies out of the way and their senior officers prepared to order an assault, they could escape their trenches and come to grips with their foe.

At 9:35 a.m. Admiral George Dewey's cruisers and gunboats opened fire against a beachside Spanish strongpoint, Fort San Antonio Abad. The 3.2-inch field guns served by Utah volunteers joined the bombardment. For fifty minutes American shells blasted the Spanish defenses. The guns fell silent and the Americans clambered from their trenches, advanced a short distance, and lay down. This was no wild charge of densely packed troops into the teeth of the enemy's breastworks in the manner of Virginia in 1864. Instead it was a carefully orchestrated, methodical assault backed by overwhelming firepower. When the soldiers lay down the navy resumed a short bombardment. Then the soldiers moved forward along the beach to within 100 yards of the Spanish position and went to ground again. For a third time the big naval guns spoke. When an eight-inch naval shell penetrated the rear wall of Fort San Antonio Abad, the Spanish garrison fled.

While one U.S. brigade pursued the Spaniards through the suburbs toward Manila, an adjacent brigade commanded by Civil War veteran Arthur MacArthur charged toward Blockhouse 14, which was barring the road to the capital. Here there was a sharp exchange of fire, costing the Americans five killed and thirty-eight wounded. MacArthur's men captured the blockhouse and pressed ahead all the way to the old walls protecting Manila. Gazing up through another tropical deluge, they saw the surprising sight of white flags flying from the city's walls. After offering token resistance, the Spanish had surrendered. Having captured the Spanish capital of the Philippine islands, the Americans turned to their second objective: keeping Aguinaldo's aroused revolutionaries from entering Manila.

THE DISEMBARKATION OF United States soldiers at the port of Cavite in Manila Bay in the summer of 1898 marked the first time in history that

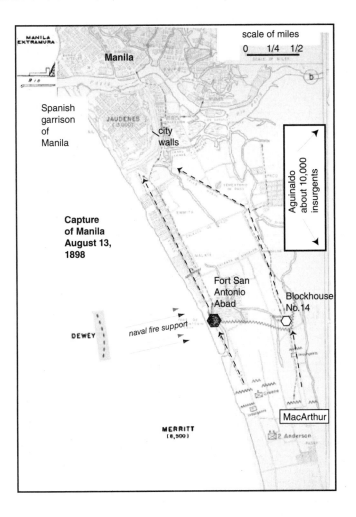

American ground forces set foot on Asian soil to fight a war. Their mission was daunting: they had volunteered to oust the Spanish but found themselves having to impose American control over the Philippines, an archipelago numbering more than 7,000 islands spread along a 1,000-mile chain. If the patriotic Westerners who filled the ranks of the volunteer regiments looked at a map they could appreciate that this was a span equivalent to the distance from Seattle to Los Angeles. But the natural obstacles were far more formidable. From mountainous interiors to swampy shorelines, individual islands presented a hostile environment featuring jungles and dense expanses of towering cogon grass pierced by rough trails that connected isolated hamlets. The threat of ambush was everywhere. Worse, heat, humidity, and terrifying tropical diseases reigned.

The Philippine islands were home to more than 7 million people. To the American soldier their behavior was a mystery. Few Americans spoke Spanish and none spoke any of the seventy-some dialects used by most Filipinos. The insurgents easily blended into the local population or hid in the interior, where they found near-perfect concealment. They were like fish swimming in a friendly sea and the American soldiers knew it.

Philippine History

In 1521 Ferdinand Magellan entered an unknown region in the South Seas while searching for a route to the Spice Islands. He came upon a chain of islands that he named the Philippines after King Philip II, of "Invincible Armada" fame. It proved his last discovery. Natives on the island of Cebu killed the great explorer, leaving it up to his second in command to complete history's first circumnavigation of the globe. The Spanish returned to Cebu in 1565 to begin a period of colonial rule that lasted until 1898.

During the great European scramble for colonies, the Philippines remained a backwater. Nonetheless, Spanish influence was great. Spain forcibly united the Filipinos into one nation for the first time in their history. The Spanish introduced Catholicism, thereby creating what to this day remains the only Christian nation in East Asia. Converting the benighted islanders to Christianity provided the cover for colonial exploitation. The great religious orders—Jesuits, Franciscans, Dominicans—owned and developed large estates where the peasants attended mass on Sunday and the rest of the time labored to produce rice, sugarcane, and hemp for the church's benefit. The Spanish zeal to perfect the natives did not extend to promoting economic development or self-government, and therein lay the seeds of insurrection.

Outside of the religious orders, few Spaniards came to the islands to live. To administer the archipelago's economy, Spanish authorities relied on select natives to occupy the lower rungs of the bureaucracy. Over time this local elite took advantage of opportunities in trade and commerce to achieve a dominant position in Filipino society. But the Spanish continued to discriminate against them when it came to appointments to important positions in the church, government, and military. By the dawn of the twentieth century, prominent, educated Filipinos, called the *ilustrados* (enlightened), had grown tired of their second-class status. As their resentment built, some *ilustrados* formed the Katipunan (Patriots' League), a secret society dedicated to overthrowing the Spanish and achieving Philippine self-rule.

The Katipunan initiated a major rebellion in 1896 in the Tagalog-speaking provinces of Luzon, the most populous island in the Philippines. The rebels quickly gained control of the area south of Manila. Then factional rivalries split the Katipunan command, leading to the execution of the movement's leader and his replacement with Emilio Aguinaldo. The quarreling allowed the Spanish to recover and counterattack. After a year of conflict, and having learned that rebellion was difficult, dangerous work, Aguinaldo and several other prominent leaders made a shrewd calculation and allowed themselves to be bought out by the Spanish. Aguinaldo went into brief exile in comfortable billets in Hong Kong.

Hostilities Erupt

The sinking of the battleship *Maine* in Havana harbor precipitated the United States' declaration of war on Spain in April 1898. Admiral George Dewey commanded the U.S. Asiatic Squadron, the spearhead of his country's Pacific thrust against Spain. Best remembered for his utterly ordinary command "You may fire when ready, Gridley," Dewey and his fleet annihilated the overmatched Spanish fleet in Manila Bay on May 1, 1898. Because he lacked sufficient ground forces to invade the Philippines, Dewey had to confine his subsequent efforts to a naval blockade of Manila. In order to avoid a total loss of momentum while he waited for the arrival of American troops, two months away, Dewey made the fateful decision to summon Aguinaldo from exile.

What exactly was said during Aguinaldo's meeting with Dewey remains controversial. Aguinaldo claimed that an American consul had already pledged that the United States would recognize Filipino independence and that Dewey reiterated this promise. Dewey claimed he said no such thing. Dewey's intention was merely to use Filipino guerrillas to pin the Spanish in Manila until an American ground force arrived to capture the capital. Toward this goal Dewey gave Aguinaldo 100 rifles and the American consul in Hong Kong purchased another 2,000 for the Filipino leader.

In a country where modern firearms were scarce, these gifts helped Aguinaldo reassert his position as leader of the Filipino independence movement. As the weeks passed, friction between the Filipino insurgents and the Americans developed. Aguinaldo had learned that the McKinley administration was coming to the view that the United States should first evict the Spanish and then retain the Philippines as a prize of war. Aguinaldo sought to preempt this effort by proclaiming himself president of a provisional government of an independent Philippine Republic. He assumed control of the insurgency and directed his forces to occupy as much territory as possible in order to give credence to the assertion that he represented the will of the Filipino people.

From the beginning, leaders from the *ilustrado* class dominated the insurgency. They were Tagalogs, racially indistinguishable from other Filipinos but separated by the language they spoke. Their homeland was the central and southern parts of the main island of Luzon. The Tagalogs did not try to mobilize support from the mass of the people. Their goal was to transfer power from the Spanish to themselves. From a peasant's perspective, this was essentially a continuation of rule by a local elite. In select areas, notably in central Luzon and the provinces south of Manila, the people enthusiastically supported the revolution. Outside of this Tagalog heartland, the peasant response to Aguinaldo's revolutionary government was tepid. However, as a contemporary American historian observed, "It is fair to presume that a people will help men of their own blood, men who speak the same language, men whose thoughts are their thoughts, rather than foreigners whose declared purposes they do not trust."[2] Despite his lack of military education and experience, Aguinaldo assumed command of the revolutionary army. By the end of June 1898, Filipino insurgents controlled most of Luzon except for Manila itself. As this point Aguinaldo believed that the United States would recognize his government. He was wrong.

On August 14, 1898, the Spanish formally surrendered to the Americans. The previous day's combat for control of Manila had been something of a sham. Guidelines over the conduct of the battle had been prearranged between the Americans and the Spanish. The subsequent show of Spanish resistance was a matter of honor, although the American casualties, 17 killed and 105 wounded, were real enough. The so-called First Battle of Manila was unusual in several respects. The nominal foes, Spain and the United States, shared a strong common interest in barring Aguinaldo's rebels from the city. The nominal allies ended the battle almost in armed conflict with each other. Hasty negotiations allowed the rebels to remain in the suburbs while the Americans controlled the city. Perhaps the least surprising outcome from the battle was the immediate collapse of army-navy harmony. Dewey told American war correspondents that he had had every-thing arranged for a bloodless transfer of power and that the army had taken unnecessary losses for glory's sake alone. The general who com-manded the assault columns responded by publishing an account of the army's storming Manila without any naval assistance.

Safely ensconced behind the walls of old Manila, the Americans issued a proclamation to inform the Filipino people that the United States had not come to wage war on them. At year's end President William McKinley reinforced this point by declaring that U.S. policy was to be based on be-nign assimilation, a paternal policy in which the knowing elder improved the child by providing education and discipline. Of course, to accomplish benign assimilation it was necessary to occupy the islands. Without real-izing the difficulty of the task, McKinley charged the U.S. Army with en-forcing "lawful rule" throughout the islands. At the same time, he ordered it to protect Filipino lives, property, and civil rights. McKinley thereby set the army a twofold task: one military and one involving civil affairs. The president was convinced that in time the Filipinos would see that Ameri-can motives for occupying the islands were pure and that this realization would end any resistance. Like Aguinaldo, McKinley was wrong in his conviction.

Following the Spanish surrender, a state of high tension persisted for almost half a year. About 14,000 American soldiers established a perime-ter defending Manila and worked fitfully to make the city a showcase for the benefits of benign assimilation. Meanwhile, Aguinaldo's newly named Army of Liberation, with about 30,000 soldiers, maintained a loose cor-don around the city while Aguinaldo, who felt betrayed by American con-duct, prepared for war. He and his *insurrectos,* as the Americans labeled them, did not intend to exchange one colonial master for another. Aguinaldo warned that his government was ready to fight if the Ameri-cans tried to take forcible possession of insurgent-controlled territory. Op-erating under McKinley's assumption that it was only a matter of time until Filipinos came to their senses, the American commander of ground forces, General Elwell Otis, avoided provoking the insurgents. Finally the inevitable occurred on the evening of February 4, 1899, when a shooting incident escalated into war.

The next day President Aguinaldo issued a proclamation to the Philip-pine people announcing the outbreak of hostilities. It explained that he had tried to avoid conflict, but "all my efforts have been useless against the

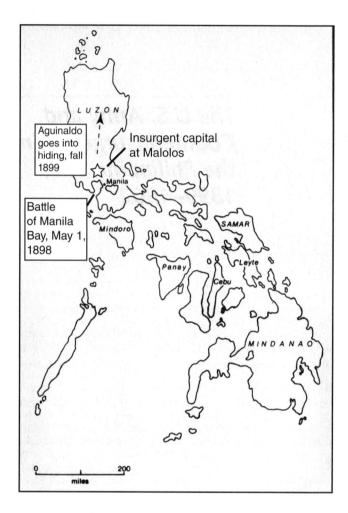

Aguinaldo goes into hiding, fall 1899

Insurgent capital at Malolos

Battle of Manila Bay, May 1, 1898

LUZON

Manila

Mindoro

SAMAR

Panay

Leyte

Cebu

MINDANAO

0   200
          miles

measureless pride of the American Government . . . who have treated me as a rebel because I defend the sacred interests of my country."[3]

On the Brink of Victory

The Philippine-American War had two distinct phases. During the first, conventional phase, from February to November 1899, Aguinaldo's soldiers operated as a regular army and fought the Americans in stand-up combat. In the absence of a coherent strategy—the revolutionary cause never bred a first-class strategist; Aguinaldo proved himself in deep over his head as a military thinker—Filipino efforts focused on defending the territory they controlled. This defense lacked imagination, amounting to little more then trying to position units between the Americans and their objectives. The U.S. Army easily dominated the conventional war. The army could reliably find the enemy and bring him to battle. Once combat began, the army's superior firepower dominated. The contest was so one-sided that General Otis reported that he could readily march a 3,000-man column anywhere in the Philippines and the insurgents could do nothing to prevent it. Conventional military history taught that when one side could not oppose the free movement of its enemy across its own territory, the war was all but over. Indeed, military pressure coupled with the army's commitment to a policy of benevolent assimilation appeared to produce decisive results in the autumn of 1899, as Otis prepared a war-winning offensive scheduled to take advantage of Luzon's dry season.

Otis worked very hard but wasted endless time supervising petty details. A journalist observed that Otis lived "in a valley and works with a micro-scope, while his proper place is on a hilltop, with a spy-glass."[4] MacArthur was even less charitable, describing the general as "a locomotive bottom side up on the track, with its wheels revolving at full speed."[5] Unfortunately, members of the Filipino elite living in Manila had the measure of the man and they told Otis what he wanted to hear, namely, that most re-spectable Filipinos desired American annexation. This fallacy reinforced Otis's instinct toward false economy, to cut corners and win the war without expending too many resources.

His plan to capture the insurgent capital in northern Luzon and de-stroy Aguinaldo's Army of Liberation was akin to a game drive writ large. One group of Americans acted as beaters, herding the Filipinos toward the waiting guns of a blocking force that had hurried into position to in-tercept the fleeing prey. By virtue of prodigious efforts—unusually heavy rains flooded the countryside, reducing one cavalry column's progress to sixteen miles in eleven days—American forces broke up the insurgent army, captured supply depots and administrative facilities, and occupied every objective. As if to confirm what the Manila elite had told Otis, sol-diers entered villages where an apparently happy people waved white flags and shouted, "*Viva Americanos.*"

An American officer, J. Franklin Bell, reported that all that remained were "small bands . . . largely composed of the flotsam and jetsam from the wreck of the insurrection."[6] Otis cabled Washington with a declaration of victory. He gave an interview to *Leslie's Weekly* in which he said: "You ask me to say when the war in the Philippines will be over and to set a limit to the men and treasure necessary to bring affairs to a satisfactory conclusion. That is impossible, for the war in the Philippines is already over."[7]

It certainly appeared that way to eighteen-year-old George C. Marshall. The volunteers of Company C, Tenth Pennsylvania, returned from the Philippines to Marshall's hometown in August 1899. Marshall recalled, "When their train brought them to Uniontown from Pittsburgh, where their regiment had been received by the President, every whistle and church bell in town blew and rang for five minutes in a pandemonium of local pride." The subsequent parade "was a grand American small-town demonstration of pride in its young men and of wholesome enthusiasm over their achievements."[8]

Victory enormously pleased the McKinley administration. Now benevolent assimilation could proceed unhindered by ugly war. The president told Congress, "No effort will be spared to build up the vast places desolated by war and by long years of misgovernment. We shall not wait for the end of strife to begin the beneficent work. We shall continue, as we have begun, to open the schools and the churches, to set the courts in operation, to foster industry and trade and agriculture." Thereby the Filipino people would clearly see that the American occupation had no selfish motive but rather was dedicated to Filipino "liberty" and "welfare."[9]

In fact, Otis and other senior leaders had completely misjudged the situation. They did not perceive that the apparent disintegration of the insurgent army was actually the result of Aguinaldo's decision to abandon conventional warfare. Instead, the ease with which the army occupied its objectives throughout the Philippines brought a false sense of security, hiding the fact that occupation and pacification—the processes of establishing peace and securing it—were not the same at all. A correspondent for the *New York Herald* traveled through southern Luzon in the spring of 1900. What he saw "hardly sustains the optimistic reports" coming from headquarters in Manila, he wrote. "There is still a good deal of fighting going on; there is a wide-spread, almost general hatred of the Americans."[10] Events would show that victory required far more men to defeat the insurgency than to disperse the regular insurgent army. Before the conflict was over, two thirds of the entire U.S. Army was in the Philippines.

How the Guerrillas Operated

Otis's offensive had been final, painful proof to the insurgent high command that they could not openly confront the Americans. Consequently, on November 19, 1899, Aguinaldo decreed that henceforth the insurgents adopt guerrilla tactics. One insurgent commander articulated guerrilla strategy in a general order to his forces: "annoy the enemy at different points" while bearing in mind that "our aim is not to vanquish them, a difficult matter to accomplish considering their superiority in numbers and arms, but to inflict on them constant losses, to the end of discouraging them and convincing them of our rights."[11] In other words, the guerrillas wanted to exploit a traditional advantage held by an insurgency, the ability to fight a prolonged war until the enemy tired and gave up.

Aguinaldo went into hiding in the mountains of northern Luzon, the location of his headquarters secret even to his own commanders. He divided the Philippines into guerrilla districts, with each commanded by a general and each subdistrict commanded by a colonel or major. Aguinaldo tried to direct the war effort by a system of codes and couriers, but this system was slow and unreliable. Because he was unable to exercise effective command and control, the district commanders operated like regional warlords. These officers commanded two types of guerrillas: former regulars now serving as full-time partisans—the military elite of the revolutionary movement—and part-time militia. Aguinaldo intended the regulars to operate in small bands numbering thirty to fifty men. In practice, they had difficulty maintaining these numbers and more often operated in much smaller groups.

The lack of arms badly hampered the guerrillas. A U.S. Navy blockade prevented them from receiving arms shipments. The weapons they had were typically obsolete and in poor condition. The ammunition was homemade from black powder and match heads encased in melted-down tin and brass. In a typical skirmish, twenty-five rifle-armed guerrillas opened fire at point-blank range against a group of American soldiers packed into native canoes. They managed to wound only two men. An American officer who surveyed the site concluded that 60 percent of the insurgents' ammunition had misfired. Although the insurgents typically had prepared the ambush site complete with their guns mounted on rests, their shooting was also notoriously poor. Not only did they lack practice because of the ammunition shortage but also they did not know how to use both the front and back sights on a rifle.

Insurgent officers were painfully aware of their deficiencies in armaments. One colonel advised a subordinate to arm his men with knives and lances or use bows and arrows. Another pleaded with his superiors for just ten rounds of ammunition for each of his guns so that he could attack a vulnerable American position. On the offensive the regulars carefully chose their moment to strike: a sniping attack against an American camp or an ambush of a supply column. After firing a few rounds they withdrew. On the defensive they seldom tried to hold their ground but instead dispersed, changed to civilian clothes, and melted into the general population.

The part-time militia, often called the Sandahatan or bolomen (the latter term referred to the machetes they carried), had different duties. They provided the regulars with money, food, supplies, and intelligence. They hid the regulars and their weapons and provided recruits to replenish losses. They also acted as enforcers on behalf of the government the insurgents established in cities, towns, and villages. The civilian arm of the insurgent movement was as important as the two combat arms. Civilian administrators acted as a shadow government. They ensured that taxes and contributions were collected and moved to hidden depots in the hinterland. In essence, the network they created and managed constituted the insurgents' line of communications and supply.

From the insurgent standpoint, the decision to disperse and wage guerrilla war placed the fate of the revolution in the hands of the people. Everything depended on the people's willingness to support and provision the insurgency. Guerrilla leaders well understood the pivotal importance of the people. They decreed it was the duty of every Filipino to give allegiance to the insurgent cause. Ethnic and regional loyalty, genuine nationalism, and a lifelong habit of obeying the gentry who composed the resistance leaders made many peasants accept this duty.

If the insurgents could not compel active support, they absolutely required silent compliance, because a single village informant could denounce an insurgent to the Americans. The guerrillas invested much effort to discourage collaboration. When appeals to patriotism failed, they employed terror. A prominent revolutionary journalist urged the infliction of "exemplary punishment on traitors to prevent the people of the towns from unworthily selling themselves for the gold of the invaders."[12] One of Aguinaldo's orders instructed subordinates to study the meaning of the verb *dukutar*—a Tagalog expression meaning "to tear something out of a hole" and widely understood to signify assassination.[13] Thereafter, numerous orders flowed from all levels of the insurgent command authorizing a full range of terror tactics to prevent civilians from cooperating with the Americans: fines, beatings, or destruction of homes for minor offenses; firing squad, kidnapping, or decapitation for Filipinos who served in American-sponsored municipal governments. However, the revolutionary high command never advocated a strategy of systematic terror against the Americans. They wanted to be recognized as civilized men with legitimate qualifications for running a civilized government and so limited terror to their own people.

As the war continued, civilians became the particular victims even though most Filipino peasants actively supported neither the guerrillas nor the Americans. As long as neither side incurred their wrath via excessive taxation, theft, destruction of property, or physical coercion, they simply continued with their daily chores and hoped that the conflict would be played out elsewhere.

The Policy of Attraction

Aguinaldo's decision to shift from conventional to guerrilla warfare forced American leaders to adapt a new strategy. During the spring and summer of 1900, northern Luzon served as a proving ground for an American counterinsurgency strategy based upon what planners called a policy of attraction. Here the military would prove that it could simultaneously implement civil government and fight the insurgency. The operating assumption was that northern Luzon was peaceful and the Filipinos accepting of American authority. This assumption was out of touch with reality. Because of insurgent terror directed against the inhabitants of towns and villages, the Americans received little useful intelligence about their foes. Thus they were completely in the dark about insurgent plans, movements, and strengths. Moreover, however peaceful the situation appeared in coastal urban areas, insurgents, criminals, and untamed mountain tribesmen dominated the interior's jungles and mountains.

Heedless of this reality, well-intentioned Americans conducted a large-scale program to eliminate smallpox by hiring Filipino doctors and providing them with vaccine. Believing that poor young men joined the insurgency out of economic need, the U.S. Army financed road repair projects to provide a legitimate income alternative. The construction of new schools served as the symbolic centerpiece of American benevolence. The emphasis on civic action meant that a second lieutenant in an isolated village or a major in a large town acted as administrator of municipal government in an alien culture. The officers fell back on what they knew. Just like the progressive reformers at home, they believed that republican institutions produced enlightened and free citizens. So they worked to alleviate society's ills by giving more people greater economic, political, and social opportunities. Their labors made real differences. Medical and sanitation teams brought cholera, smallpox, and plague under control and reduced the incidence of malaria. New water and sewage systems also improved public health. But none of these efforts tamped down the insurgency.

It became apparent that Otis's victory claim was premature. As soon as the rainy season ended in northern Luzon the insurgents began a new offensive. During the next three months, they inflicted 50 percent more casualties on the Americans compared to any other time during the guerrilla war. They cut down vital telegraph lines faster than the lines could be repaired. They repeatedly attacked the rafts that provided the main source of American supply. When U.S. soldiers tried to clear the riverbanks they encountered significant guerrilla opposition. As alarming as all of this was— and it was sufficient to panic the district commander, Brigadier General Samuel Young, into writing his superiors that defeat might be at hand— perhaps worse was the ability of the insurgency to prevent Filipino cooperation with the American vision of civil government.

A guerrilla armed with an obsolete firearm might not be able to engage the Americans on equal terms but his gun allowed him to intimidate unarmed civilians. Better still, in the interest of revolutionary justice, a collaborator hacked to death with a bolo in a village market made a powerful impression and saved scarce ammunition. During 1900 the Americans recorded 350 known assassinations and 442 assaults. The actual numbers were doubtless much higher.

The ability of the guerrillas to terrorize anyone who contemplated cooperation with the Americans made it impossible for the United States to create a civil government. Among many garrison commanders, Major Matt Steele tried to implement his orders and dutifully called for elections. He candidly wrote his wife that he did "not expect a single person to vote" because "the edge of a bolo and the hand of an assassin are the price they would pay for taking that oath and holding office under American rule."[14] An insightful American colonel came to the realization that the "best assistance the Military authorities can now give to the schools is to guarantee to the towns a stable government and to the people personal safety."[15]

With a strength of some 60,000 men, the U.S. Army lacked the manpower to garrison enough places to maintain law and order. Furthermore, the units in the garrison and in the field could not obtain useful intelligence about the enemy. They lacked guides to lead them along obscure jungle and mountain trails. They did not have the language skills to communicate with the local people. Everyone appreciated that efficient Filipino auxiliary forces could solve these problems. Indeed, colonial empires from imperial Rome to British India had rested on the backs of native soldiers. But which natives to trust seemed unknowable.

TWO

Chastising the *Insurrectos*

The Failure of Attraction

THE U.S. ARMY THAT FOUGHT THE guerrilla war in the Philippines comprised regular infantry and cavalry regiments made up of veteran, professional soldiers. Supplementing the professionals were the National Guard and volunteer regiments, "the Boys of '98," commanded by officers who had distinguished themselves during the Spanish-American War. The equipment and training inadequacies that had hampered the fight against the Spanish in Cuba had been corrected. Notably, both regulars and volunteers now received rigorous training. Consequently, they were tough, capable soldiers. Although few enlisted men and junior officers had seen combat prior to 1898, they displayed one of the hallmarks of the American soldier: a willingness to learn by trial and error.

The senior officers from regimental command on up were combat veterans, having fought in either the Civil War or the Indian Wars, if not both. The legacies of these conflicts blended to shape the conduct of the guerrilla war in the Philippines. The Civil War officers were prepared for stern measures. They remembered Sherman's March to the Sea and Sheridan's torching of the Shenandoah Valley. The Indian War officers were comfortable with small-unit warfare, a style of command that involved a high level of command autonomy and rewarded individual initiative and aggressiveness.

For officers and enlisted men alike, the guerrilla war was sporadic and highly localized. During the entire war, no fighting took place in thirty-four of the seventy-seven provinces in the Philippines. In some of the contested provinces, the Americans operated with a light touch. In Albay, on Luzon's southern tip, Filipinos were more concerned with their export economy than with revolutionary slogans. Their lack of firm resistance gave the Americans time to disprove revolutionary propaganda. Contrary to that propaganda, Americans did not kill, enslave, or forcibly convert insurgent prisoners from Catholicism to Protestantism. Instead, they offered peace, the prospect of economic recovery, and amnesty to insurgent fighters. True, the American soldiers often drank to excess, but so did many locals, hence this behavior was tolerable. Albay proved to be one of many places where the Americans merely had to demonstrate that they were better than the Spanish to become tolerated if not welcomed.

Because the insurgent menace was initially slight in many places such as Albay, military service in the Philippines often featured a boring routine of uneventful guard duty interrupted by occasional, usually ineffectual, insurgent sniper attacks. Soldiers could leave camp to swim, forage, visit town, or even take horseback rides across the country without fear. But as Private Edwin Segerstrom of the Colorado National Guard observed, "You can't trust them though, for in the daytime they may be friendly when you meet them and have your gun along, but in the night they are different I guess."[1]

In the unpacified provinces, American officers at all levels of command found themselves thrust into the unfamiliar task of establishing civil government as the occupation made the transition from military to civilian rule. Yet they still had to fight the insurgents. In order to accomplish this, the army dispersed into small garrisons. In November 1899—at a time when the insurgents were still trying to fight as a regular military force—some 43,000 American effectives occupied 53 dispersed bases (called stations in official reports). In response to the outbreak of guerrilla warfare, reinforcements arrived, increasing American strength to about 70,000 effectives. As of October 1900 they manned 413 stations.

In other words, to contest dispersed guerrillas the Americans also had to spread out, and by so doing they encountered a classic counterinsurgency conundrum. To provide civilian security and find the guerrillas, the army had to operate in the most remote, inhospitable terrain. Garrisons in such places could not live without supplies from the main bases. Supply convoys, in turn, moved along narrow, unpaved roads through jungle and densely planted cropland. Numerous rivers and streams bisected the landscape, funneling the convoys onto primitive bridges, a natural choke point for ambushes. When it rained, which was often, the so-called roads dissolved into deep, cloying mud. Then, soldiers had to substitute themselves for weary draft animals to haul bogged wagons from the mud. All of these factors made supply convoys so vulnerable that they became the insurgent target of choice. In response, U.S. commanders had to increase the number of men providing security along the lines of communication, which took away from the number available to hunt for the guerrillas.

Regardless of whether they were occupying a remote station or guarding supply bases and escorting convoys, young American soldiers found such routine duties unappealing. They had either volunteered for military duty or chosen the military as a profession and did so with the expectation that they had joined a fighting service. Instead they "were confronted with conditions utterly alien to their experience . . . They found themselves living in native houses or church buildings in the middle of large towns, in many cases of four or five thousand people, whose language they did not speak, whose thoughts were not their thoughts."[2] The natives' lack of enthusiasm and support for their earnest efforts initially perplexed the American soldiers. Then came frustration. They had given the gift of American-style democracy and met indifference or resistance. The only possible explanation was that the natives were too primitive, too foreign, too different to appreciate the benefits of American-sponsored civilization. The strong words the American soldiers used for Filipinos—"niggers," "gugas"—betrayed their disdain for the local population.

The Guerrillas Adapt

From the American strategic viewpoint, the dispersion of the Army of Liberation into guerrilla bands had pluses and minuses. A big advantage was that guerrilla leaders had great difficulty communicating across districts because terrain and American patrols made the ability of a courier to deliver a message highly problematic. Thus there was little strategic coordination among insurgent bands. Each operated in a near-vacuum of information about the activities of bands outside the district, so they were unable to mass for powerful attacks against isolated American garrisons. Consequently the Americans could disperse to occupy the countryside without fear of being overrun. However, on the negative side, the decentralized nature of the resistance meant that there was neither one place to capture nor one leader to kill to cripple the insurgency. In effect, the resistance had mutated from a recognizable entity with a spine and a central brain into something more primitive that could endure the loss of an appendage or a nerve bundle and survive.

The typical American combat operation involved a small patrol searching the countryside for guerrillas and their bases. The soldiers called these operations "hikes." In order to march light, they discarded heavy packs and extra gear and severed reliance upon traditional supply trains. They used mule pack trains and native bearers. To increase mobility they formed picked detachments of mounted infantry and scouts. Whenever they possessed useful intelligence, these mounted detachments hounded insurgent bands relentlessly. However, most hikes failed to find the guerrillas. Insurgent spies and civilian sympathizers often forewarned the enemy. Moreover, the rugged jungle and mountain terrain provided excellent concealment. One typical hike traversed what the soldiers called the "Infernal Trail," a rugged, mountainous path only eighteen inches wide that zigzagged through jungle and forest and ascended steep slopes where a misstep meant a 300-foot fall into a cliffside ravine.

In such terrain a typical encounter began when guerrillas hidden in thick bamboo alongside a trail or concealed in a mountain gorge fired at an American patrol or supply column. This first fire invariably came as a surprise. After discharging a few shots the guerrillas scattered. The entire event usually ended within a matter of seconds. Such combats were enormously frustrating to the American soldiers. General Arthur MacArthur later testified that because it was so difficult to find the insurgents and because their shooting was so wild, American officers regarded "a contact under any conditions as a great advantage."[3] A new arrival to the Philippines, Captain David Mitchell, certainly held this view and it cost him his life.

Mitchell commanded Company L, Fifteenth Infantry, based in Laguna Province in southern Luzon. This was the home territory of the insurgent leader General Juan Cailles. Cailles sent the local American commander, Colonel Benjamin Cheatham, a message that Cheatham regarded as "insolent." Cheatham resolved to make Cailles "eat his words" and sent two infantry companies to attack Cailles's stronghold in the village of Mabitac.[4] On the morning of September 17, 1900, Mitchell encountered Cailles's men defending the approaches to Mabitac. Cheatham's plan called for Mitchell's 134-man company to create a diversion while a flanking company maneuvered into position.

Although Cailles's force apparently numbered about 800 men, Mitchell cared not. In Mitchell's mind the difficult part of the operation, finding the insurgents, was over. Now all he needed do was kill them. The terrain heavily favored the insurgents. The end of the monsoon season had flooded the countryside. The only way to get at the enemy was by advancing along a narrow causeway leading to Mabitac. Under such conditions even the notoriously poor insurgent marksmanship proved deadly. Their first volleys killed most of Mitchell's advance party. None of Mitchell's men had ever been under fire before and the survivors refused to charge into the hail of bullets. Mitchell and his subordinates exposed themselves recklessly to encourage the men to advance. Some soldiers tried to deploy off the causeway only to encounter waist-deep water. Meanwhile, deep water prevented the flanking column from providing assistance. Limited to an advance over the fire-swept causeway, the Americans had nothing except naked courage. It was not enough. After eighty minutes the battered Americans withdrew.

Mitchell and twenty-three of his men lost their lives. Another nineteen Americans were wounded. In his report to Washington, MacArthur put the best light possible on this pointless carnage, asserting that the 33 percent loss rate was a sign of the "fearless leadership of officers and splendid response of men." MacArthur privately acknowledged that if Mitchell had not been killed he would have been court-martialed for his reckless conduct. When U.S. forces returned the next day to resume the fight, the enemy had disappeared. MacArthur explained that Cailles's men had undoubtedly escaped to nearby *barrios*, where they would pose as "peaceful amigos" until summoned to fight again.[5] MacArthur mentioned neither that Cailles had returned the bodies of eight of Mitchell's soldiers along with all their private property nor that Cailles claimed to have suffered only ten casualties.

In the fight against Mitchell's regulars, the insurgents had enjoyed a commanding position that turned the combat into a virtual turkey shoot. Consequently they willingly held their ground to inflict the maximum number of casualties. More commonly the insurgents avoided large American forces and instead struck isolated, vulnerable detachments. There was no pattern to the timing of the contacts and they could take place anywhere. An American regimental commander explained that the insurgent strategy thus gave the guerrillas a preeminent advantage since they could act the role of either *insurrecto* or *amigo* according to circumstances.

MacArthur described the insurgents' tactics: "At one time they are in the ranks as soldiers, and immediately thereafter are within the American

lines in the attitude of peaceful natives, absorbed in a dense mass of sympathetic people."[6] Captain John Jordan described how his patrols entered a
village to encounter people greeting "you with kindly expressions, while
the same ones slip away, go out into the bushes, get their guns, and waylay
you further down the road. You rout them & Scatter them; they hide their
guns and take to their houses & claim to be amigos."[7] The insurgent-amigo
act infuriated American soldiers. They could tolerate the common civilian
attitude of sullen indifference. But treachery and betrayal were something
else. A Manila-based journalist, Albert Robinson, wrote, "We have found
many of them who were believed to be honestly friendly, but time has
proved that they were simulating. Some of our most promising local presi-
dentes [mayors] have been found guilty of the rankest treachery toward the
Americans."[8]

American conduct also stoked the insurgency. There were the inevitable
unfortunate encounters between intoxicated soldiers and civilians. In addition, soldiers supplemented their often deplorable rations by taking from
civilians. But there was also something deeper. Most American soldiers
had enlisted to fight. They generally regarded Filipinos as the enemy and
believed that an enemy was someone who should be killed. Journalist
Robinson noted, "The enlisted man of the army to-day is not a philanthro-
pist with a broad love for his fellow men . . . Many enlisted for the avowed
purpose of 'killing niggers' and such have neither intent nor desire to return without having done their errand."[9] Although the army sometimes
tried to punish abusive behavior, the deterrent effect was problematic. And
there were routine cover-ups, as when soldiers in the Thirty-eighth Volunteers found a comrade's decapitated body and retaliated by burning down a
large section of the nearest town. Army investigators concluded that Filipinos had started the blaze.

As 1900 progressed, increasing numbers of Filipinos who had been
displaced by the war returned to their homes. They began living among
the Americans, which gravely worried insurgent leaders. A guerrilla colonel warned that because of the American "policy of attraction" regular
civilian contact "with our enemies may cause the gravest damage to our
sacred cause."[10]

It is impossible to make a sweeping generalization about the impact
of building schools, conducting classes, and providing a host of other
civil services. They probably influenced events in the 44 percent of the
provinces where no conflict occurred. Within insurgent strongholds

they had little effect. Under American duress, municipal officials would perform their American-directed duties by day and at night cooperate with the insurgents. It was a logical human choice given that neither side could adequately protect them from the sanctions of the opponent.

The ability of the Americans to defeat the insurgents with ease in open battle had awed the insurgents. The American inability to capitalize upon their conventional victories gave the insurgent leadership hope. At least one farsighted American colonel perceived this. He warned his superiors, "It seems to me that the people have less respect for the United States' authority than they had six months ago. They still have the same appreciation of their incapacity to meet its military power, but they have learned what they did not know, that it can be evaded, and how this can be done. I say this with profound regret."[11]

Presidential Politics

As the pacification strategy based on a policy of attraction faltered, the upcoming American presidential election dominated events in the Philippines. Aguinaldo and his lieutenants invested great hope in the election's outcome. They thought that if they inflicted some sensational losses then the American public would turn against McKinley and elect Democrat William Jennings Bryan.

Had the Democratic Party nominated a different candidate this strategy might have been effective. But in 1900 American voters were enjoying economic recovery from the depression of 1896. Consequently, Bryan's "Free Silver" economic policy, which had seemed appealing four years earlier during Bryan's first contest against McKinley, failed to compete with the Republican slogan, "Four more years of the Full Dinner Pail." This left Bryan with only his opposition to the annexation of the Philippines as a reason to attract voters and it proved not enough.

However, in the summer of 1900 Aguinaldo did not perceive that Bryan was virtually unelectable. In June Aguinaldo issued a general order calling for "heavy blows" against the Americans during the summer months.[12] His subordinates echoed his call. In August General Cailles ordered "constant combats, ambuscades, surprises and encounters" to "aid the triumph of the candidacy of Bryan who is our hope for the declaration of the independence of our country."[13]

Like their Filipino counterparts, American generals understood the significance of the election in determining the war's outcome. Civil War veterans recalled their encounters with a press corps filled with anti-Lincoln and antiwar journalists. In the Philippines in 1900, as in Virginia and Georgia in 1864, they knew that military setbacks would provide political ammunition for the administration's opponents if someone could deliver that ammunition. War correspondents in Manila tried to fulfill this role. To thwart them, the military leadership in the Philippines imposed strict censorship. An Associated Press reporter complained that this was more "unreasonable" and "stringent" than at any prior time and that censors "suppressed" his report about "incontrovertible military occurrences," "delayed" controversial reports, rewrote political news, and "prohibited" the word *ambush*.[14]

To influence the election, the military also exaggerated its accomplishments and inflated reports to make it appear that the war was progressing smoothly. In a war in which the capture of modern rifles was a crucial metric of progress, an official army bulletin announced the surrender of 800 insurgents and their firearms in the province of Bayombon. On the surface this appeared to be a notable victory. A diligent correspondent investigated and determined that in fact only forty rifles had been captured. The army had included in its count obsolete weapons and unimportant handguns found in private homes and also inflated the total to match the number of prisoners. The discrepancy between number of prisoners and number of firearms raised the question of how many of the prisoners were actual insurgents.

Correspondents correctly believed that linguistic manipulation—such as forbidding the use of the word *ambush*—coupled with official censorship and exaggeration had political motives. However, when confronted by a military willing and able to control the flow of news there was little they could do about it. Only after the election did information emerge that would have brought into sharp question the administration's veracity regarding the war's progress.

Taft and MacArthur

The effort to muzzle the press during the run-up to the election consumed time that officers would have preferred to spend in actual military operations. But they understood that the fight against the insurgents had an important domestic political component. Reinforcing this point was the arrival of another distraction; a high-ranking, politically well-connected civil commission headed by William H. Taft. A fat man—schoolmates had nicknamed him "Big Lub"—whose appearance disguised his gifts, Taft was contentedly serving as a federal judge when he received an unexpected summons to the White House. McKinley still believed that the best way to undermine the insurgency was to demonstrate America's benign intent. His vehicle for accomplishing this was a five-man Philippine Commission chaired by Taft.

His offer of the chair floored Taft. "He might as well have told me that he wanted me to take a flying machine," Taft related. The offer seemed a perilous career detour, so Taft equivocated. Secretary of War Elihu Root applied the necessary suasion. He told the forty-three-year-old Ohioan, "You have had an easy time of it holding office since you were twenty-one. Now your country needs you. This is a task worthy of any man. This is the parting of the ways. You may go on holding the job you have in a hum-drum, mediocre way. But here is something that will test you . . . and the question is, will you take the harder or the easier task?"[15]

For a parochial Ohio boy, the Philippines presented a novel challenge. Taft observed to his half brother, "The situation in Manila is perplexing. You meet men who are completely discouraged at it; you meet men who are conservative but very hopeful of good results; and you meet men who have roseate views of the situation."[16] In Taft's mind, the commission's goal was clear: to gain the confidence of the Filipino people by providing them with the best government possible.[17] In September 1900 the Philippine Commission assumed legislative and executive duties for the islands. In practice, civilian rule, as represented by the Philippine Commission, re-placed military authority as soon as the army declared a province pacified. Then the commission established municipal and provincial governments. Over time, the commission could boast of a rare accomplishment: it con-ducted a steady transfer of power that amounted to a self-liquidating colo-nial management. But at the start success seemed a distant mirage because Taft and his fellow commissioners met a wall of resistance erected by Otis's successor, Arthur MacArthur.

A Wisconsin native, MacArthur compiled a distinguished combat record in the Civil War. Thereafter he spent twenty-three years languish-ing as a captain in the regular army until finally receiving the recognition he craved. He lacked the tactical flair some possessed. But he was unusu-ally well-read in military matters and put his learning into practice as he deliberated over alternative plans. Some called him slow and not particularly bright, while others judged him "thoughtful" with particular talent for "efficient strategical movement."[18] Regardless of what others thought, MacArthur was much convinced of his own brilliance and also was a tireless self-promoter, two characteristics he would pass on to his son Douglas. Like many other officers, he keenly resented the notion that civilian government could be put in place in the Philippines while the fighting still raged. MacArthur considered Taft and his fellow civilians annoyances best ignored.

Taft also served as a convenient lightning rod for the enlisted men's frustrations. After Taft characterized the Filipino as "our little brown brother" who merely required American compassion to improve his lot, field soldiers replied with new lyrics to a popular tune:

> *I'm only a common soldier-man in the blasted Philippines.*
> *They say I got Brown Brothers here, but I dunno what it means.*
> *I like the word Fraternity, but I still draw the line;*
> *He may be a brother of William H. Taft, but he ain't no friend of mine.*[19]

Indeed, the song made light of a significant problem. As one American general observed around this time, "The most serious obstacle in the way of complete pacification of the islands now lies in the mutual distrust between the troops and the inhabitants."[20]

THREE

The War Is Won Again

Lieutenant William T. Johnston Goes to Work

THE INSURGENTS' PREELECTION OFFENSIVE focused attention on combat encounters between American soldiers and guerrillas while obscuring
the more important battle to control the civilian population. Americans
were learning that benign assimilation in the face of an insurgency able
and willing to terrorize the civilian population was impossible. Among
them was William Taft. By now Taft had visited some of the islands' safer
regions—including in his baggage an outsized bathtub since he could not
fit into the local ones—and reached the conclusion that most Filipinos
wanted peace but were too frightened by the insurgents' systematic terror
campaign to act. An American colonel concurred, observing that civilians
"would gladly take their oaths of allegiance if assured that our troops
would remain to protect them."[1] But the Americans were unable to provide adequate security.

General Lloyd Wheaton, the commander of the Department of Northern Luzon, studied the problem and concluded that the insurgents had
prepared carefully for the American arrival. They selected loyal delegates
to confer with the Americans and participate in the American-sponsored
elections. Thus they controlled the municipal government. A vice mayor's
official duties included fulfilling contracts to supply the Americans. He
siphoned off half the profits for the insurgency. An insurgent colonel organized the police force. The police force's most important duty was to inform the insurgents about American movements. Their second duty was
to mislead the Americans regarding the whereabouts of the guerrillas. In

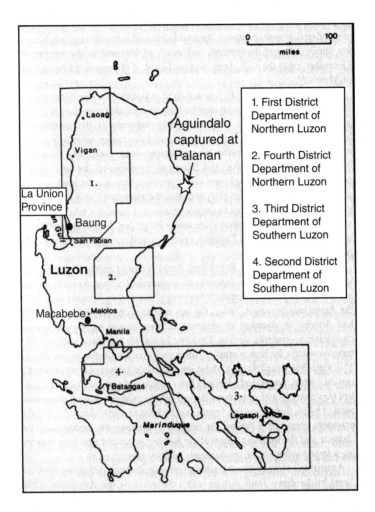

sum, the insurgents had established an embedded infrastructure, what later generations would call a shadow government. Wheaton himself did not hold such a sophisticated view. He concluded that the policy of "benevolent assimilation" was not working because the Filipinos were "semicivilized natives belonging to a race whose every impulse is to treachery and perfidy."[2]

The extent of the continued Filipino resistance surprised the man at the top, General MacArthur. He had originally thought that Aguinaldo's fighters represented a distinct minority. However, "contact with both insurrectos and amigos" had taught him that in fact most Filipinos on the main island of Luzon supported Aguinaldo.[3] MacArthur had reached a different conclusion than Taft regarding Filipino motivations. MacArthur concluded that the Filipinos were quite happy to accept the material benefits flowing from the American pacification effort while continuing to support the insurgents with money, supplies, shelter, and new recruits. As MacArthur pondered what to do, Lieutenant William T. Johnston produced a brilliant analysis titled "Methods Adopted by the Insurgents for Organizing and Maintaining a Guerrilla Force."[4] It arrived on MacArthur's desk at the end of June 1900 and proved a shocking appraisal of past pacification efforts.

To date no American had systematically studied the infrastructure that supported the insurgency. Johnston set to work diligently investigating towns and villages in the province of La Union, some 170 miles northwest of Manila. Painstaking interviews with local Filipino officials convinced Johnston that a very active insurgent shadow government was operating right under the noses of the American garrisons. Just how active and how close he did not know until a stroke of fortune produced an invaluable informant. This was Crispulo Patajo, a suspected outlaw delivered to the Americans by the mayor of Bauang. Patajo turned out to be a disgruntled leader of a minor religious cult, the Guardia de Honor. The cult had long been in conflict with Filipino authorities. Patajo took the opportunity of his arrest to seek revenge against his cult's oppressors. He told Johnston that among others the mayor of Bauang was a member of the insurgency. He offered to prove his accusation by exposing the region's entire guerrilla network.

Johnston, in turn, pursued the matter like a detective investigating a crime. He gave Patajo the opportunity to establish his bona fides by revealing the locations of hidden insurgent supply depots. At his first test, Patajo led the Americans into a supposedly pacified town, denounced several men who turned out to be insurgent officers, and found a stockpile of guns. Encouraged by this demonstration, Johnston unleashed Patajo on Bauang. In short order, Johnston reported, "Bauang was cleaned up and the presidente [mayor] made to see the error of his ways."[5] With a huge assist from Patajo, in less then three months Johnston assembled a complete picture of insurgent operations in the region. Among his findings was the startling fact that insurgent leaders routinely circulated among multiple safe houses in the midst of American-garrisoned towns and villages. Here they regularly met with civil authorities including mayors and police chiefs. Those officials handed over tax receipts and forced requisitions as well as monies siphoned off from American aid programs. If they needed muscle to enforce their demands, the insurgents summoned guerrillas from secure camps located within two miles of a an American garrison. Indeed, the presence of American forces did little to deter the insurgents. Johnston learned that insurgent shadow governments operated even in places occupied by substantial American garrisons. Here as elsewhere, men serving the insurgent cause had been installed by the Americans to serve in the American-sponsored municipal government.

Armed with this knowledge, Colonel William P. Duvall, the officer commanding La Union, set to work. Duvall melded Johnston's talents, Patajo's offer to provide anti-insurgent volunteer militia, and a handful of rebel turncoats into a comprehensive intelligence system that produced dramatic results. Duvall appointed Patajo chief of detectives for the entire province and allowed him to recruit from within his own cult. Patajo quickly raised some 400 to 500 volunteers who accompanied American patrols. The volunteers proved their worth by guiding the Americans to guerrilla hideouts or operating on their own. At the end of March, Patajo's men attacked an insurgent force, capturing officers, men, and guns while they rested in their safe houses. This was a feat the Americans alone could not accomplish.

Patajo handed the prisoners over to the Americans, who gave them the choice of prison or freedom if they betrayed their comrades. From an American perspective, the beauty of this approach was that once a guerrilla became a turncoat, he also became highly motivated to fight the insurgency since he well knew that he had become a marked man. Indeed, the local guerrilla commander offered a large reward for killing the "terrible Americanista" Patajo, to no avail. Worse from an insurgent standpoint, once Patajo's men rooted out the shadow government and replaced it with their own, the insurgents found that they could not regain control of the towns.

Higher in the chain of command, Colonel Duvall's decision to rely on Patajo and his cult was problematic. It went against official policy, upset the region's Filipino elite, and alarmed American civil authorities. Taft reported to the secretary of war that Duvall had merely replaced insurgent terrorism with a different system of terrorism. Taft warned that this approach would ultimately harm American pacification efforts. However, there could be no denying results. As Johnston noted, Patajo's men "are the only ones who have ever told us where we could find insurrectos and

guns, and who voluntarily went and helped find them."[6] By exploiting ethnic and religious differences, the Americans in La Union were able to
sever the connection between the insurgent bands and the towns that supported them. In a matter of months, the province that MacArthur's predecessor had called the worst part of the Philippine islands was pacified.

At the end of June 1900, when MacArthur read Johnston's eye-opening
analysis, he praised it as the best description of the insurgency he had seen.
He concluded that the extent and strength of the insurgency demanded a
major strategic shift. But if he announced such a shift, he would give ammunition to the opponents of the McKinley administration four months
before the presidential election. Consequently, MacArthur bided his time
and warned the War Department that the war had entered a new phase that
was likely to persist for a long time. The general relied upon his censors to
keep this information from the American public.

THE PHILIPPINES EXPLODED into violence as the insurgents began a general offensive timed to influence the American election. In spite of the
censors' efforts, as the presidential election entered its decisive weeks,
events in the Philippines assumed center stage. McKinley responded to
fierce domestic political attacks against his Philippine policy by appealing
to patriotism and asserting that victory was very near if only the country
stood to the task. He did not reveal MacArthur's altogether different assessment. Republican advocates equated support for Bryan with support
for the insurgents. Secretary of War Root openly called into question the
patriotism of the anti-imperialists, saying that insurgents firing from ambush and the anti-imperialists were allies in the same cause. Other politicians quoted letters from servicemen saying that the only reason the
Filipinos continued to fight was because of reports from the American
press that undermined the administration. The pro-administration *New
York Tribune* charged that Bryan was more of an insurgent leader than
Aguinaldo and "every American soldier that is killed during these
months can be laid directly to his door."[7]

On election day 1900, William McKinley won reelection with 52 percent of the popular vote and almost twice the number of electoral votes
as Bryan. In this, his second contest against Bryan, his margin of victory
was substantially higher than it had been four years before.

For the Filipino insurgents, this result spelled disaster. They had always suffered from a scarcity of military resources and from indifferent popular support. They invested both assets heavily on the prospect of Bryan's election. McKinley's overwhelming victory saw their hopes dashed and their assets depleted. It also allowed the Americans to take off the gloves and begin a much crueler war.

The Laws of War

One of the army's hard men, Major Matt Batson, greeted McKinley's re-election with great satisfaction. He told his wife:

> The time has come when it is necessary to conduct this warfare with the utmost vigor . . . But the numerous, so styled, humane societies, and poisonous press, makes it difficult to follow this policy if reported to the world, so what I write to you regarding these matters is not to fall into the hands of the newspaper men. At the present we are destroying everything before us. I have three columns out, and their course is easily traced from the church tower by the smoke from burning houses . . . there will be but little mercy shown to those who are carrying on guerrilla warfare, or giving them aid.[8]

The soldiers doing the burning were Filipinos recruited from the town of Macabebe. The Macabebes had a tradition of military service to Spain and detested the Tagalogs. Batson organized a five-company battalion named Batson's Macabebe Scouts. As time went on the Macabebes usefully provided scouts, guides, and interpreters, but they and their leader really excelled at small-unit counterinsurgency operations. During the unit's first week of existence Batson proudly wrote his wife: "With my battalion of Macabebe Scouts I am spreading terror among the Insurrectos. They may be wily but they have found their equal, I think. Word reaches a place that Macabebes are coming and every Tagalog hunts his hole."[9]

Exploiting ethnic divisions to squash an insurgency had long historical roots. The Romans had been masters of this approach. In the Philippines, the success of Batson's Macabebe Scouts encouraged the U.S. Army to take advantage of the archipelago's ethnic rivalries and recruit some 15,000 native auxiliaries. Employing natives was a helpful step but in MacArthur's mind it was not enough. Like almost all of his veteran officers, the commanding general believed that for too long American policy had been mistakenly tilted in the direction of attraction. Even MacArthur's offer of a general amnesty—in his mind a nonpareil exemplar of benign assimilation—had failed. MacArthur complained that the routine reluctance of even the most active pro-Americans to give useful intelligence was one of the greatest problems. Yet MacArthur judged that this reluctance was merely a manifestation of a deeper problem.

According to MacArthur, the insurgency received widespread popular support by "a strange combination of loyalty, apathy, ignorance, and timidity."[10] So strong was the insurgent hold that civilians marked for death by the insurgent command accepted their fate without appealing for American protection. Something had to be done to detach the towns from the insurgents in the field. In MacArthur's view, looming strategic defeat required a "new and more stringent policy."[11] The new policy's legal basis derived from an order drafted and adopted by the Lincoln administration in 1863. At that time the Union army was occupying areas of the Confederacy where partisans waged an increasingly effective guerrilla war. The rebels had extended the cloak of legitimacy to guerrillas who operated in civilian dress. The guerrillas' ability to blend into the civilian background frustrated the U.S. Army. In response, the army's commanding general asked a noted legal scholar, Dr. Francis Lieber, for his views.

The result was General Order 100, "Instructions for the Government of Armies of the United States in the Field," a synthesis of the laws of war as they had evolved by the mid-nineteenth century. Its central theme was that the object of war was restoration of peace, not the death of one's foes. It included a long list of moderating guidelines for an occupying army. However, toleration had limits and irregulars who fought out of uniform could be treated summarily as pirates rather than as legitimate combatants. For active guerrilla sympathizers, legitimate sanctions included exile, relocation, imprisonment, fines, and confiscation. Because of its realistic blend of moderation and severity, General Order 100 gained international acceptance and served as the basis for the first formal international agreements on the laws of war. On December 20, 1900, with the American presidential election comfortably past, MacArthur informed the Filipino people of his new policy. Written in English, Spanish, and Tagalog, his proclamation stated that the insurgents and their supporters were "collectively and individually" guilty of violating the laws of war as encoded in General Order 100.[12] They would eventually be brought to justice. The proclamation's special focus was on the most successful guerrilla elements, namely, those who kidnapped and assassinated American collaborators, participated in the guerrilla's shadow government that operated in American-occupied towns, or fought without belonging to an organized military unit. MacArthur pledged to counter their deeds with exemplary punishments as determined by American military tribunals. He noted that the excuse that someone was acting because of intimidation by the insurgents would rarely be accepted.

MacArthur took additional steps permitted by General Order 100. He sent into exile prominent Filipino leaders. He ended the misguided policy of automatically releasing prisoners. He authorized his provost marshals to arrest and detain suspects without evidence. MacArthur specifically warned that insurgent leaders involved with assassinations would be forbidden from returning to normal civil life once the fighting ended. This threat gave insurgent leaders pause. They had grown up as members of the islands' upper class and heretofore had assumed that, win or lose, when the conflict ended they would resume their privileged lives.

Prior to MacArthur's proclamation to the Filipino people, many American officers such as Matt Batson had already regarded General Order 100 as justification for burning crops and buildings, incarcerating suspects, imposing curfews that authorized shooting on sight anyone found near a telegraph line, and executing prisoners. In one sense, MacArthur was merely providing official acknowledgment for practices already widely employed. However, most American military men had a different sense of what MacArthur's new policy implied. They understood that going forward they had official sanction for waging a much harder war. General Samuel S. Sumner explained, "I am aware that this is a severe and stringent measure and will entail hardships and suffering on the inhabitants, but it seems the only practical means at hand."[13]

MacArthur's new counterinsurgency strategy coincided with a surprising decline in American popular support for the war. The anti-imperialists were enraged that first the McKinley administration had waited until after the election to acknowledge the extent of the Philippine insurgency and then implemented a much harsher policy. Anti-imperialist headlines announced that MacArthur intended to show no mercy, telling Filipinos to "Be Good or Be Shot."[14] As discouraging reports of violence and killing continued, opposition to the war spread beyond the anti-imperialists. On the second day of 1901, the formerly supportive *New York Times* presented an opinion that spoke for many:

> The American people are plainly tired of the Philippine War. The administration must be aware that the case of its enemies is not weakened nor the confidence of its friends augmented by the daily reading about all this cost and killing. To kill rebellion by inches and trust to patience and slow time to bring back peace and contentment is not a humane or wise policy. It cannot be the lack of money. Is it the lack of troops, supplies, transportation, ammunition, artillery? Is it the lack of a competent commander? The public simply does not know where the trouble lies. It does know that there is trouble somewhere. Where is it? How long is this Philippine War going to last?[15]

The continuing insurgent resistance bemused some: "It seems strange to Americans that the Filipinos—or so many of them—are bitterly opposed to our sovereignty. They must know it is likely to be a great improvement over former conditions . . . Nevertheless they fight on." Critics of the administration asked, "Is it not time to confess the whole policy a hideous blunder?"[16]

The Federal Party

MacArthur's decision for sterner war coincided with the peak of U.S. troop strength during the entire war. Freed from political worries and with the rainy season over, MacArthur began 1901 by committing 70,000 veterans to an offensive. His focus was the main island of Luzon. Win there, he argued, and the rest of the islands would fall into place. For the next seven months elite task forces conducted lightning assaults on insurgent bases. Conventional forces made larger sweeps through the jungles, swamps, and mountains that shielded the insurgents. In the countryside, American soldiers burned crops and buildings owned by suspected insurgent sympathizers. In the towns, the Americans made mass arrests, paraded the suspects in front of collaborators who identified the insurgents, and incarcerated the betrayed. Using investigative methods developed in La Union by William Johnston, the Americans purged the civil administration of insurgent sympathizers and broke up the shadow governments.

Simultaneously, an important segment of the local population decided to put their lives on the line in support of the American cause. They called themselves the Federal Party. With the support of MacArthur and Taft, a prominent group of Manila *ilustrados* and former revolutionary officials formed the party in December 1900. The party's basic plank was recognition that the Philippines was under U.S. sovereignty and belief that this was only a temporary state of affairs leading to eventual independence. Of course, their decision had a strong component of self-interest. The founders of the Federal Party had concluded that after McKinley's reelection the Americans were in the Philippines for the indefinite future. Prolonged warfare would tear the islands apart, which was good neither for the nation nor for themselves. If against all odds the insurgents ultimately triumphed, the status of the *ilustrados* in society was still likely to change for the worse because the underclasses would demand more change. On the other hand, if the Americans triumphed, then those who had supported them would have a seat at the table during the national restructuring.

While the Federal Party may not have been dominated by selfless patriots, its ranks included hundreds of very brave individuals. They traveled around the islands to speak out in favor of U.S. policies. They also used their contacts with the insurgency to try to convince insurgent leaders to give up. Increasing numbers of guerrillas, including some prominent senior officers, heeded the call of the Federal Party and came down from the mountains to surrender. They did all of this at considerable personal risk. Aguinaldo reacted to the rise of the Federal Party and the emergence of other collaborators by ordering their capture and trial by drumhead court-martial followed by execution.[17] More broadly, anyone who held a position in the American civil administration continued to face punishment ranging from a $100 fine to death.

In spite of increasing use of terror tactics against civilians, the insurgents found their support eroding. Because of the change in American strategy and the assistance of the Federal Party, as 1901 progressed the Americans enjoyed growing help from the civilian population. Guides became available when before there were none. Town dwellers denounced insurgent tax collectors. Rural people led Americans to supply caches. Filipino militia and police accepted the burden of defending themselves against revolutionary terror. Then, as if to confirm that victory was within reach, came the capture of the insurgent supreme commander, Emilio Aguinaldo.

A Spectacular Raid

Starting in the autumn of 1899, the time Aguinaldo decided to inaugurate guerrilla war, the Filipino leader became a marked man. American units vied with one another for the glory of capturing the insurgent leader. None surpassed the zeal of Batson's Macabebe Scouts. "I hunted one of his Generals to his hole the other night," Batson wrote his wife, "and captured all his effects as well as his two daughters."[18] Such relentless pursuit forced Aguinaldo to keep on the move. He and his small band of loyal staff endured exhausting treks across rugged terrain. They were often hungry, reduced to foraging for wild legumes supplemented by infrequent meat eaten without salt. Sickness and desertion reduced their ranks. Aguinaldo's response was periodic exemplary punishments, drumhead courts-martial, firing squads, and reprisal raids against villages that either collaborated with the Americans or failed to support the insurgents. "Ah, what a costly thing is independence!" lamented Aguinaldo's chief of staff.[19]

Aguinaldo took solace from the occasional contact with the outside. In February 1900 he received a bundle of letters including a report that the war was going well with the Americans suffering "disastrous" political and military defeats. A correspondent in Manila affirmed that the people "were ready to drink the enemy's blood."[20] The high command's ignorance of outside events was startling. For example, Aguinaldo and his party learned from a visitor that five nations had recognized Philippine independence. However, his chief of staff reported that "we do not know who these five nations are."[21] Indeed, the chief of staff candidly recorded that since fleeing into the mountains "we have remained in complete ignorance of what is going on in the present war."[22]

During his exodus Aguinaldo was unable to exercise effective command of his far-flung forces. This did not change after he sought refuge in the remote mountain town of Palanan in northern Luzon. All Aguinaldo could do was write general instructions to his subordinates and issue exhortations to the Philippine people. His efforts had scant effect on the war. What was important was his mere existence. He was the living symbol of Filipino nationalism. In addition—and this mattered to the *ilustrados* who managed the war at the regional and local levels—as long as he remained free the insurgents could say that they fought on behalf of a legitimate national government.

Aguinaldo's efforts to maintain a semblance of command authority led to his downfall. In January 1901 an insurgent courier, Cecilio Sigismundo, asked a town mayor for help getting through American lines. His request was standard practice. The mayor's response was not. He happened to be loyal to the Americans and persuaded the courier to surrender. Sigismundo carried twenty letters from Aguinaldo to guerrilla commanders. Two days of intense labor broke the code and revealed that one of the letters was addressed to Aguinaldo's cousin. It requested that reinforcements be sent to Aguinaldo's mountain hideout in Palanan. This request gave Brigadier General Fred Funston an idea.

Funston interviewed Sigismundo to learn details about Aguinaldo's headquarters (and, according to Aguinaldo, subjected him to the "water cure," an old Spanish torture whereby soldiers forced water down a prisoner's throat and then applied pressure to the distended stomach until the prisoner either "confessed" or vomited; in the latter case the process started again).[23] Palanan was ten miles from the coast, connected to the outside world by a single jungle trail. Although Americans had never operated in this region, obviously the trail would be watched. Funston conceived a bold, hugely risky scheme to capture the insurgent leader. He selected eighty Tagalog-speaking Macabebes who disguised themselves as insurgents coming to reinforce Aguinaldo. Funston armed them with Mauser and Remington rifles, typical weapons for the undergunned insurgents. To make the reinforcements seem more believable, four Tagalog turncoats performed the role of insurgent officers. To make the bait even more enticing, five American officers acted as prisoners and accompanied the column. Nothing if not personally brave—he had earned the Congressional Medal of Honor in 1899—Funston was one of the five.

MacArthur approved of the desperate plan—his chief of staff wrote the secretary of war that he did not expect ever to see Funston again—and on March 6, 1901, a navy gunboat sailed from Manila Bay to deposit the raiding party on a deserted Luzon beach sixty straight-line miles from Palanan. So began the most celebrated operation of the guerrilla war. No mission like this could unfold seamlessly. A harrowing 100-mile trek that called upon physical stamina and quick-witted improvisation brought the column to Palanan on March 23, 1901. To allay any possible suspicions, Funston sent runners ahead to deliver two convincing cover letters. They were written on stationery that had been captured at an insurgent base. Not only did they bear the letterhead "Brigade Lacuna" but they were signed by the brigade's commander, an officer whose writing Aguinaldo was certain to recognize. In fact a master Filipino forger who worked for the Americans had signed the letters. The letters informed Aguinaldo of the impending arrival of the reinforcements he had requested along with a special bonus of captured American officers.

While Funston and his fellow officers hid in the nearby jungle, the column's sham insurgent officers went ahead. A last obstacle remained: the unfordable Palanan River. Two "officers" crossed in a canoe and gave instructions for the Macabebes to follow. The two "officers" approached Aguinaldo's headquarters to see a uniformed honor guard formed to greet them. The cover letter had done its work. Aguinaldo was completely deceived. For a very nervous thirty minutes the two "officers" regaled the insurgent commander with stories about their recent ordeal. Finally the Macabebes arrived. They formed up across from the honor guard as if in preparation to salute Aguinaldo. Then at a signal they opened fire at the startled headquarters guards. Inside Aguinaldo's headquarters, the two "officers" seized Aguinaldo. Meanwhile, Funston and his band emerged from the jungle to take charge. The effect of the surprise was so overwhelming that Funston's commandos managed to escape with their prize and rendezvous with the waiting gunboat.

Funston took Aguinaldo to Manila, where MacArthur treated him with great courtesy, even to the point of having his staff dine with the insurgent leader. Within a few days Aguinaldo was exploring terms of surrender. Within a month he issued a proclamation calling on all insurgents to surrender and for Filipinos to accept United States rule.

In a campaign suffering from slow and indeterminate results, Aguinaldo's conversion was something concrete. MacArthur and the War Department took full advantage, proclaiming the incident the most important single military event of the year. Among the skeptics were the midshipmen of the Naval Academy standing in the left-field bleachers at the first Army-Navy baseball game ever played. Arthur MacArthur's son Douglas was Army's left fielder. The midshipmen heckled Douglas with the chant:

MacArthur! MacArthur!
Are you the Governor General
Or a hobo?
Who is the boss of this show?
Is it you or Emilio Aguinaldo?[24]

Indeed, the claim that Aguinaldo's capture was decisive overstated the facts. Instead, although it was not clearly apparent at the time, MacArthur's stern policies had already begun to erode insurgent strength significantly. While his conversion did inspire the surrender of five prominent insurgent generals, and hundreds of soldiers either turned themselves in or ceased active operations, his removal from the scene had little practical impact for many insurgents. They were accustomed to recognizing the authority of their local commanders. Those commanders, in turn, had been acting like regional warlords for some time and consequently were used to a high level of autonomy.

Aguinaldo's capture was a brilliantly conceived and boldly executed coup. As had been the case when Otis proclaimed victory after dispersing the regular insurgent forces, senior American leaders anticipated a prompt end to the war. Unfamiliar with the ambiguous nature of counterinsurgency, they again overestimated the value of a single "decisive" success. On July 4, 1901, as MacArthur neared the end of his tour of duty in the Philippines, he reported that the armed insurrection was almost entirely suppressed. The army had squashed armed resistance in nearly two thirds of the hostile provinces. In the United States a pleased President McKinley began a domestic victory tour designed to heal the sharp political divisions created by the war.

Again the general commanding the field forces and the commander in chief were wrong. The insurgency survived the loss of its leader and persisted for more than another year.

FOUR

The Policy of Destruction

The Response to Massacre

IT FELL TO MACARTHUR'S SUCCESSOR, Major General Adna Chaffee, to bring the war to a close. When he assumed command in September 1901 it appeared that the endgame was in hand. Chaffee identified three remaining areas where the insurgents were active: southwestern Luzon, Samar, and Cebu. Chaffee was perfectly happy to cede control of everywhere else to the Philippine Commission and get out of the pacification business. The velocity of this transition was a problem. An officer serving in Samar, one of the lingering trouble spots, caustically questioned whether the time for civil government had really arrived given the commissioners still required strong security detachments around their Manila residences. He complained that the Filipinos "cannot be conquered, civilized, and taught to love us in a year."[1] He concluded that it was a mistake for impatient Americans to force the expansion of civil government in places where security was problematic.

Chaffee cared not. In his view, for too long junior officers had operated outside the scrutiny of their betters and it was time to reel them in. With the guerrilla war all but won, he wanted soldiers to return to real soldiering. Then, "like a clap of thunder out of a clear sky," came the Balangiga Massacre on September 28, 1901.[2]

The small port of Balangiga was on the southern coast of Samar. Samar, in turn, was the home island of a ferocious, untamed insurgency. To date, small American garrisons had seldom ventured inland from their coastal enclaves and were ignorant of all that transpired outside range of their

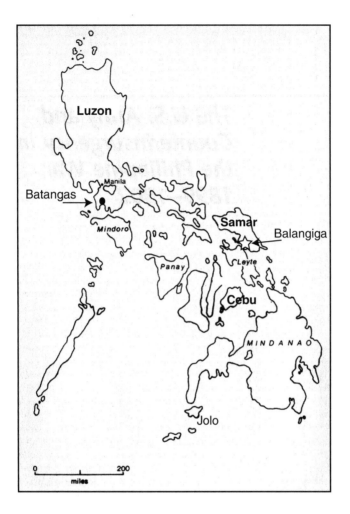

Krag-Jorgensen rifles. The mayor of Balangiga had invited an American garrison to protect his town from Moro pirates. Better American intelligence would have revealed that pirate raids against coastal Samar had all but ended more than fifty years earlier. Instead, Company C, Ninth U.S. Infantry, came to Balangiga to provide security. Company C was a veteran outfit. One soldier had served aboard Dewey's flagship, the *Olympia*, at the battle of Manila Bay. Most had fought insurgents on Luzon and all had traveled to China to fight the Boxers. But their return to the Philippines and occupation of Balangiga was not happy. The company commander, Thomas Connell, was insensitive to local mores. He insisted that the villagers work to trim back the jungle to eliminate concealment, he tried to

ban the popular cockfights, and he attempted to keep his men from frater-
nizing with young girls. Ugly incidents of abuse and rape ensued. To limit
conflict with the villagers, Connell forbade any save his sentries from carrying weapons. Meanwhile, the village mayor informed the insurgents
about the Americans' habits and routines.

Around midnight on September 26, numerous women began deliver-
ing small caskets to the central church. A suspicious American sergeant
glanced inside one casket, saw a child's body, and allowed the women to
pass. Although he noted that the women wore heavy clothes in spite of
the warm night, the sergeant was well aware of his captain's demand for
strict conduct in the wake of the rape incidents, so he did not investigate
further. Had he done so he would have found that the clothes concealed
machetes and that the caskets actually held drugged children lying atop
hidden weapons.

On Sunday morning, an apparently friendly Filipino police chief
paused to chat with a sentry and then seized his rifle and shot him. The
church bells began pealing, the signal for bolomen to emerge from hiding
to cut down the remaining sentries. Simultaneously several hundred
machete-wielding men emerged from the church to overrun the officers'
quarters and murder the Americans in their beds. Connell leaped from a
window into the street, where insurgents hacked him to death in full view
of his regulars. The first surge killed some fifty soldiers. A sergeant rallied
thirty-eight survivors around the arsenal, including eight too hurt to fight,
and managed to fight off the bolomen. They made their way to three
dugout canoes to begin paddling to the nearest American post while pursued by insurgents as well as swarming sharks attracted to the blood seep-
ing into the water. Only six regulars escaped unharmed. A total of
fifty-nine were killed and twenty-three were wounded.[3] It was the heaviest
American loss of any action during the entire war.

The next day came the American reprisal. After a gunboat blasted
Balangiga with Gatling guns and cannon fire, an infantry column stormed
ashore. They beheld the mutilated bodies of their comrades. They saw a
trench filled with the Filipino casualties from the previous day's action. Apparently the Americans had interrupted the burial service. A patrol caught
twenty unarmed men and the officer in charge handed them over to the six
unharmed American survivors. The six proceeded to gun down the prisoners. After burning the town the Americans departed.

In the United States, a hysterical press promoted an atmosphere of panic by calling the massacre a Philippine version of Custer's Last Stand. In Manila, the civilian commissioner Taft retained a balanced perspective. He recognized the event as a discouraging blow but told the secretary of war that "there will be no shadow of turning from the course we have marked."[4] The military man, Chaffee, exhibited less balance. The massacre seemed to fly in the face of the claim by the Philippine Commission and the Federal Party that the insurgents were on their last legs. Instead, Chaffee listened to his intelligence service, which now reported that the insurgents were regrouping in preparation for widespread uprisings in January 1902. Their warnings convinced Chaffee that he was sitting on a powder keg that was about to explode.

In this climate of high emotion and fear, Chaffee insisted on a harder war against the remaining insurgents. As a twenty-two-year-old second lieutenant, he had participated in Sheridan's razing of the Shenandoah Valley in 1864. Given that a policy of massive property destruction was acceptable against fellow Americans, Chaffee saw no reason it should not be used against Asians. To fight this harder war, he called upon two hard men. He assigned Brigadier General J. Franklin Bell, his most accomplished counterinsurgency general, to squash the rebels in Luzon's Batangas Province once and for all. To remote Samar he sent Brigadier General Jacob Smith.

In Samar, insurgents operated from jungle sanctuaries in the roadless interior and confined the Americans to a handful of coastal enclaves. Their victory at Balangiga had increased their strength. Whomever Chaffee had assigned to Samar would have faced tremendous problems, including the need to keep the American troops firmly in hand because the lurid memories of the "treachery" at Balangiga were foremost in their minds and they wanted revenge. Unfortunately the sixty-one-year old Smith possessed few qualifications beyond a savage instinct—he would be best remembered for allegedly ordering a subordinate to reduce Samar's interior to a "howling wilderness"—and his loose control led to some of the worst American atrocities of the war.[5]

Smith knew war. He carried a Confederate minié ball in his hip, a legacy of his valiant conduct at the Battle of Shiloh. His subsequent behavior during a three-year recuperation revealed a less attractive side to his personality. While serving as a recruiting agent, he invested ignorant recruits' bounties for personal gain. Cashiered for insubordination during the 1880s and then reinstated, Smith again displayed valor at the Battle of

El Caney in Cuba, where the Spanish defenders shot him in the chest. Transferred to the Philippines, Smith found himself in independent command at a level he had never before experienced. He enthusiastically complied with Chaffee's demands to employ the harshest methods on Samar. He ordered his brigade to wage hard war, telling subordinates the more killing and burning the better, and reminded them that not even civilized war could be carried out "on a humanitarian basis."[6] He then set to work by ordering the concentration of Samar's inhabitants into protected zones on the coast. He treated the rest of the island as enemy territory. Smith sent his forces, including a battalion of U.S. Marines, inland, where they killed opponents, real and imagined, burned houses and crops, and slaughtered livestock. Many of his subordinates kidnapped civilians and routinely applied physical abuse to extract intelligence. Eventually, a comprehensive starvation policy forced the insurgents to spend most of their time searching for food. Meanwhile, uncounted numbers of civilians also perished. The capture of an emaciated and sick Vicente Lukban, Samar's insurgent leader, on February 18, 1902, led to mass desertion among the remaining insurgents and marked the collapse of resistance against American occupation on Samar.

After the last guerrilla bands on Samar surrendered, a series of courts-martial ensued. Revelations of gross misconduct, including murder and torture, emerged. Allegedly when an officer asked Smith to define the age limit for killing, he replied, "Everything over 10."[7] The judge advocate general of the army noted that only the good sense exhibited by the majority of Smith's subordinates had prevented a complete reign of terror on Samar. The fact that Chaffee's fearful overreaction to the Balangiga Massacre had created a climate where such conduct could occur escaped scrutiny. Smith had conducted a savage campaign well outside even the stern norm of American operations elsewhere in the islands. His legacy was to tarnish horribly the history of the American war in the Philippines.

The Real Terror of the Philippines

In contrast to Smith, Brigadier General J. Franklin Bell conducted his Batangas campaign within the boundaries of what the military considered acceptable. Indeed, he employed counterinsurgency methods that he and others had successfully demonstrated in previous campaigns.

Nonetheless, for many Filipinos the consequences looked very much the same as those endured by the inhabitants of Samar.

Bell was forty-five years old when he took over the Third Separate Brigade in Batangas. He was one of the army's comers, a West Point graduate who arrived in the Philippines as a first lieutenant in the regular army and then ascended rapidly.[8] A contemporary described him as "robust, vigorous, energetic."[9] He raised, trained, and commanded the Thirty-sixth Infantry, U.S. Volunteers. The regiment comprised soldiers who had come to the Philippines as volunteers in the state regiments, discovered that they rather liked being soldiers, and opted to remain when their units returned home. They were tough, spirited men who found a kindred spirit in Colonel Bell. A subordinate whose long career would extend through World War I wrote, "In all my service since, I have never known an officer who was held in such high regard by the officers and men of his command as was Colonel Bell."[10]

During the campaign in northern Luzon, Bell repeatedly conducted daring reconnaissance missions. He was personally brave to the point of recklessness. In one famous combat, he led a scouting party into the teeth of a much larger insurgent force. Ignoring the fire from insurgents concealed in a nearby bamboo grove, Bell drew his revolver, charged seven *insurrectos*, and single-handedly captured three of them. His combat courage later won him the Congressional Medal of Honor. Transferred to Manila, he served as provost marshal. At the time the capital served as an insurgent sanctuary, with numerous safe houses where guerrillas could find food and shelter and recover from the strain of active campaigning in the hinterland. Six months of Bell's stern rule changed everything. His success at clearing the capital of the insurgents won praise from civilians and soldiers alike.

Promoted to brigadier general, at the time the youngest man to hold this rank, Bell went to northern Luzon. Here his solution to the insurgency was to make the civilians feel "the full hardship of War" in order to make them not only stop helping the insurgents but also take an active role in defeating them.[11] Success in northern Luzon enhanced his reputation. William Taft was one admirer. Taft told Secretary of War Root that if Chaffee would send Bell into Batangas, the general would "make things so uncomfortable for the people who are supporting the insurrection that the men in the field [the guerrillas] would soon be brought in."[12]

Batangas was a particularly tough nut to crack. Located in southwestern

Luzon, it was a large, densely populated province with wretched terrain ranging from rice paddies and swamps to jungles and volcanic mountains. Filipinos living in the Batangas region had been in revolt since the uprising against Spain in 1896. This was the Tagalog heartland, from where a majority of the important revolutionary leaders emerged. In Batangas, guerrilla leaders avoided direct combat with the Americans. Instead, they concentrated on maintaining support in American-occupied towns by enforcing orders against Filipino participation in American civil government. Regional, ethnic, and family ties accounted for much of the support given to Aguinaldo and his successor, Miguel Malvar. Revolutionary terror—threats, property destruction, kidnapping, assassination—kept those inclined to support, or at least tolerate, the Americans in check. As was the case in Samar, to date American pacification efforts had failed here.

Bell assumed command in Batangas eight months after Aguinaldo's surrender. He understood the difficulty of the challenge, observing that the revolution appeared destined to meet its death "in the place of its birth and to die hard."[13] Like most American soldiers, he was contemptuous of the natives. In particular, he considered them peerless liars totally unfit for self-government. Along with his racial bigotry, Bell also possessed a sharp analytical mind. More than any other American general, he had studied the insurgency and gained a comprehensive understanding of how it operated. He explained the beliefs undergirding his strategy in a circular order to all his station commanders: "The insurrection in this brigade continues because the greater part of the people, especially the wealthy ones, pretend to desire, but in reality do not want peace." Bell continued that as soon as the people wanted peace, peace would come quickly. Based on his experience in northern Luzon, Bell concluded that clearly the correct policy was to "make the people want peace, and want it badly."[14]

On December 8, 1901, Bell gave his most controversial order. Some years back Bell had interrupted his military career to study law and pass the Illinois bar. Now his legal eye examined General Order 100 and focused on the mandate requiring an occupying force to protect the people from undue hardship. This duty to protect the people became his justification to concentrate them into secure camps. He ordered post commanders to establish protected zones for the safety of all Filipinos who desired peace. The peace-loving people had twenty days to move their families, food, and possessions into the protected zones. Thereafter, all territory outside of the zones would be treated as enemy territory. Here all property could be confiscated or destroyed and all males subject to arrest. If they tried to evade they would be shot. Bell informed his subordinates that General Order 100 "authorizes the starving of unarmed hostile belligerents as well as armed ones, provided it leads to a speedier subjection of the enemy."[15]

Bell was correct that General Order 100 allowed the "withholding of all sustenance or means of life from the enemy." Indeed, this was well within accepted military practice. From earliest recorded times, starvation was the method by which a besieging force compelled the surrender of a castle or fortress town. Senior American officers were well aware that the starving of the people of Vicksburg had led to its surrender to the Union army commanded by U. S. Grant. Likewise, the practice of forcibly separating civilians from insurgents was not a novel solution. In South Africa the British were using concentration camps in their battle against the Boers. During the American Civil War, something of this sort had been done on a smaller scale and had been a key ingredient in ending Confederate guerrilla operations in northern Arkansas. But the policy had most recently been employed by the Spanish in Cuba and this was not a happy comparison in American minds.

Spanish general Valeriano Weyler and his Cuban *reconcentrado* policy had drawn widespread condemnation in the American press. During the buildup to the war with Spain, he was routinely described as "Butcher Weyler." Press accounts of the Cuban victims of Butcher Weyler's concentration camps had been instrumental in turning American public opinion against Spain. With this in mind, heretofore the U.S. Army had concealed its concentration camps by calling them "colonies" and "zones of protection." Chaffee tried to maintain this fiction, going so far as to ask the adjutant general of the army to hand-deliver news of Bell's plan to the secretary of war and then destroy it. Chaffee explained that he did not "care to place on file in the Department any paper of the kind, which would be evidence of what may be considered in the United States as harsh measures."[16]

In the event, a concentration policy of the scale employed in Batangas could not be concealed. The *Philadelphia Ledger* compared Bell with Butcher Weyler and asked, "Who would have supposed . . . that the same policy would be, only four years later, adopted and pursued as the policy of the United States in the Philippines?" The *Baltimore American* expressed astonishment "that a general of our army in the far-off Philippines has actually aped Weyler." It continued, "We have actually come to a thing we went to war to banish."

The imperialist press counterattacked. It wrote that comparisons between Bell and Weyler were mendacious because Bell, unlike Weyler, did not intend to starve the people. It asserted that complaints about Bell's policy stemmed from either partisan politics or, as the *Army and Navy Journal* explained, sheer ignorance: "The things which the civilian critics in the United States don't know about military affairs in the Philippines would make a whole library of war history."[17]

FAR REMOVED FROM this highly charged domestic debate, American officers in southwestern Luzon implemented Bell's directive, concentrating about 300,000 Filipinos inside the protected zones. The extent of the protected zones depended upon the size of the U.S. garrison. Small garrisons controlled areas limited by the range of their Krag-Jorgensen rifles. The larger garrisons, in towns such as Batangas, established zones one or two miles wide and six miles long. A perimeter 300 to 800 yards wide surrounded each zone. This was known as the "dead line," beyond where soldiers had orders to shoot to kill anyone who strayed without permission.

Many officers used their local knowledge to apply commonsense interpretations of Bell's directive. They told their men to avoid shooting women, children, and the aged and to exhibit restraint at all events. In addition, the Americans properly considered it their duty to feed the Filipinos who inhabited the protected zones. But the purpose of the concentration order was to separate them from the insurgents and then destroy all food outside the camps in order to starve out the insurgents. The soldiers focused on this task.

Prisoner interrogations indicated that the insurgents had hidden a two-year supply of food. Bell intended to find and destroy these caches even though it meant searching "every ravine and mountain top."[18] And as long as they were in the field, Bell wanted the soldiers to kill all the animals they could not bring back to the towns so that nothing edible remained to nourish the guerrillas. To cripple further the insurgent ability to find food, the army closed all ports in Batangas and in an adjacent province. Bell banned the movement of merchandise by land inside these provinces. No civilian was allowed to travel within the province without a special pass. Able-bodied males did not get passes.

No longer would individuals or town councils be allowed to straddle the divide between the Americans and the insurgents: "No person should be given credit for loyalty simply because he takes the oath of allegiance or secretly conveys to Americans worthless information." Henceforth, the only acceptable measure was public acts that "commit them irrevocably to the side of Americans by arousing the animosity and opposition of the insurgent element." Examples of such acts included leading American troops to enemy camps, identifying insurgents, and denouncing members of the insurgent shadow government. Civilian neutrality was no longer acceptable. Either a person demonstrated by deed, not word, that he opposed Malvar's insurgents or he was considered hostile. No person was to receive credit merely for doing nothing against the Americans.[19]

Within two weeks of launching his campaign, Bell called for increasingly harsh measures in order to apply extreme pressure against the region's elites. Bell knew that since the beginning of the insurgency the *ilustrado* class had provided both revolutionary leadership and vital material support. What he did not realize was that the insurgency in Batangas now extended beyond this class. So in a special "confidential" telegraphic order—Bell recognized the howls of protest this order would produce if exposed to the public—he attacked what he thought was the root of the insurgency by ordering the arrest of all municipal officials, priests, and policemen who failed to perform unmistakable acts against the insurgents. If a mayor had denounced an enemy agent, if a policeman had guided the Americans to a food cache, he was considered loyal. Everyone else was given the choice to do the same or go to prison. Another tactic was to arrest the relatives of prominent guerrilla leaders and hold them hostage for the conduct of the insurgents. Of course it was desirable to have "proof" before making such arrests, but in the absence of evidence a well-founded suspicion was acceptable grounds for arrest and indefinite confinement.[20]

More of the same followed. What was good for the gentry was good for all. Bell ordered that captured insurgents, meaning any males outside the zones, be brought to trial for violation of the laws of war unless they provided useful intelligence about the insurgency. Faced with the prospect of a military trial, certain imprisonment, and possible execution, many prisoners turned collaborator. The American pressure brought a recurring problem of false denunciations. Bell responded by ordering military trials for anyone strongly suspected of this behavior. He authorized burning of dwellings near where telegraph lines were cut or bridges burned. On the day before Christmas he brought back the old Spanish law of forced work to compel the able-bodied men concentrated in towns to earn food for themselves and their families.[21] He imposed universal curfews from 8:00 p.m. to daybreak. If people refused to meet food and fuel requisitions, the town leaders were to be arrested and forced to work harvesting crops and cutting wood until the villagers complied. Likewise, if the town leaders refused to provide guides, they themselves were to be installed at the front of American patrols and forced to lead.

On December 24, 1901, Bell reiterated that the entire Filipino population was at heart opposed to the Americans. Therefore, he reminded his officers, it was necessary "to make the state of war as insupportable as possible, and there is no more efficacious way of accomplishing this than by keeping the minds of the people in such a state of anxiety and apprehension that living under such conditions will soon become unbearable."[22]

Bell was too smart merely to impose benevolent assimilation with threat, armed might, and rough treatment of prisoners. He also understood the salient importance of timely intelligence. So Bell created a nimble intelligence machine that passed information obtained from captured documents, informers, and interrogations rapidly up and down the chain of command. Each garrison had a post intelligence officer whose task was to maintain updated information about his region and its inhabitants. These officers exchanged lists of known and suspected insurgents, often annotated with physical descriptions or even photographs. When American intelligence pinpointed an insurgent column, fast-moving cavalry set off to engage them. In most cases Filipino scouts, local militia, or rebel turncoats acted as guides.

While Bell's provost marshals dismantled the insurgents' clandestine infrastructure within the concentration zones, patrols crisscrossed the hinterland. Bell believed that he had to combine pressure against civilians with relentless pressure against the armed insurgents in order to wear them down. Toward that goal, at any one time about half of Bell's manpower, 4,000 men or so, was engaged in field operations. This was "hard war" writ large. Bell issued orders to kill or capture any able-bodied man encountered, round up everyone else, and "destroy everything I find outside of the towns." Bell added, "These people need a thrashing to teach them some good common sense, and they should have it for the good of all concerned."[23] A typical large-scale operation began on the night of January 31, 1901, when 1,800 Americans established a cordon stretching about ten miles from the outskirts of Batangas. The next morning they began moving slowly like a line of army ants devouring every animal, crop, and structure encountered. The soldiers commanded by Colonel Almond Wells—about half the total—kept meticulous records of the destruction: more then 500 tons of rice and corn burned; 200 water buffalo, 800 cattle, and 680 horses killed; uncounted thousands of hogs, chickens, and goats killed; more than 6,000 houses burned.

In addition to the larger sweeps, small American patrols flooded the interior. Bell's tactical instructions encouraged aggressive response to all contacts with the insurgents. Even in the event of an ambush he wanted his men to respond with bold attacks. He judged that because of his soldiers' superior firepower and training they had achieved a moral superiority over the guerrillas and such aggressive tactics would be rewarded. In a typical operation, individual companies established a base interdicting a trail. Bell was so confident in his soldiers' superiority that he authorized the detachments to secure their bases with only one or two soldiers while everyone else went out on patrol. Detachments fanned out from this base to interdict guerrilla movement and comb through the hinterland.

Bell had warned his officers that, "inasmuch as the change of policy which has recently taken place is calculated to arouse strong resentment on the part of the enemy," the likelihood of aggressive response was high.[24] Bell overestimated insurgent capacities. Malvar's entire force numbered about 2,500 rifle-armed men. But they could not operate in large enough units to challenge even the smallest American detachment. Relentless American pressure forced the insurgents to move constantly. Seldom could they remain in place for more than a day. If they had any spare time, the desire to seek revenge paled against the need to rest and find food.

Back on December 18, 1901, General Chaffee had written, "I can't say how long it will take us to beat Malvar into surrendering, and if no surrender, can't say how long it will take us to make a wilderness of that country, but one or the other will eventually take place."[25] Indeed, the remaining hard-core guerrillas faced bleak prospects. Their supporters and relatives were in prison or living in the protected zones, where they were unable to plant and harvest and faced famine and disease. Instead of sending the guerrillas money and food, the former supporters sent messages begging them to surrender. Outside of the protected zones, too little strength remained to prevent the Americans from destroying the countryside.

During February, guerrilla demoralization spread. Some bands killed their officers and surrendered. Others abandoned their weapons and went into hiding. American troops hounded Malvar, forcing him to be "constantly on the move."[26] Malvar's fighting courage was now at odds with his intellect, which told him that continued resistance was futile. His friends and former soldiers begged him to give up. When his wife fell dangerously ill, he sent Bell a letter requesting a suspension of hostilities. Upon receipt of Bell's pledge of fair treatment, Malvar surrendered on April 16, 1902. The remaining insurgents quickly followed suit.

A dedicated *insurrecto* leader who resisted until the end was interviewed after his surrender. When asked what caused his forces to disperse and surrender he replied, "They could get no money to spend or food to eat and they had no clothes to put on."[27] Likewise, another guerrilla officer related that his command had been doing well until "the American troops began to reconcentrate the people" while continuing their relentless hunt.[28] American interrogators asked one insurgent, Norberto Mayo, why he had surrendered. Mayo spoke for many who had pledged to resist until winning independence: "They surrendered for various things; some because they were tired of staying in the field; some through fear and because they lost hope; because some of them had been injured or lost their health through life in the field; and some because their families obliged them to surrender."[29]

FIVE

Why the Americans Won

The Cost of War

THEN AND THEREAFTER THE VICTORY achieved by policies of J. Franklin Bell was controversial. His concentration policy had successfully isolated Malvar's guerrillas from the noncombatants. During a four-month campaign, four Americans soldiers were killed and nineteen wounded. The insurgents suffered 147 killed, 104 wounded, and 821 captured, and 2,934 surrendered.[1] For many Americans the testimony of Malvar's brother-in-law, who was also a province commander, vindicated Bell's strategy: "The means used in reconcentrating the people, I think, were the only ones by which war could be stopped and peace brought about in the province."[2] However, there was the troubling fact that Bell's policies also caused the deaths of about 11,000 civilians.

The problem of civilian deaths emerged by mid-January 1902 when it became apparent that civilians concentrated inside the protected zones faced famine. One American station commander reported that 30,000 civilians had been herded into an area that normally supported 5,000. Bell understood that General Order 100 decreed that the occupying army provide for the occupied. Accordingly, Bell issued orders to make the people cultivate crops inside the zones. He ordered the importation of a tremendous quantity of rice to feed civilians. He ordered his subordinates to bring food from outside the zones back to the towns. At the time he worried that these measures "might possibly create in the minds of some an impression that greater leniency in enforcing" past policies was desired.[3] Not so, he hastened to assure his subordinates.

American food distribution efforts failed to stop the dying. Large numbers of people still went hungry because of the confluence of multiple factors: a natural plague had decimated the water buffalo, the draft animal indispensable for agricultural pursuits; American troops had slaughtered surviving water buffalo wherever they found them outside the zones; the imported rice was thiamine-deficient polished rice that compromised people's immune systems; field commanders found it difficult to transport food from remote mountain hiding places back to the towns and often ignored this part of Bell's instructions.

People inside the zones did not starve to death. Rather, the lack of food and the poor nutritional value of what food there was weakened them, making them susceptible to the real killers: the anopheles mosquitos. The mosquitos normally preferred water buffalo blood. Deprived of their usual prey, they turned to human targets, which, by virtue of Bell's concentration policy, they found conveniently herded in dense masses. Malaria killed thousands. In addition, overcrowded conditions and extremely poor sanitation promoted the killing transmission of measles, dysentery, and eventually cholera. Civilian deaths in Batangas were an unintended consequence of Bell's policy of concentration and food destruction.

ON JULY 4, 1902, President Theodore Roosevelt, who became president after McKinley's assassination, declared the Philippine Insurrection over and civil government restored. Roosevelt did make a caveat regarding Moro territory, a handful of southern Philippine islands dominated by an Islamic people, but in the general glow of victory few noticed. He issued a fulsome thanks to the army, noting that they had fought with courage and fortitude in the face of enormous obstacles: "Bound themselves by the laws of war, our soldiers were called upon to meet every device of unscrupulous treachery and to contemplate without reprisal the infliction of barbarous cruelties upon their comrades and friendly natives. They were instructed, while punishing armed resistance, to conciliate the friendship of the peaceful, yet had to do with a population among whom it was impossible to distinguish friend from foe, and who in countless instances used a false appearance of friendship for ambush and assassination."[4]

Roosevelt's effusive praise not withstanding, the brutality of Bell's campaign along with Smith's crueler campaign fought on the island of

Samar brought a Senate inquiry into army misconduct. On May 23, 1902, a senator read a letter purportedly written by a West Point graduate serving in the Philippines that described a *reconcentrado* pen with a dead line outside. A "corpse-carcass stench" wafted into the writer's nostrils as he wrote. "At nightfall clouds of vampire bats softly swirl out on their orgies over the dead."[5]

Roosevelt pledged a full investigation. His adjutant general established the principle for the investigation: "Great as the provocation had been in dealing with foes who habitually resort to treachery, murder, and torture against our men, nothing can justify . . . the use of torture or inhuman conduct of any kind on the part of the American Army."[6] The subsequent investigation provided sensational allegations supported by extensive testimony. It became clear that torture had taken place and everyone knew it. One major candidly wrote a comrade, "You, as well as I, know that in bringing to a successful issue [the war] certain things will take place not intended by the higher authorities."[7] Numerous witnesses testified to the use of the "water cure." A veteran composed "The Water Cure in the P.I.," sung to the tune of "The Battle Cry of Freedom," one verse of which went:

> We've come across the bounding main to kindly spread around
> Sweet liberty whenever there are rebels to be found.
> So hurry with the syringe boys. We've got him down and bound,
> Shouting the battle cry of freedom.[8]

The shooting of unarmed men and the execution of wounded and prisoners also proved to be commonplace. A Maine soldier in the Forty-third Infantry wrote to his local newspaper that "eighteen of my company killed seventy-five nigger bolomen and ten of the nigger gunners . . . When we find one that is not dead, we have bayonets."[9] The official War Department report for 1900 revealed how widespread was the practice of finishing off wounded insurgents. The U.S. Army had killed 14,643 insurgents and wounded a mere 3,297. This ratio was the inverse of military experience dating back to the American Civil War and could only be explained by the slaughter of the wounded. When asked about this during the Senate inquiry, MacArthur blithely explained that it was due to the superior marksmanship of the well-trained U.S. soldiers.[10]

MacArthur, like the other senior commanders in the Philippines, had

issued orders and guidelines against coercive behavior while acknowledging that sometimes field conditions required extraordinary behavior.
The senators accepted this explanation. In the end, the Senate inquiry
documented frequent American excursions outside the bounds of behavior permitted by the laws of war while whitewashing the conduct of the
officers in charge. This conclusion satisfied Roosevelt, who had promised
to back the army wherever it operated lawfully and legitimately. Thereafter, Roosevelt kept faith with the hard men of the Philippines. During
his administration he named Adna Chaffee and later J. Franklin Bell to
the army's highest post, chief of staff of the U.S. Army. For Chaffee it represented an unprecedented climb that began as a Civil War private. For
Bell, it represented vindication after the humiliating Senate inquiry.

Anatomy of Victory

The collapse of the organized insurgency in the Philippines removed the
islands from the forefront of American consciousness. The tactics employed to squash the guerrillas disillusioned Americans and most were
happy to forget about the distant islands as soon as possible. Thereafter
American history recalled the sinking of the battleship *Maine*, Teddy Roosevelt's Rough Riders, and the "Splendid Little War" against Spain. Yet
the Spanish-American War had lasted only months, while the Philippine
Insurrection officially persisted for more than three years and involved
four times as many American soldiers. Regardless, few Americans paid
attention to what had transpired in the Philippines until forty years later
when a new event, Arthur MacArthur's son Douglas's doomed defense of
the islands against Japanese invasion, superseded all else. Subsequently,
even military historians largely disregarded the Philippine Insurrection
until American involvement in Vietnam compelled renewed interest in
how to fight Asian guerrillas.

By 1902, officers who served in the Philippines came to a near unani-
mous conclusion that commitment to a policy of attraction had prolonged
the conflict. Colonel Arthur Murray expressed a combat soldier's view.
When he first assumed regimental command, Murray opposed punitive
measures because they caused innocent people to suffer and turned potentially friendly people into insurgents. His experience on the ground
changed his mind: "If I had my work out there to do over again, I would

do possibly a little more killing and considerably more burning than I did."[11] Most officers concluded that the key to a successful counterinsurgency was decisive military action employing severe policies of chastisement. To their minds, the Filipino insurgents had given up the fight for the same reasons Robert E. Lee surrendered: both were unwilling to endure the pain that continued resistance would bring. As an inhabitant of Batangas explained in an interview decades after the conflict had ended, "When the people realized that they were overpowered they were forced to accept the Americans."[12]

When the Americans invaded in 1899, victory depended upon the suppression of violent opposition to the United States by replacing the control exercised by the Philippine revolutionary government with American control. The American solution had three components. First was to persuade the Filipinos that they were better off under the American vision of their future. This effort came quite naturally because Americans sincerely believed it. In American minds, the Spanish had exploited the islands. The revolutionary government continued both the exploitation and the entrenched, Spanish-style inefficiency and corruption. The Americans had no particular insight into Filipino "hearts and minds." Without any extensive thought, they assumed that Filipinos—indeed, all reasonable people—wanted what Americans wanted. So both military officers and civilian administrators worked hard to make real physical improvements to show the Filipinos that their future was brighter under American rule. This notion guided the policy of attraction.

The second component of American pacification emerged when American leaders realized that attraction alone was insufficient. The military had to devise a way to end the insurgent hold on the people. In some areas the Americans were able to exploit ethnic, religious, or class differences to enlist native support. With the help of collaborators, the Americans identified and eliminated insurgent operatives. But in areas where resistance was the fiercest and the fear of insurgent retaliation too high, collaborators did not appear. So the American pacification effort forcibly separated the insurgents from the people by concentrating them in the so-called protected zones.

The third component of American pacification was military field operations. The field operations were essential to prevent guerrillas from massing against isolated American outposts and to deny them opportunities to rest and recover. Naturally most officers preferred such operations because they better represented the war for which they had trained. Likewise, their soldiers, particularly the volunteers who had come seeking adventure and fighting, preferred "chastisement" to attraction. As one lieutenant noted, the American soldier was a poor "peace soldier" but a mighty "war soldier." Victory in the field came from the skilled practice of recognized military craft: scouting, march security, aggressive small-unit action. The American three-part strategy was like a tripod: without any one of the three legs it would collapse.

On a strategic level, the Philippine Insurrection highlighted the vital role of the civilian population. An insurgency could not be suppressed as long as the insurgents readily blended into a supportive general population. Accordingly, the army used a variety of measures to control the population while destroying the insurgent infrastructure, the shadow government. This destruction could not progress without Filipino assistance. In most areas, the people waited until they saw that the American army could protect them from insurgent terror before they supported the Americans. In southern Luzon, J. Franklin Bell found ways to compel civilian collaboration by extreme force, thereby proving himself to be, in the words of Matt Batson, "the real terror of the Philippines."[13]

An analysis of how the Americans won must recognize notable weaknesses and blunders committed by the insurgent leadership. Simply stated, the man at the top, Emilio Aguinaldo, was an inept military commander. After losing a conventional war to the Spanish, Aguinaldo and his subordinates adopted the same approach to fight the Americans. The result was an unbroken chain of tactical defeats that wiped out the best insurgent units. Only then did Aguinaldo opt for what always was his best strategic choice, guerrilla warfare.

The *ilustrado* class chose not to appeal to latent Filipino nationalism because they feared losing their hold on society. Consequently, the revolution of 1898 did not change the lives of most Filipinos. For centuries Filipinos had been forced by the Spanish to accommodate a colonial culture. Before the revolution a local elite had controlled the peasants' daily life. The transition from Spanish to revolutionary government did not change this essential fact of life. The Americans came and made their own, but hardly new, set of demands. Now both the revolutionary government and the Americans levied taxes, administered justice, and used force as the ultimate suasion. A Filipino, poor or rich, assessed his prospects and either picked a side or tried to stay removed from the fray. The most adroit straddled both sides, portraying themselves as supporters of whichever side presented the most immediate peril. In the words of Glenn May, one of the conflict's foremost modern historians, for an insurgency "to win any war with lukewarm public support is difficult enough; to win a guerrilla war on one's own soil under those circumstances is virtually impossible."[14]

The insurgents suffered from a crippling lack of firearms and ammunition. Although the Filipinos tried to purchase weapons from other countries, they were seldom successful. Geography played a role. The U.S. Navy interdicted most vessels trying to deliver supplies for the insurgents, an operation made easy by the fact that no foreign government became involved in the supply effort. In addition, the navy prevented cooperation among the Filipino leaders on different islands. The Americans also benefited hugely from the fact that their enemy had no secure areas, no sanctuaries that were out of bounds to American intervention.

Throughout the war, the Americans could and did isolate the battlefield and bring overwhelming firepower to bear. This was not the indiscriminate firepower of a B-52 bomber or a battery of 155 mm howitzers. Rather, it was most often the firepower of a foot soldier sighting his Krag-Jorgensen rifle. Against the massive American superiority, the guerrillas could conduct pinprick raids but there was nothing they could do to change the calculus of battle. Their only chance was that the American public might turn against the war. At first the insurgents invested great hope that Bryan would defeat McKinley. While there was a spirited anti-imperialist movement at the turn of the century, it never achieved wide political support among voting Americans.

McKinley's reelection reduced the anti-imperialists to harassing the administration without being able to change national strategy. It left the insurgents with only the hope that America would grow war-weary and abandon the struggle. American soldiers fighting in the Philippines keenly understood the vital importance of domestic support for the war. Brigadier General Robert P. Hughes, who served as provost marshal of Manila, told the Senate committee that it was the universal opinion of everyone who went to the Philippines "that the main element in pacifying the Philippines is a settled policy in America."[15]

The Senate Committee in January 1902 asked Taft if a safe and honorable method for withdrawal from the Philippines could be devised. He replied no and elaborated that at the present moment an assessment of the effort to end the insurgency was too bound up in politics. However, "when the facts become known, as they will be known within a decade . . . history will show, and when I say history I mean the accepted judgment of the people . . . that the course we are now pursuing is the only course possible."[16]

Afterward

While most American historians cite the campaign in the Philippines as an outstanding counterinsurgency success, little mention is made of what took place after Roosevelt declared the war over on July 4, 1902. Five years after the declaration of peace, 20 percent of the entire U.S. Army still remained in the Philippines. American involvement in the islands was costing American taxpayers millions of dollars a year in an era when $1 million represented an enormous sum.

The U.S. Army handed responsibility for keeping the peace to the Philippine Constabulary, who found that they had their hands very full indeed. In all guerrilla wars, the distinction between insurgents and bandits becomes blurred. In the war's aftermath, armed men accustomed to preying on the civilian population to obtain their material needs often find it difficult to stop. Jesse James comes to mind. In the Philippines this class of men were known as *ladrones*, or brigands.

The *ladrones* had been active before the Americans came; some became notable participants in the fight against the Americans, and many continued to operate after the peace. They imposed their will through intimidation and terror while specializing in rustling, extortion, and robbery. In the province of Albay, on Luzon's southern tip, armed resistance resumed in the middle of 1902. The Americans insisted on calling them "bandits," although their numbers peaked at some 1,500 men and they operated according to a military structure. The "bandits" held out for more than a year in the face of a brutal counterinsurgency campaign fought by members of the Philippine Constabulary and Philippine Scouts commanded by American officers. Elsewhere, a former guerrilla proclaimed the "Republic of Katagalugan" with the goal of opposing U.S. sovereignty. He surrendered in July 1906 and was duly executed. As late as 1910, Constabulary agents in Batangas warned that a shadowy organization whose roots stemmed from the fight against the Americans was preparing a new insurrection.

In Samar, late in 1902 armed bands again descended from the mountainous interior to raid coastal villages. They were a mix of *ladrones*, never-say-die common soldiers, and a bizarre mystical sect. The Constabulary fought a losing battle against them until 1904, at which point the U.S. Army intervened. The subsequent fighting on Samar became so tough that American insurance companies refused policies to junior officers bound for this region. The violence continued until 1911.

Roosevelt's proclamation of peace had little impact on the Moros, a collection of some ten different ethnic groups who lived among the southern islands and followed the Islamic faith. They constituted about 10 percent of the Philippine population and were not racially different from other Filipinos but had been long separated due to their Islamic beliefs. Their conflict with ruling powers, in particularly Christians and Tagalogs, went back centuries. On Mindanao and Jolo in particular, they battled against the U.S. occupation troops in an effort to establish a separate sovereignty. A three-year campaign involving Captain John J. Pershing among others officially ended the so-called Moro Rebellion. Yet here too fighting continued past the official close of the conflict. Indeed, close-quarter combat convinced the army to introduce the Colt .45 automatic pistol in 1911, a weapon with enough stopping power to drop in his tracks the fanatical Muslim tribesman. Fighting persisted through 1913 but the Moro dream of sovereignty did not die with the advent of peace. This dream again spawned an insurgency in the 1960s, this time directed against the Philippine government. The violence continues to this day as the Moro Islamic Liberation Front struggles with the Philippine government and Al Qaeda–linked groups maintain training centers on the island of Jolo and elsewhere.[17] Thus, the dictates of the worldwide "War on Terror" send U.S. Special Forces to the same areas that witnessed the Moro Rebellion.

While the Philippine insurgency still raged, two insightful men, one a war correspondent, the other an army colonel, contemplated the future for both Americans and Filipinos. The war correspondent, Albert Robinson, respected the Filipinos and deeply believed that they deserved self-rule. But he recognized this would not come easily. He thought that aspiring Filipino politicians lacked balance, a feat achieved in America by virtue of the embedded checks and balances in the Constitution as well as a cultural tradition. In time, he judged, the Filipinos would acquire this balance, but until that time the United States was "morally committed" to protecting "against disorder arising out of struggle for leadership." This protection required American cultural sensitivity in the form of tact and restraint: "The great danger in American interference in Filipino affairs

lies in the idea that American ways are best and right, and regardless of
established habit, custom, and belief, these ways must be accepted by any
and all people."[18]

At the end of 1901 a colonel who had served as military governor of
Cebu wrote eloquently about the possibility that the Philippines would
one day enjoy the American promise of government for and by the people. Toward that lofty goal it was necessary to work hard to educate the
Filipinos about self-government. Such education would take time: "We,
and they, will be fortunate if it be secured in a generation." He warned
that many Americans underestimated Filipino mistrust of Americans
and misunderstood how Filipino nationalism motivated their opposition
to U.S. controls. The colonel observed that "too many Americans are inclined to think the struggle over" and the work of establishing a stable,
just government nearly completed. They were wrong, he claimed, and
added that guerrilla warfare would persist for years. He asserted that the
correct American response was the sincere promotion of justice coupled
with patience. This goal required the selection of "Americans of character, learning, experience and integrity" to implement civil government.
"The islands are now ours, for better or worse," he wrote. "Let us make
it for the better by looking the future bravely in the face, without for one
moment losing interest in our work. Above all, let it be a national and
not a party question."[19]

During the war almost every unit in the United States Army served at
one time or another in the Philippines. Here the army enjoyed its greatest
counterinsurgency success in its history. Yet then and thereafter the army
was not particularly enamored with its victory. Since its birth during the
American Revolution, the army had measured itself against conventional
European armies. With this mind-set, it viewed the Philippine Insurrection as an exception, something distasteful and outside its true role.
Henceforth, it was more than willing to cede responsibility for fighting
the nation's "small wars" to a rival service, the United States Marine Corps.
So the hard-earned lessons of a nasty fight against Filipino insurgents
were quickly forgotten as army planners refocused on conventional warfare against European foes.

PART TWO

The War in Algeria

SIX

Terror on All Saints' Day

This is not Indochina. This is not Korea.
But it is a nasty piece of work.

—A French captain on patrol in Algeria[1]

The French Challenge

IN 1827 THE DEY OF ALGIERS ALLEGEDLY struck the French consul with a fly whisk. The insult provided a convenient pretext for France to maintain a naval blockade of Algiers. The failure of economic pressure, the blockade, and the failure of "diplomacy" in the form of three years spent ineffectually plotting to overthrow the uppity dey convinced French leaders to invade Algeria in 1830. They explained to the natives that they came not to war against the people but rather to expel their Turkish rulers and allow the Arabs to be masters of their own country. In fact, politicians in France had concluded that a foreign military adventure would solidify army support for the restoration regime of Charles X. This calculation proved erroneous. A few weeks after the invasion Charles X's regime fell. But by then the French army controlled Algiers and its leaders were eager to colonize the rest of the country. It was a decision that led to an occupation that lasted for the next 132 years.

Before the French invaded, the country the French called Algeria had no history of nationhood or self-rule. The Carthaginians, Romans, and

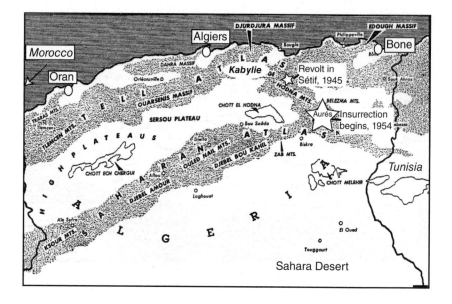

Vandals all preceded the Arab conquest that came in A.D. 643. Before the sixteenth-century Ottoman conquest, the western part of Algeria was often closely associated with Morocco while the eastern part followed the lead set by Tunisia. The few home-grown Muslim dynasties that developed in Algeria did not last long. However, history, language, custom, and the practice of Islam made the native people an integral part of the larger Arab world.

All would-be rulers discovered that geography made Algeria a difficult country to control. It had an area three times the size of Texas. Large mountain chains formed barriers to north-south communication. The formidable Sahara Desert extended along Algeria's southern border, while the lack of good natural harbors along the Mediterranean shoreline limited access from the sea to the hinterlands. Most people lived along the Mediterranean coastal strip, where fertile soil and rain allowed agriculture, and it was here that the Europeans settled as well.

From the beginning many of the natives resented the French presence. A series of rebellions against the "Christian invasion" failed, but the embers of revolt remained to ignite subsequent struggle. The inhabitants of the rugged Kabylie (or Kabylia), a non-Arab regional minority, proved particularly difficult to subdue. Not until 1871 did the French suppress their last, great rebellion. Thereafter, for an elite subset of French bureaucrats and military officers, the preservation of the conquest became a profound matter of honor.

The elimination of native resistance and confiscation of the best land opened the way to European colonization. Thousands came from Spain to live around the great port of Oran, while Italians, Maltese, and French settled farther east around Algiers and Bone. But in the eyes of French administrators, Algeria was destined to be a French colony pure and simple. In 1848 settlers converted the three Turkish provinces to departments on the French model and colonization expanded rapidly. The colonists soon established political, economic, and social domination. The Arabs who saw the first French settlers arrive collectively nicknamed them *pieds-noirs* (black feet), apparently in reference to their wearing black leather shoes. The *pieds-noirs* modernized Algeria, building roads, railroads, hospitals, and schools where select natives were allowed to learn French language, history, and culture. The Europeans created prosperous agricultural plantations along the Mediterranean coast where grains, olives, and grapes grew in a favored environment of fertile soil, sun, and water. By 1945, some 1 million Europeans, of whom fewer than 20 percent were of pure French descent, lived in Algeria. By now Algeria was jurisdictionally a part of France, which added to the power of the *pieds-noirs* since they sent delegates to the French parliament. For most *pieds-noirs*, particularly those on the top rungs of the economic ladder, life was good and the future appeared bright.

The Rise of the FLN

In 1945 thousands of Muslim inhabitants of the Algerian town of Sétif revolted against French rule and massacred more than 100 European settlers. In French eyes the attack was unprovoked. The French military responded with brutal repression, subjecting suspect Muslim villages to systematic punishment called *ratissage*, literally a "raking-over." An unknown number of killings ensued, with the total undoubtedly higher than the official French report of 1,800. It proved a watershed moment. The excessive French reprisal alienated a population that might not otherwise have sided with the rebels. A liberal Algerian poet, Kateb Yacine, was sixteen years old at the time. He spoke for the Muslim majority when he recalled that the "pitiless" French reprisal marked the "moment my nationalism took definite form."[2]

Although largely unnoticed by the general population in France, the

Sétif incident alarmed the French political class. In 1947 the French assembly passed a new "bill of rights" for Algeria. It responded to Muslim demands with important reforms including the recognition that Muslims would be considered as full French citizens with the right to work in France. However, the creation of an Algerian assembly with 120 deputies revealed the maintenance of colonial rule. Some 370,000 Europeans and 60,000 "assimilated" Muslims elected half the deputies. The country's other legal voters, some 1.3 million Muslims, also elected half of the deputies. Thus, the Algerian assembly was a far cry from representative government. Moreover, the *pieds-noirs* blocked the implementation of most reforms. The 1948 elections for the new Algerian assembly featured widespread fraud. Subsequently, 9 million native Algerians, most of whom were Muslim, understood that the legal path to reform was closed to them. *Pied-noir* intransigence drove them toward the path of violence.

There were several nationalist movements inside Algeria but only one advocated the use of all necessary means to end French rule. This movement coalesced into the Front de libération nationale (FLN). The typical FLN leader was a male in his early thirties, of modest origin, education, and prospects. Many, like Ahmed Ben Bella, the man who became the movement's principal leader, were former members of the French army. Some had returned from World War II festooned with French military medals. Ben Bella had earned the Croix de Guerre in 1940 and the Médaille Militaire in 1944. Ben Bella and his fellow combat veterans contrasted their war experience—the equality of shared danger in the bitter mountain fighting against German fortifications during the Italian campaign—with the open discrimination they found in postwar Algeria. Ben Bella was among the many who saw the rigged election of 1948 as final proof that any hope of achieving independence at the voting booth was illusory. The revolutionaries did not view the world according to a set political ideology. What united them was opposition to French rule. What separated them from the thousands of similar men who lived in Algeria during the 1950s was their willingness to fight to the finish to accomplish this goal and their willingness to sacrifice their lives. The FLN objective was the restoration of a sovereign Algerian state. It advocated social democracy within an Islamic framework.

When FLN leaders contemplated strategy they appreciated that the Communist Chinese formula for anticolonial insurgencies began with the creation of a strong revolutionary party. The construction of this necessary foundation took time. Once the foundation was set, the revolutionary front could proceed to terrorist violence and initiate guerrilla warfare. The ensuing disruption would produce opportunities to acquire base areas, or liberated zones. Here the front would organize a regular army to begin conventional war.

The insurgent leadership in Algeria were impatient strategists. They decided to take a shortcut by beginning with violence and seeing what ensued. In the spring of 1954, Ben Bella and other Algerian nationalists convened in Cairo, where, with the full support of the aspiring leader of the pan-Arab nationalist movement, Egyptian president Gamal Abdel Nasser, they formed the Revolutionary Committee for Unity and Action. The committee ignored existing Algerian nationalist groups and instead decided on bold, decisive action to drive the French out of Algeria and install themselves in power.

An event in faraway Vietnam, the surrender of the French garrison of Dien Bien Phu on May 7, 1954, after an epic fifty-six-day siege, galvanized Algerian militants. Before, only a handful of nationalists supported the notion of military struggle with France. The task seemed too daunting. Dien Bien Phu demonstrated French vulnerability and emboldened Algerians to conceive that they could successfully fight their way to independence. Using the French Resistance as their model, FLN leaders prepared an Algerian resistance movement. It relied on one military weapon and one political weapon. The military weapon was domestic guerrilla warfare featuring hit-and-run raids, ambushes, and sabotage. The political weapon relied upon the international climate that in the wake of World War II nominally favored self-determination. The FLN intended to assert the right of self-determination on the international stage, particularly at the United Nations. FLN leaders expected this assertion to garner support from other Arab nations. They also intended to capitalize on Cold War schisms to receive support from the Communist bloc.

FLN leaders selected the Aurès massif, a mountain chain extending across eastern Algeria, as the most promising region to launch their campaign. The rugged Aurès mountains, with their razorback ridges separated by deep ravines and scattered pine, live oak, and cedar forests, were a traditional refuge for men fleeing invaders or the law. Even by Algerian standards the Aurès was a poverty-stricken region where subsistence farmers lived in mud-daubed villages. Banditry was nearly as common as sheep herding. Three times in the past hundred years the Aurès had re- volted against the French. The FLN calculated that such people would happily support a fourth revolt. Moreover, a native revolutionary of the re- gion, Belkacem Krim, already had an organized and armed guerrilla band hidden in the heartland of the Aurès mountains. Better still, in 1954 in all the massif only seven gendarmes were present to represent French law.

Couriers carried instructions across Algeria: "Arm, train and prepare." In the crowded Muslim quarter of Algiers, the infamous Casbah, a dedi- cated terrorist named Zoubir Bouadjadj set up a network of bomb- making factories. Elsewhere, insurgents smuggled firearms past police outposts, everything from World War I–era bolt action rifles to weapons carelessly lost by American GIs during the 1942 invasion of North Africa. Most fighters had to be content with unreliable hunting guns better suited for shooting a feral goat than a French regular.

The effort to create a revolutionary infrastructure without solid prepa- ration did not work. Recruitment for the *djounoud*, the "soldiers of faith," failed to attract many candidates; most people chose to wait and see what happened before choosing sides. The FLN leadership cared not. Inspired by news of French failure in Indochina, they wanted to strike while oppor- tunity beckoned. D-Day for the simultaneous outbreak of rebellion would be one minute after midnight on November 1, 1954, the day France, and most especially the staunchly Catholic *pieds-noirs*, celebrated as All Saints' Day.

The Counterinsurgency Begins

During World War II, diverse French political parties had forged bonds of mutual self-interest in order to oppose the Germans. After the war those bonds became unstable as shaky coalition governments collapsed one after another. Military men disdainfully spoke of striving politicians while French citizens took solace in the fact that a strong and competent bureaucracy administered the country regardless of the political circus at the top. However, short-lived coalitions could not muster a coherent national response if trouble arose in the colonies. The postwar rise of nationalism in Africa brought that trouble barely six months after Dien Bien Phu's surrender.

The number of Algerian rebels who participated in the All Saints' Day revolt probably did not exceed 700. They conducted seventy simultaneous attacks at scattered places throughout Algeria, killing seven people and wounding four. This was hardly a devastating blow. It made a minimal first impression in France, where few suspected that a war had begun. Indeed, the rebels lacked firearms, their homemade explosive devices were unreliable, and there were simply too few insurgents ready to start fighting. The poverty of resources was such that although the FLN leaders had ambitiously divided Algeria into six military-political districts, or *wilayas*, for almost a year following the All Saints' Day revolt three of the district chiefs had neither followers nor weapons.

In Algeria, when the Europeans recovered from their initial shock and assessed the situation, they quickly perceived the rebels' weaknesses. Among the *pieds-noirs* a deep sense of outrage replaced initial fears. The FLN campaign slogan calling on the Europeans to leave or risk death, "The suitcase or the coffin," amazed them. For generations they had made this country their home and it was inconceivable that anyone should challenge their right to call themselves Algerians.

In France itself, the All Saints' Day revolt presented a major political challenge. There were two alternatives to war: rapid and fair integration of Algeria into metropolitan France and disengagement. Neither choice was politically acceptable. Ethnic, religious, cultural, and racial divisions between French and Algerians made equitable integration a nonstarter. Disengagement was psychologically difficult. French leaders, the army, and the people still reeled from the humiliating events of 1940, when a German blitzkrieg overran the fatherland. Postwar loss of the colonial empire threatened to reduce France to second-rate status. The gallant but futile defense of Dien Bien Phu was still very much in everyone's mind. France's Algerian lobby and the army were powerful political influences and neither body could countenance losing another valuable and prestige-conferring colony. The politicians bent with the prevailing wind.

French determination to hold Algeria arose from the interplay of multiple factors, the most salient of which were the presence of close to a million settlers, the legal fiction that Algeria was an integral part of France, wounded pride, and last but not least the discovery of oil in the Sahara desert in Algeria's far south.

For these reasons the mandate to retain Algeria as part of metropolitan France extended across political parties. The French premier representing the Radical Party, Pierre Mendès-France, told the National Assembly in November 1954 that Algeria was part of France and that it was inconceivable that it should be otherwise. He emphasized that a "blow struck at the French of Algeria, be they Moslem or European, is a blow struck at the whole nation." Applause from delegates of all stripes greeted his words as he emotionally intoned there could be no compromise when it came to "defending the internal peace of the nation and the integrity of the Republic."[3] Mendès-France pledged to send massive military reinforcements to restore order. His minister of the interior, François Mitterrand, a member of the left wing, added that "the only possible negotiation is war."[4] Later, Mendès-France's successor, the Socialist premier Guy Mollet, said, "France without Algeria would be no longer France."[5]

This viewpoint and its undergirding logic dictated how France responded to the crisis. For the duration of the conflict the French government treated the insurgents as citizens engaged in outlaw behavior. They were subject to the law in the same way a citizen of Paris or Marseilles was subject to the law. The government sent the military to Algeria to restore and maintain order in the same way it dispatched riot police to a city on the mainland. This legal distinction that described Algeria as part of metropolitan France carried significant implications. In the arena of foreign affairs, no international law prevented a government from suppressing an internal rebellion. No foreign power could legitimately support the rebels or intervene on their behalf. In the arena of French military conduct, counterinsurgency efforts were nominally subject to French law. This would be observed in the breach, with the government itself permitting and encouraging extralegal measures with a wink and a nod.

The French Military

From a military standpoint, the outbreak of terror in Algeria came at a bad time. The army's most experienced guerrilla fighters were still in slow transit from Indochina. Troubles in neighboring Morocco and Tunisia, both of which were also asserting their right to self-rule, tied down another 140,000 men. Commitment to NATO occupied additional divisions. Few

trained reserves remained. In Algeria itself, there were about 49,000 security forces of all types among whom a mere 3,500 were combat effective
soldiers. The available air transport was indicative of the military's poor
state of combat readiness: eight leftover World War II–era Junkers transport planes, a type already obsolete ten years earlier, and one helicopter.
Given that the insurgents' tactic of choice was terror, the role of the police
would be crucial. Yet the total number of police in Algeria barely exceeded
the size of the Parisian police force. The logical answer to the manpower
shortage was to recall French reserves, but such strong medicine was politically unpalatable.

Instead, French authorities brazenly dismissed the initial wave of terrorist acts as "ordinary banditry." This failure to appreciate the true challenge enabled the rebels to pass through the revolution's precarious first
stage. Henceforth, its spread became inevitable. By the time French authorities recognized the rebellion for what it was, there was no easy re-
course. Firm, even bold political and military action was the only possible
strategy for victory. Instead, the succession of weak French governments
tried hastily devised reforms to undercut the insurgents. These economic
and social reforms only hardened the insurgents' resolve and encouraged
the FLN to limit the alternatives they presented to the French colonists to
two: "the suitcase or the coffin."

IN ALGERIA THE initial official response to the outbreak of violence was
the predictable overreaction of an embarrassed administration. First came
heavy-handed, indiscriminate arrests of suspects, thereby converting neutrals to the cause of the insurgency. Next came French government resistance to reform, a stance widely acclaimed by hard-liners in France and
the *pieds-noirs*. And then, too late, came official proposals for meaningful
reform.

During the winter of 1954–55, the French army conducted several
clumsy operations featuring conventional, large-scale pincer operations
designed to trap and eliminate the guerrillas. The insurgents were seldom
to be found. Somehow their intelligence network—the Arab "bush telegraph," using beacon fires lit from peak to peak—outpaced both the
French mechanized columns and their foot-slogging brethren. It was
soon apparent that in the battle for intelligence the insurgents held a big
edge. Worse, the large scale sweeps proved counterproductive. One French

analyst caustically observed, "To send in tank units, to destroy villages, to
bombard certain zones, this is no longer the fine comb [*ratissage*]; it is using a sledgehammer to kill fleas. And what is much more serious, it is to
encourage the young—and sometimes the less young—to go into the
maquis."[6] Indeed, an FLN leader confirmed that this style of French operations was "our best recruiting agent."[7] After one typical French military
operation caused the death of an innocent Muslim woman, an FLN leader
remarked, "*Voilà*, we've won another battle. They hate the French a little
more now. The stupid bastards are winning the war for us."[8]

At this time French leaders still failed to understand thoroughly the political dimensions of the struggle. FLN appeals to nationalism were useful
insurgent tools in the competition for popular support inside Algeria.
More effective was the endless repetition of a potent propaganda message
delivered to Algerian Muslims who sat on the fence: "The French swore
they would never leave Indochina; they left. Now they pledge to never
abandon Algeria." In 1956, after France announced the independence of
neighboring Morocco and Tunisia, revolutionary propagandists had two
examples much closer to home of France reneging on its solemn vows.

Jacques Soustelle, soon to be appointed governor-general to Algeria,
described the essential question asked by all French sympathizers: " 'Are
you leaving or staying?' There is no officer, who assuming command of
his post in a village . . . has not been asked this question by the local notables. What it meant was: 'If the village raises the French flag, if this or that
family head agrees to become mayor, if we send our sons and daughters to
school, if we hand out weapons of self-defense, if we refuse to supply the
fellaghas roaming around the djebel with barley, sheep and money, will
you, the army, be here to defend us from reprisals?' "[9]

If armed French regulars possessed too much firepower for the insurgents to risk an attack and European civilians were not yet on the target list, French sympathizers among the Muslim population remained
vulnerable. A village policeman found with his throat slit—a particularly
humiliating death normally reserved for slaughtering sheep and goats—
and an FLN placard pinned to his corpse, an Algerian vineyard manager
employed by a French owner found tortured and killed, and an outspo-
ken pro-French village elder subjected to slow death within a few hundred yards of a French army base, all conveyed the terrorist message to
cease collaborating with the French.

Targeted terrorism also sought to drive a wedge between the Muslim and the French population by compelling rural Muslims to burn schools and destroy public properties in order to bring French repression. The FLN also worked to raise Muslim political consciousness by rigid enforcement of Islamic rites. One notable tactic was to enforce a ban on public tobacco consumption. A few public chastisements where a smoker's nose was cut off went a long way toward enforcing a national tobacco boycott. The Front also organized local political cadres whose main job was to collect taxes to support the insurgency. Having initially made the strategic error of impatience, the FLN focused on building revolutionary infrastructure by mobilizing the population through persuasion and terror.

SEVEN

Terror Without Limits

The Philippeville Massacre

THE STRATEGY PROMOTED BY FRENCH president Mendès-France called for simultaneous reform and military pressure. When the insurrection began there were 2,000 employees in the general government of Algeria. Eight were Muslims. To help redress this imbalance a new school of administration gave Muslim Algerians access to public sector management positions. Nationwide, only 15 percent of Muslim children attended school. Proposed educational measures addressed this issue. The average European's salary was twenty-eight times that of the Muslim. Economic measures sought to reduce the gap between Algerian and European salaries. In sum, comprehensive economic and social reforms would give Algeria more equal standing within France's political structure. The problem with this approach was obvious: it threatened the *pieds-noirs*, who wanted to preserve the status quo, but failed to satisfy the FLN, which wanted nothing less than full independence. Lack of progress in Algeria and fierce opposition from the Algerian lobby brought down the Mendès-France government in February 1955. The Algerian lobby in France and many *pieds-noirs* celebrated the government's collapse. In their view, now could begin the proper employment of force. FLN leaders likewise welcomed Mendès-France's ouster. They regarded his promise of liberal reform as a dire political threat to their goal of total independence.

One of Mendès-France's last acts before his ouster was to appoint a new governor-general for Algeria, Jacques Soustelle. Soustelle was a remarkable man who by age forty-three had already enjoyed an outstanding

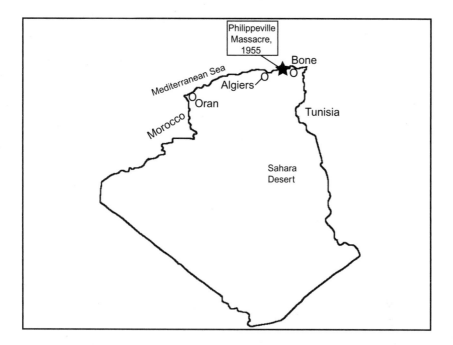

career as academic, political thinker, administrator, and World War II partisan. In February 1955 Soustelle toured Algeria and quickly saw that the situation was much worse than metropolitan France realized. The French military had understood the paramount importance of recruiting and employing large numbers of Muslims. In turn, the guerrillas made examples of these "loyal" Muslims, subjecting them to torture, mutilation, and death. Soustelle realized that FLN terror had driven the Muslim majority into fearful neutrality. "The Administration and the Army," Soustelle wrote, "had seen information dry up . . . Fear closed mouths and hardened faces."[1]

Soustelle represented the school of thought that poverty breeds revolution. His response, the so-called Soustelle Plan, and its subsequent variants sought to combat the insurrection through social and economic reforms. This school of analysis had superficial validity. The impoverished peasants of the Aurès mountains had little to lose by joining the insurrection. However, the urban poor were equally destitute yet did not initially participate in the insurrection. A grand strategy based on the wrong diagnosis could not succeed. Expensive social and economic reforms designed to conquer poverty were of limited value when the conflict was really about politics. The FLN did not fight to banish poverty; they fought to banish French rule.

The arrival of substantial French reinforcements in Algeria frustrated the insurgents' hopes for a quick victory. French military pressure drove many guerrilla bands into hiding, where the hard winter of 1954–55 seriously depleted their ranks. In March 1955 Soustelle asked the government for the right to adapt legislation to wartime conditions. At month's end the National Assembly, while refusing to use the word *war*, voted for a state of emergency that strengthened the powers of the army. But these powers applied only to a limited zone of the Aurès. The National Assembly also authorized the first population regroupments in order to move "contaminated" populations to "settlement camps."[2]

During this time the insurgents continued to have trouble obtaining arms and ammunition—probably only half of the guerrillas who had participated in the All Saints' Day attacks were armed—so they could not openly challenge French security forces. FLN leaders realized that there would be no war-winning Algerian version of Dien Bien Phu. Henceforth, insurgent strategy relied upon fighting a low-level war of attrition that pitted their scarce armed manpower and ammunition against French national will.

Yet they had to be seen to remain active in order to prevent the Muslim population from rallying to the French cause and to encourage foreign support. So the FLN lifted restrictions on attacks against European civilians and embarked on a terror campaign without limits. Civilians became targets for indiscriminate bombings and shootings. The goal was to provoke repressive French military responses in order to alienate both the Algerian and the French people. A hand grenade tossed into a crowded cafe or a homemade bomb detonated on a school bus carrying French children could be expected to bring furious reprisals against the local Muslim population. The new policy came into sharp focus on August 20, 1955, in and around the harbor city of Philippeville.

The man who had the covert assignment of identifying and eliminating the FLN in Philippeville was Paul Aussaresses. He was a Special Services intelligence officer and a veteran of clandestine operations in World War II and Indochina—in other words, an experienced, discreet officer perfectly at ease with following orders and keeping his mouth shut. He had killed men and had participated in interrogations but up to this time never tortured anyone. That was about to change.

The Philippeville police, whose ranks composed exclusively *pieds-noirs* and "assimilated" Muslims, told him that the terrorists were up to something but that no one knew precisely what. They matter-of-factly stated that the only way to extract information from unobliging prisoners was torture. They asserted that torture was legitimate to obtain information that would save lives. Specifically, if they arrested a suspect who was involved in preparing a terrorist act such as setting a time bomb in a French grade school, a forced confession could foil the plot. Their logic persuaded Aussaresses and men like him: it was better to torture a suspected terrorist, to make a single person suffer, than to allow scores of innocent people be killed and maimed.

Aussaresses patiently assembled a list of FLN members and sympathizers. Many were common criminals, which made his job easier. When they refused to talk the police took charge. Often a beating was enough. For particularly stubborn suspects the police used a field radio as a power source and attached electrodes to the ears and testicles, the infamous *gégène*. Regardless of outcome, when the interrogation was over Aussaresses ordered the prisoners executed. He justified summary executions on the basis that the regular justice system was suitable for a peacetime situation in metropolitan France but this was Algeria, where a war of terror was under way.

In spite of Aussaresses' efforts, FLN guerrillas goaded the civilian population in and around Philippeville into indiscriminate acts of violence. Some of the worst atrocities came in the mining town of El-Halia, where Muslim workers who had seemed to enjoy a rare degree of equality with the French mine managers brutally turned on the small European community. The village constables were conveniently absent, so the attack came as a complete surprise. Guided by mineworkers, guerrillas first isolated the village by cutting telegraph lines and disabling the emergency radio transmitter. Then attackers went house to house, slaughtering Europeans without regard to age or sex. The terrorist mob entered homes and used billhooks and pitchforks to commit acts of unspeakable savagery, including ripping open the bellies of nursing mothers and hurling their infants against the wall until their brains spilled out. Thirty-seven settlers including ten children under fifteen years of age perished.

Elsewhere, purportedly urged on by chants from mobs of Muslim women and muezzins' broadcasts from the minarets exhorting the attackers to slaughter Europeans in the cause of "holy war," similar scenes of savagery played out. The victims of August 20, 1955, included seventy-one Europeans and fifty Algerians killed and scores of others maimed. What was particularly notable about the butchery was the careful planning that took place involving so many Muslims whom the French community regarded as friendly. The sense of betrayal coupled with the many sites of blood-soaked horror produced a brutal French retaliation.

When paratroopers belonging to a crack French regiment arrived in Philippeville, they beheld the mob continuing the slaughter. Under such circumstances the paratroopers had little interest in separating the insurgents from the civilians, a difficult task under any circumstance. They fired on whoever ran. Later, they rounded up prisoners, lined them up against the wall, and opened fire with machine guns. There were so many killed that burial teams used bulldozers to inter the corpses. French sources acknowledged killing 1,273 "insurgents." The actual figure is unknowable.

What is certain is that the Philippeville Massacre, as it became known, had profound consequences for the war. The rebel atrocities implacably hardened the hearts of the *pieds-noirs* and forever altered the behavior of many members of the French army and security forces. But it was the retaliation that mattered most. It handed the insurgents a victory and provided confirmation going forward for their strategy of indiscriminate terror. All the terrorists needed to do was to create an incident and await the predictable French overreaction. The greatest threat to the FLN strategic goal of full independence had been French political reform such as the measures proposed by Governor Soustelle that led to Muslim integration into a French political entity. The French reprisal at Philippeville caused moderate Muslims to repudiate integration. Guerrilla recruitment soared.

When he first heard the news, Soustelle flew to the scene of the massacre. The savagery inflicted on French women and children, the suffering of the mutilated in the hospitals—fingers hacked off, throats half slit as a warning—sickened Soustelle. From this time on his ideal of liberal reform became a remote priority, superseded by his determination to crush the rebellion. Nonetheless, Soustelle was wise enough to understand that the massacre was a victory for the FLN because it created an abyss separating the European and Muslim communities "through which flowed a river of blood."[3]

ON THE INTERNATIONAL front, the Philippeville Massacre caused the United Nations to address the Algerian problem for the first time. This was an important political victory for the FLN. The insurgents received material and propaganda support from the Communist bloc, from Iraq and Egypt, and most importantly from neighboring Morocco and Tunisia. At the United Nations it was easy for France's enemies to portray Algerian terrorists as nationalists striving to depose their colonial oppressors. An examination of a graph showing FLN activity since the start of the insurgency revealed regular peaks in November-December for the years 1955 to 1957. French intelligence called these peaks "United Nations fever" since they corresponded to the time the UN General Assembly met to discuss the situation in Algeria.

In France, the Philippeville Massacre also led to a new Socialist government in January 1956, headed by Premier Guy Mollet. Mollet's policy toward Algeria was first to win the war and then to implement reforms. Mollet and like-minded French politicians understood the vital importance of national will in murky counterinsurgency warfare. He acceded to the army's request for reinforcements by taking the important step of calling up a large number of reservists and extending the term of service for conscripts by 50 percent, from nineteen to twenty-seven months. These measures effectively nationalized the war by putting more citizens, instead of exclusively the military professionals, in harm's way. By so doing, Mollet hoped to engage the French people, to make it really matter to them who won in Algeria. He explained his calculation to a French newspaper in April 1956: "The action for Algeria will be effective only with the confident support of the entire nation, with its total commitment."[4]

Mollet also appointed Robert Lacoste, a popular veteran of both world wars, to replace Soustelle as governor-general. The strength of the army in Algeria swelled from around 50,000 in 1954 to more than half a million men by 1958, the largest overseas military commitment in French history. Mollet's emphasis on military action before political action notably shackled Lacoste. Nonetheless, Lacoste raised the Algerian minimum wage, pushed land redistribution for Algeria's land-hungry peasants, improved education, and decreed that half of all vacancies in public service go to Muslims.

Had these measures been implemented a decade earlier they might have changed history. Instead, coming in the wake of the Philippeville Massacre, most Muslims saw them as a tardy response to FLN pressure. By the summer of 1956 the rebels had won over a majority of previously uncommitted political leaders. These were the men France had depended on to help them win the battle for the hearts and minds of the Muslim masses. Then in October 1956 came an electrifying French intelligence coup.

France had decided to grant full independence to Morocco and Tunisia while concentrating its resources on retaining Algeria. In an effort to find an acceptable compromise for Algeria, the Moroccan sultan and Tunisian premier invited five principal FLN leaders, including most notably Ahmed Ben Bella, to fly to Tunis for a meeting aboard a plane chartered by the Moroccan government. In a flagrant breach of international law, French intelligence officers diverted the plane to Algiers.

Aboard the plane, the FLN leaders were totally deceived. As the plane descended, one Algerian saw the large crowd on the tarmac and exclaimed, "Why, they've organized a very handsome reception for us!" Instead the "crowd" was composed of French security forces, including tanks and armored cars. Although Ben Bella carried a pistol, he realized resistance was futile. The French arrested the leaders and confined them to prison in France. In Algeria the *pieds-noirs* rejoiced. In France one radio commentator said with deep approval, "At last France has dared!"[5]

However, the capture of the FLN's senior leaders had little effect on the direction of the rebellion. Quite simply the movement was too diffuse, too loosely organized, to crumple from this blow. Within the FLN the loss of senior leadership merely eliminated obstacles in the path of ambitious junior leaders and allowed them to climb toward the top. Still, although few realized it, a turning point had occurred. This supreme demonstration of French perfidy eliminated the possibility of a negotiated compromise. Henceforth only the military option remained.

Confronting Revolutionary Warfare

Although political instability in metropolitan France led to an erratic military response to the insurgency, 1955 witnessed a gradual military buildup in Algeria as veterans returned from Indochina. For the French Foreign Legion it marked a return to its birthplace. Because service in Algeria had been unpopular among soldiers of the regular army, in 1831 the French government designated Algeria the home base for the newly created Foreign Legion. The government's intention was to put a disruptive element of society—failed revolutionaries, criminals on the run, soldiers of fortune—to useful work for the benefit of France. During its first years in Algeria, "useful work" meant the most remote and dangerous assignments in bandit-infested mountains and Saharan oases. As the decades passed, the Legion bonded around its motto—"The Legion Is Our Homeland"—and became an elite fighting organization composed exclusively of volunteers. The coming years of service in Algeria would forge a new bond between the Legion and those who resisted the insurgents and ironically lead to the Legion participating in a rebellion against the French government.

The year 1956 saw the Foreign Legion joined by a massive deployment of reinforcements as three entire divisions, including the Seventh Mechanized Reserve and two marine infantry divisions, transferred from France to Algeria. At first neither the Indochina veterans nor the regulars and conscripts from France adapted well to Algeria. For the Legionnaires and the veterans, the experience of Indochina, both a conventional war against regular Communist units and a counterinsurgency at the village level, had formed the veterans' thoughts and habits. They took their resentments, memories, and lessons from Indochina and initially refused to recognize that many aspects of the war in Algeria were different. On the other hand, the regulars and conscripts fresh from France had no notion how to wage a counterinsurgency. Not only were many soldiers ill-suited to Algerian operational requirements but the grand tactics imposed by senior leadership were flawed. In sum, the first two years of French military response to the insurgency featured inappropriate, conventional large-scale operations. In the words of David Galula, at the time an infantry company commander operating against insurgent strongholds in the Aurès mountains, "We encircled, we combed, we raided, with little result."[6]

The standard army pacification method utilized the so-called quadrillage (framework or grid) approach. The term referred to the neatly ruled map grids that divided Algeria into seventy-five sectors. Security forces entered each grid sector and secured the major towns, garrisoned lesser communities with small forces, actively patrolled the region between the garrisons, and worked to expand the number of places held. The military had the particular duty of defending the European farmers and their labor force from terrorist strikes. The static garrison forces also had the responsibility to eliminate the embedded insurgents and convert their sympathizers. Because the static forces remained in one place for an extended period, they developed considerable local knowledge, an indispensable feel for how a small community operated in the presence and absence of guerrillas.

To identify and root out the embedded infrastructure, garrisons needed to work closely with civil affairs officers called Specialized Administrative Sections (SAS). As part of his comprehensive reform efforts, Governor-General Soustelle had established the SAS in May 1955. Soustelle described their mission as bridging "the yawning gap between the administration and the poorer inhabitants."[7] One hundred ten years earlier the commander of the first French conquest of Algeria, Marshal Thomas Bugeaud, had established a similar organization, the Bureaux Arabes, for the same purpose, to act as liaison officers between the French army and the native population. In 1844 the officers' mission was to assist ongoing military operations by collecting political and military intelligence. Thereafter, they turned to pacification duties with the specific focus on bringing the benefits of French government to the natives. The duties of the SAS were remarkably similar.

The SAS officers were all Arabic-speaking volunteers. The best of them had spent their careers in the colonies working as native affairs officers. Like the American Special Forces or Green Berets, the SAS officers, called the *képis bleus* after their distinctive hats, operated in remote villages where there was no French presence. Here they taught schools, helped farmers, and provided basic health care as well as a military presence, both to keep the rebels from dominating the village and to prevent the French army from wrecking it.

An SAS team consisted of an officer (usually a lieutenant), a secretary, an interpreter (the Kabyles, for example, spoke a Berber language), a radio, a vehicle, and a small security force, to be replaced by native auxiliaries as quickly as possible. The first twenty-six teams went out into remote outposts in the Kabylie with instructions to pacify their zone. Naturally, they quickly became the special targets of the insurgency. From time to time came chilling accounts of their native security details turning on them or of formed guerrilla units overrunning an SAS outpost and wiping the team out. Because the SAS had the extra assignment of collecting intelligence, there were reports that they engaged in torture.

Working in isolated regions, in command of predominantly Muslim units, the SAS officers became the only concrete representative of the central government. Gradually they shifted from an advisory role and assumed most civilian administrative functions and became responsible for their village's health and well-being. The SAS officers assured Muslims that France would protect them always from FLN reprisals, a statement made more powerful by the fact that the officers truly believed it. They formed cooperative and sometimes even friendly relationships with the villagers in their area while building health clinics, markets, and schools where, to ease the natives' future assimilation, children learned French history and its heroes such as Joan of Arc and Napoleon rather than Arab history and Abd-el-Kadr and Abd el-Krim.

Although their ultimate goal was to promote French bureaucratic control, at the time the SAS was seen by many to be a beacon of light in a dark war. A British journalist described them as attempting "to tidy up the mess of war before the war is over."[8] Later analysts suggested that had this approach been performed on a large scale, the war's outcome would have been different. Eventually the SAS expanded to some 5,000 personnel, but in 1955 there were too few and it took precious time for the program to get up to speed.[9]

IN TIME THE French military adapted to the special requirements of war in Algeria. To combat what the theorists called revolutionary warfare required new thinking that reversed the conventional emphasis on purely military action. Military action had to take "a back seat to psychological action."[10] This was a new way of thinking, and one widely resisted throughout the French military hierarchy. That hierarchy wanted to focus on waging conventional war. Indicative of this bias were the attitudes of the instructors at the prestigious École de Guerre, who routinely criticized their officer-students whose service in Indochina had "deformed" their military judgment.[11] In the "deformed" minds of the reformists, psychological action—which they understood to include propaganda, the collection and exploitation of political as well as military intelligence, police measures, and personal contact with the local people, as well as social and economic programs—trumped purely military action. What was needed was a unified strategy featuring both destruction and construction. As General Jacques Allard explained, "These two terms are inseparable. To destroy without building up would mean useless labor; to build without first destroying would be a delusion."[12]

To help put these new ideas into practice the army established a special counterinsurgency school in 1956. During its first year of operation the school stressed marksmanship, detection of booby traps and mines, and combat communications. In the summer of 1957, Lieutenant Colonel Bruge, an officer who had served in France's colonial army and spent time as a prisoner of war after the fall of Dien Bien Phu, reformed the curriculum. Bruge's experiences at the hands of Communist interrogators and propagandists had given him a deep understanding of revolutionary warfare. He believed that persuading "the future leaders of the pacification effort that regaining the population's adherence to France constitutes the ultimate stake" was the school's true mission.[13] Toward that goal the new curriculum focused on the psychological foundations of guerrilla warfare, the destruction of insurgent infrastructure, pacification, psychological action and psychological warfare, and knowledge of Algerian and Muslim sociology. During the time of reform, more than 7,000 French officers passed through the school. A graduate of the Arzew Training Center observed, "I discovered here that to be victorious in the Algerian war, the vital battles that we have to win are those to be won with the head and heart, and not with a machine-pistol."[14]

EIGHT

The Question of Morality

Paths to Victory

IN THE FRENCH ARMY, LIKE ALL OTHERS, the accepted path to promotion was combat experience. Ambitious officers did not want to be shunted off to backwater assignments dealing with civil affairs and pacification duties. Consequently, in Algeria pacification became the dumping ground of the second-rate, elderly, drunken, or simply dumb. Such men all too often filled staff positions in civil affairs, propaganda, and even intelligence. One exception was David Galula.

That Galula marched to a different drummer was hardly surprising. A graduate of Saint-Cyr, the prestigious French military academy, Galula was purged from the officer corps in 1941 according to the "Statute on Jews of the Vichy State." After living in North Africa, he joined the Free French Army in time to be wounded while participating in the liberation of France in 1944. Thereafter, he served as a French military attaché and traveled widely in nations experiencing rebellion and insurgency. His life's experiences informed his theories of counterinsurgency.

Galula's company occupied a guerrilla-dominated region of the Aurès mountains. Galula perceived that the true battle was for the population and he understood that insurgent terror dominated the rural villages. When he interrogated civilians they candidly described their situation. They were not afraid of the French because, as French citizens, the worst fate that could befall them was jail. The insurgents, on the other hand, would cut their throats. Consequently, even the potentially pro-French chose not to cooperate. Thus Galula described the challenge: "Under what conditions would our potential supporters emerge from their present silence? How much risk were they prepared to take?"[1]

Galula concluded that the only way to make progress was to eliminate the insurgents' Political and Administrative Organization (OPA). At the village level, the OPA consisted of a Communist-style three-man cell. One military affairs member provided intelligence for the guerrillas. Another member dealt with administration and justice, while a third collected taxes to support the insurgency.

Identifying members of the village cell proved very difficult. In one village it seemed that an army-sponsored school was making a favorable impression until one day a soldier-teacher asked a young student if everything was all right. The boy responded positively but added that things would be much better if they had guns and ammunition because then they could drive the French out.

Extracting information from prisoners became an overarching challenge. A stroke of good fortune brought an elderly and disgruntled Kabyle who informed on his nephew, a village cell boss. A dawn raid caught the nephew and several other suspects. Over a period of days, Galula reduced the suspects' food until they received water only. Still, patient interrogation revealed nothing until a sergeant reported that one of the suspects was ready to talk. The sergeant had put the suspect in a bakery oven and threatened to light a fire under the oven if the suspect failed to cooperate. Ten minutes of being shut inside the oven broke the suspect. Thereafter, Galula authorized harsh interrogation methods and acknowledged he felt no more moral compunction than if he had been a World War II bomber pilot carpet-bombing a city.

Confessions led to the capture of new suspects and their confessions, in turn, had a cascading effect, allowing Galula to compile a list of OPA operatives. The reward came after a successful "purge" of an entire village OPA cell. The elimination of this cell produced a sea change in villagers' attitudes and behavior. They began to volunteer intelligence. A sure sign of success was the fact that villagers dared, in violation of the FLN ban, to smoke in public.

With experience Galula systematized his pacification approach into three steps. The first step involved intelligence collection utilizing threats and harsh treatment in order to identify OPA agents. Next came their arrest. Then an army garrison occupied the village to prevent the terrorists from recruiting new agents. Although it alarmed his conventional-minded superiors, Galula widely dispersed his company into small garrisons while keeping a reserve as a reaction force. And it worked. Galula converted a guerrilla stronghold into one of the quietest regions in all of Algeria. But, to his immense frustration, the blueprint for victory that he believed he had drawn proved of limited value. In Algeria, the French military declined to promulgate his policy. In France, political instability thwarted bold policy changes. Consequently, "no matter how much effort was devoted to pacification locally, we would find sooner or later that we had reached a plateau above which we could not rise."[2]

Moreover, Galula's success proved fragile. When military authorities redrew areas of responsibility, new units and new commanders took over villages that Galula's unit had pacified. The new commanders, having ignored the population in their previous assignments, continued their policy of neglect. Because all seemed quiet they did not continue Galula's policy of regular nocturnal ambushes. Soon the terrorists returned and the villages reverted. As Galula viewed the situation, "we were caught in the classic vicious circle of an insurgency: because of the repeated and costly operations, the Kabyle population was solidly against us; because of the attitude of the population, our soldiers tended to treat every civilian as an enemy."[3]

By the end of 1956 the French military presence in Algeria surpassed the 400,000 mark. There was a clear division of labor among them. The real fighting fell to only 10 percent of the army, the elite professionals in the paratroops and Foreign Legion units, who regularly conducted field operations. Designated as "units of intervention," this elite chased the guerrillas through mountain and forest, relying increasingly on helicopters to carry them into battle. Celebrated by the French press and most importantly by the *pieds-noirs*, the elite—who already carried bitter memories of abandoning their native allies in Indochina—reciprocated by identifying with increasing fervor with the settlers' plight. In the minds of elite Indochina veterans, defeat in Algeria could come only from political failure on the home front. When they looked at the shaky coalition governments in France they saw "the embodiment of irresolution."[4] For this reason many veterans grew to resent their own national government.

The draftees, reservists, and less capable regular forces mostly served in static roles. They guarded important national infrastructure: roads, railroads, ports, power stations. Many guarded settlers' farms or provided security for "pacified" villages. A domestic political calculation influenced how and where troops served. The French government calculated that it could regulate combat casualties by assigning its draftees and reservists to duties that seldom exposed them to losses. It did not anticipate that these men would refuse to witness silently army atrocities and that instead they would inform the French public through letters to their families and published accounts in the popular media.

Most officers expected the draftees to be poor soldiers uncommitted to a colonial war, particularly given that 25 percent of the French population voted Communist. The Parisian draftees who composed the majority of the 228th Infantry Battalion were of this sort. As a train conveyed them south across France, the unhappy draftees vandalized a train station. Thereafter riot police accompanied them until they landed in Algeria. Sent to the remote south deep in the Sahara desert, the men seethed with resentment and continued to wreck army property and loot civilian stores. They seldom ventured outside of their camp, which became an island in an alien environment. The high command finally sent a seasoned professional, Major Jean Pouget, to deal with these demoralized, poorly disciplined men.

Pouget addressed the troops: "Neither you nor I had a choice. We are [on] the same team and the match has started. I hate losing."[5] By force of character, insightful man management, and energy, Pouget restored the battalion's military effectiveness.

Pouget was another of the celebrated paratrooper heroes of Dien Bien Phu. Formed by his experience as a prisoner of war at the hands of the Viet Minh, Pouget, in contrast to most French veterans, insisted on treating prisoners decently. He firmly believed that it was both the right thing to do and the best way to obtain intelligence. He extended his notion of "soft" war to the task of pacifying his region. However, he fully understood that the first requirement was security: his battalion had to show it could protect the people, and particularly his SAS officers, from the terrorists. Toward this goal he ordered his battalion to flood the inhabited areas of his sector with frequent patrols. But he knew that these patrols would fail to contact the insurgents unless they had timely intelligence. To obtain this intelligence he worked hard to cooperate with the SAS officers and to treat the local population respectfully.

When one of his SAS lieutenants put his arm around the waist of the daughter of a local dignitary, Pouget publically rebuked him and sentenced the lieutenant to fifteen days of menial labor. He also paid a reparation to the offended father to help restore his daughter's honor. Pouget insisted that everyone in his battalion deal honestly with civilians, thereby eliminating the payment of bribes, the Arab's traditional baksheesh. Pouget also authorized economic assistance measures, such as acquiring chemical washes to disinfect the local flocks of sheep, and social programs, including starting schools.

The way Pouget treated Ain Melah, the largest village in his district, showed him to be completely different from most French officers. Everyone knew Ain Melah was dominated by the insurgents. Pouget met with the village elders, who assured him that the village was devoid of insurgents. Pouget told them that they were liars but that he completely understood their motives; all they were doing was trying to preserve peace in the village. All Pouget asked of them was to allow him to send a medical team once a week and to restart an irrigation project. The elders agreed.

Even when the terrorists killed a French soldier who taught at a school in Ain Melah, Pouget forbade retaliation. After this seminal event, the village elders requested a French garrison to help protect the population. Thereafter, the villagers provided a wealth of intelligence and thirty-five of them volunteered for the village militia, or *harki* (literally, Arabic for "movement"). For a time it appeared that Ain Melah was successfully pacified. The French intelligence lieutenant who managed the village's pacification program walked about the village unarmed. A captured enemy report acknowledged that the village had turned against the insurgents. The insurgents sent a team to assassinate the French lieutenant. They succeeded, but the villagers assisted the French in hunting down the killers.

Pouget and his battalion created an island of stability in a region of instability dominated by the insurgents. He practiced an approach to pacification enormously different from that of most French officers. It was not a systematic program like the one conceived by David Galula, but rather one inspired by a strongly held code of personal ethics. Like Galula's approach, it depended hugely on one man's personal leadership. Because neither Galula's nor Pouget's policies fit well within the French army's conventional mind-set, their successes remained isolated exceptions.

FRENCH MILITARY CAPACITY throughout Algeria improved dramatically. Veterans of the Indochina War assumed important command positions. These leaders substituted innovative, flexible tactics for the clumsy large-scale operations of the past. Reinforcements flowed to Algeria, including numerous crack paratroop and Foreign Legion formations. They possessed new equipment, including American-supplied helicopters. French morale soared.

However, conventional operations brought French soldiers face-to-face with two grim realities. The first was that an area remained secure only as long as French forces were present and vigilant. When the French sentries turned their backs, honorable old men, their chests laden with decorations earned while fighting for the French during two world wars, would grab their weapons and open fire against the French. A second realization was that rebel intelligence always seemed to be a step ahead of French intelligence. Superior intelligence allowed the guerrillas to evade battle and melt into the urban population or the remote interior. The French could not reliably separate the guerrillas from the general population. Conventional interrogation revealed nothing useful.

The Indochina veterans understood Maoist principles and strategy. In particular, they appreciated the notion that guerrillas had to swim like Mao's fish in the water of the uncommitted masses. One prominent Indochina veteran explained that it was little use merely destroying dispersed guerrilla bands. Instead, the French aim had to be to find and eradicate the entire clandestine political organization that supported the guerrillas. More ominously, the Indochina veterans appreciated how guerrillas used force to influence the civilian population. They believed that counterrevolutionary forces had to employ the same methods and so they did.

This produced military results. By the end of 1956 FLN leaders understood that they could not contend in open battle with the French. There would be no war-winning Algerian version of Dien Bien Phu. But they believed that by maintaining a military presence—even if that meant small guerrilla bands scattered in remote mountain hiding places—and continuing their domination of the people by terror tactics, they could avoid losing. And, in spite of French efforts, the FLN had made some notable achievements. They had recruited and armed some 20,000 men from a population largely uninterested in revolutionary rhetoric. They had established a political-military infrastructure across a vast area. They had impressively increased the number of violent actions—ranging from cutting down a telephone line to shooting a Muslim constable to ambushing a French patrol—from 200 a month in April 1955 to 2,624 in March 1956. Their major target continued to be Muslim "traitors," civilians known to have co-operated with the French or suspected of having done so. For the first thirty months of the conflict, terrorists killed an estimated 6,353 Muslims against 1,035 Europeans.

Having regrouped from their earlier mistakes, FLN leaders again showed their strategic impatience by seeking decisive results in the country's capital city, Algiers.

The Battle for Algiers

The FLN judged the capital city as the decisive battle zone. If they could routinely conduct terror operations inside Algiers, then they could discredit or perhaps even paralyze French rule. Ever since March 1956, Algiers had experienced occasional terrorist incidents. In August 1956 the FLN leadership decided to change the war's focus and inflict on the capital an orchestra of terror, featuring a steady drumbeat of detonating high explosives. It ordered its commander in Algiers, Yacef Saadi, to begin a relentless campaign of urban terrorism to undermine France's capacity to provide public order and security.

Yacef coordinated welders who made bomb casings, explosive experts who had learned their trade in the French army, and drivers to convey the bombs to secret depots. Then Yacef dispatched the bomb planters to targets he had personally selected. The planters typically were young, educated, stylish Algerian women who easily passed as Europeans as they deposited their bombs at popular nightspots frequented by young pieds-noirs. On September 30, bombs detonated inside the Milk-Bar, just across from French army headquarters, and at La Cafétéria. On November 13, terrorists hurled a bomb into a bus, inflicting thirty-six casualties, and planted another in a department store and a third at the rail station. A well-coordinated attack on November 28 detonated three large bombs simultaneously in downtown Algiers. Just before Christmas a school bus bombing killed or maimed several children. The terrorists followed this up by assassinating two prominent political leaders.

Europeans who ventured onto the streets carried concealed firearms and saw a possible assassin in the face of every Muslim. Terrorist violence produced brutal reprisals, the infamous *ratonnades* (Arab-bashings). Intimidated by the possibility of random *pied-noir* reprisal, cowed by Yacef's long arm of terror, the city's Muslim population also lived in fear. Exposed to frequent and seemingly unstoppable terror bombings and assassinations, Algiers quickly descended into chaos.

French authorities concluded that it was impossible to prevent urban terrorism through normal police and judicial procedures. On January 7, 1957, Governor-General Robert Lacoste summoned General Jacques Massu to his office. He told Massu that since the city's 1,500 police could neither prevent terrorist outrages nor control retaliation by *pied-noir* mobs, he was giving Massu carte blanche to use the his 4,600-strong Tenth Paratroop Division to restore order in the capital. General Massu was like the Napoleonic marshal Michel Ney: a man of action who responded to resistance by conducting a head-down charge. Events in Algiers immediately tested his command style.

Massu's paratroopers entered the city just in time to confront a nationwide strike the FLN had called to begin on January 28, 1957, the opening day of the United Nations debates on Algeria. The FLN goal was to discredit the French assertion that the rebellion enjoyed little popular support. As the sun rose, it appeared that the FLN was correct. Algiers was dead. Muslim schoolchildren stayed at home. Shops did not open for business. Muslim employees who worked in essential services at power plants and water pumping stations failed to report. Massu responded by ordering his paratroopers to open shops by force and compel workers to report. Soldiers attached cables to the steel shutters securing the closed shops and armored vehicles dragged them from their hinges. Paratroopers rounded up public workers and conducted them to the power plants and telegraph offices. Within forty-eight hours Massu's men had broken the strike.

But terror bombings continued. Massu remembered Paul Aussaresses' performance as an intelligence officer in Philippeville and summoned him to serve in Algiers. Massu told Aussaresses that the job was going to be hard and "we'll have to be implacable."[6] Aussaresses understood this meant using torture and summary executions. Massu shared his understanding. Massu sought legal latitude from the French government in hopes of overturning the laws that banned torture. When the government failed to oblige, Massu simply denied the supremacy of civil law in Algeria. He asserted that because Algiers was under military authority, civil law did not apply.

Aussaresses cared little about such fine distinctions. Police files provided him with a list of suspects. Mass arrests followed by interrogations, which usually meant torture, often began with the small fry and the question "Who is the district tax collector?" Disclosure led the French security forces to new names, new arrests, and new interrogations: "To whom do you turn in your money?" So the French traced the bomb-making network, climbing up command levels to find the terror chiefs.

Meanwhile, Massu divided the city into four quadrants, each under the control of one paratroop regiment. The paratroop officers were almost all veterans of the Indochina War. Massu's chief of staff, Yves Godard, had commanded the Eleventh Shock, the so-called dirty-tricks battalion answerable directly to the prime minister. Formed by the paratroop establishment and the French secret service, the Eleventh Shock in Indochina had been part of the column attempting to relieve Dien Bien Phu. In Algiers the Eleventh Shock performed many of the "delicate" missions that no French official wanted to acknowledge. Among the other hard men were regimental commander Lieutenant Colonel Roger Trinquier, who had commanded an airborne combat brigade with the mission of collecting intelligence behind Viet Minh lines. Lieutenant Colonel Pierre Jeanpierre, who had survived both a German concentration camp and a devastating Viet Minh ambush, commanded another regiment. Then there was the brave, ruthless Lieutenant Colonel Marcel Bigeard, celebrated for his conduct at Dien Bien Phu. Collectively these men were determined to avoid the "mistake" of lack of firmness exhibited in that war. They set out to prove that they were willing to be more extreme than the terrorists.

Henceforth, the Muslim population of Algeria lived in a city subdivided by barbed-wire barriers illuminated by searchlight beams. The focal point of the urban insurgency was the Casbah, a thickly packed slum home to some 80,000 Algerians. The Casbah was a confusing matrix of extremely narrow streets and alleys overlooked by old stone buildings. Europeans had long ago abandoned this sector and the absence of French authority allowed the FLN free rein. The Casbah was the command

center for Yacef's bomb-making network, now using much more powerful plastic explosive packages only slightly larger than a pack of ciga-
rettes. Operating from secure safe houses, Yacef plotted his terror
campaign. Yacef sent his cadre of young girls to place a bomb in the female lavatory at a student hangout called the Otomatic and for a second
time at the popular bistro La Cafétéria; when diners at the nearby
brasserie rushed to the window to see what had happened, a third bomb,
placed beneath a table, detonated, sending fragments slicing through
the crowd.

Massu assigned the sector containing the Casbah to Colonel Bigeard's
Third Regiment. He and his men worked closely with Aussaresses. Aussaresses had the paratroopers perform a detailed census by asking the old-
est inhabitant of a house to name all the people living in the house. Police
cross-checked this information with statements made by the neighbors. If
someone was missing, he or she became a suspect. If the suspect returned home, police hauled in him or her for interrogation. In Aussaresses' words, "The results of the interrogations and comparisons of
various sources allowed the patrols to set up reliable lists of persons we
should be looking for."[7]

Conventional detective and forensic work contributed to closing in on
Yacef's bomb-making network. A waiter gave a detailed description of a
woman who had sat at the table shortly before the detonation. Careful
examination of a clothing fragment found at one bombing site led to the
arrests. Henceforth Bigeard's paratroopers carefully searched all women
leaving the Casbah. Throughout the city the paratroopers established a
curfew and began shooting on sight anything that moved. Thus began
an intense and brutal nine-month military campaign.

Much of the action took place at night when the paratroopers donned
their jungle camouflage uniforms and took to the streets to make their
arrests. The goal was to be done by midnight in order to leave plenty of
time for interrogations. Aussaresses boasted, "I was responsible for the
decisions regarding all the suspects arrested inside the city of Algiers."
The vast majority had weak links to the FLN, having joined out of fear.
These people were sent to prison camps. Eventually more than 20,000
people, or 3 percent of the entire population of Algiers, passed through
these camps. Aussaresses focused on the prime suspects, flitting among
the four paratroop headquarters inside Algiers to make godlike snap

decisions literally involving life and death, with the pendulum of justice heavily weighed toward the latter: "We would hold on to the others who were either positively dangerous or thought to be so and make them talk quickly before executing them."[8] An estimated 3,000 Muslims "disappeared" during the Battle of Algiers.

The policy of counterterror sharply reduced the number of terrorist incidents as the months passed. But Massu's chief of staff, Godard, wanted more. He understood that most of the lower-level operatives— bomb transporters, lookouts, and even bomb planters—were easily replaceable. Killing them would not completely end the terrorists' ability to sow terror. Indeed, on February 10, 1957, the terrorists showed they still had teeth when nearly simultaneously they detonated two large bombs at two soccer stadiums while matches were being played. The bombs destroyed the stadiums' grandstands, killing 11 and seriously wounding 146 more. Godard compiled all information to replicate the bombers' organizational hierarchy. For a long time the name of the head of the organization remained unknown.

Indeed, Yacef took exceptional care to conceal himself. Purportedly he changed hideouts fifteen times on the day the general strike began. He disguised himself as a woman in order to personally scout public places to detonate bombs. But as the paratroopers systematically rolled up the FLN terror network, Yacef's personal security and that of his remaining chiefs became doubtful. The remaining senior leadership in Algiers dispersed, leaving Yacef to continue the campaign as best he could. Following a long lull during which time he partially reconstructed his bomb network, Yacef ordered a new campaign to begin. Four terrorists disguised in the uniform of public works personnel placed time bombs inside several streetlights next to a crowded bus stop. A fifteen-year-old Muslim employee of a popular casino set a bomb underneath the orchestra platform, killing nine and wounding eighty-five.

The French responded by clamping down even harder on the Casbah and intensifying the search for Yacef, who they now knew was the head of the bomb network. Acting on pinpoint intelligence, at 5:00 a.m. on September 24, 1957, paratroopers sealed off rue Caton in the heart of the Casbah. They went to Yacef's safe house, broke into his hidey-hole built into a small space between staircase and bathroom, dodged the hand grenade thrown by Yacef, and captured the terror chieftain. To the frustration of many in the security service, most notably Paul Aussaresses, the French prime minister demanded that Yacef not be mistreated.

In their zeal to capture Yacef, the paratroopers had overlooked his alternative safe house on the rue Caton. From here three of Yacef's subordinates fled to another safe house. After realizing their mistake, French security forces relentlessly tracked the subordinates until they cornered and killed them in the Casbah on the night of October 8. With this final blow, the Battle of Algiers came to a close. The military result of the Battle for Algiers was the clear defeat of the FLN. Bombings and other acts of terror virtually ceased inside the capital. For the remainder of the war the FLN abandoned large-scale urban terrorism inside Algeria.

But the French victory had unforeseen consequences. Before the Battle of Algiers there had been occasional reports of torture and other abuses. As early as January 15, 1955, an article in *L'Express* entitled "The Question" raised doubts about French conduct. On December 20, 1955, *L'Express* displayed photographs depicting the execution of an Algerian "rebel" by an auxiliary gendarme. The photographs did not quite have the impact of the famous image capturing the moment of impact when the South Vietnamese police chief executed a Viet Cong suspect in the streets of Saigon during the Tet Offensive in 1968, but it did provide a powerful image that prompted some Frenchmen to question their nation's behavior in Algeria. The Battle of Algiers changed questions to moral certainties and henceforth, as one historian observed, the "rivulet of allegations . . . swelled to a flood" and became imprinted upon the French consciousness.[9]

Two groups held in high moral esteem by the French people, clergymen and veterans of the French resistance against the Nazis, began to question openly French conduct. When the French press published disturbing accounts reported by conscripts and reservists, the ethical issue of how the army conducted the fight in Algeria became crucial to the war's outcome. Writers asked if the French army had descended to the level of the Gestapo.[10] Politicians began to criticize the army's conduct. These criticisms, in turn, cemented the army's loathing for the politicians of the Fourth Republic. Right-wing extremists began plotting to overthrow the Fourth Republic and to replace it with a tougher regime.

Meanwhile, the paratroopers in Algiers enjoyed their newfound adulation among the city's young female *pieds-noirs*. Their officers found satisfaction in a dirty job well done and looked forward to some cleaner, real soldiering out in the hinterland against main-force insurgent units. In the words of Colonel Bigeard, counterinsurgency operations in Algiers had been a battle of "blood and shit."[11]

NINE

The Enclosed Hunting Preserve

The Battle on the Frontiers

FRENCH DECREES ISSUED IN THE spring of 1956 divided Algeria into three zones: a zone of operation, a pacification zone, and a forbidden zone. The allocation of counterinsurgency forces logically followed this division. The zone of operations was the killing ground where elite mobile French forces relentlessly pursued guerrilla bands with the objective of eliminating them. In the pacification zones, which embraced the most populous and fertile areas, French conscript and reserve formations tried to protect the civilian population, European and Muslim alike, from terrorist attacks. Here security was accompanied by major economic reforms, education, and propaganda indoctrination. French strategists designated sparsely populated areas that were adjacent to the pacification zones as forbidden zones (*zones interdites*). The strategic intent was to separate the rebels from their sources of supplies and recruits while providing security for the pacification zones. They were beyond the pale, a region from where the population was evacuated and relocated in settlement camps controlled by the army. Thereafter, the army was permitted to fire on anyone seen moving in the forbidden zones.

Having established the parameters by which it would operate, the French military went to work. It employed overwhelming force to drive the FLN's military organization, the Armée de Libération Nationale (ALN), out of Algeria. Most ALN fighters took refuge in the neighboring countries of

Morocco and Tunisia. Those who continued the fight inside Algeria became dependent on external supply sources. The French recognized this vulnerability and concentrated on isolating Algeria. Nourished by good intelligence, the French navy intercepted ships carrying arms to Algeria. They also blocked aerial resupply of the guerrillas. Outside of Algeria, French secret agents waged a successful intimidation campaign, including targeted assassinations, against international arms dealers. Because of these measures, the insurgents remained starved for effective firearms and munitions.

Inside Algeria, the French organized *harki* units of "loyal" Algerians. A farsighted settler, Jean Servier, had overcome official resistance to organize light companies from FLN defectors. Servier insisted that these *harki* units serve near their homes so they could protect their own families from FLN retaliation. Armed with shotguns, intimately familiar with the local environment, Servier's *harkis* soon demonstrated their worth by eliminating local insurgents. News about the opportunity for regular employment spread rapidly and French-loyal village elders began organizing their own *harki* units. They were essentially miniature tribal armies. Over a two-year period beginning in 1957, the number of these lightly armed native forces serving as village militia rose to involve some 60,000 Algerians. When associated with skilled French SAS leaders the *harkis* proved to be very effective in denying the insurgents access to rural people.

However, the Algerian borders were open to infiltration from guerrilla sanctuaries in Morocco and Tunisia. The recent memory of Indochina, where Communist guerrillas enjoyed free passage across international borders, persuaded the French to tackle this challenge decisively. The French utilized a classic counterinsurgency approach that the Romans who constructed Hadrian's Wall would have admired. The French built extensive fortified barriers along 500 miles of the Moroccan border in the west. But it was in the east along the Tunisian border where they erected a state-of-the-art defensive barrier. This was the famous Morice Line, named after the French defense minister, a 200-mile-long line extending from the sea to the Sahara desert. An eight-foot-high electrified wire barrier carrying 5,000 volts ran through the middle of a wide minefield overlooked by regularly spaced watchtowers. When the guerrillas tried to break through the fence, detection devices triggered an alarm system. Of critical importance, the Morice Line, like Hadrian's Wall, was not simply a passive defense

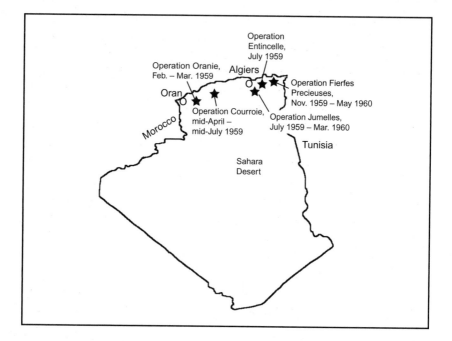

system. Rather, both worked in association with mobile combat formations who met insurgent breakthroughs wherever they occurred. Precalibrated artillery fire rained down wherever automatic devices detected a breach, while mobile combat patrols rushed along a purpose built highway that ran along most of the Algerian side of the barrier to deal with the penetration. If a breach occurred in the roadless, remote southern sector, helicopters flew the reaction force to the scene of the incident. The entire system involved 80,000 soldiers, watching and waiting for any FLN attempt to reinforce their beleaguered fighters in Algeria.

The challenge came soon. Raiders probed the Morice Line looking for weaknesses. They employed high-tension wire cutters purchased in Germany, insulated ramps, tunnels, and blasting charges. After opening a breach the raiders tried to hold the nearby terrain to permit the passage of reinforcements and supplies before the French resealed the border. Nothing worked. Infiltration parties attempting to outflank the line at its southern end found themselves exposed to French air power in the open Sahara and were slaughtered. So the armed wing of the FLN, the ALN regulars, tried a series of escalating conventional attacks against the Morice Line.

A large ALN force fought through the Morice Line in May 1958 only to encounter the reconnaissance group of the First Foreign Legion Parachute Regiment. Colonel Pierre Jeanpierre, one of Massu's paratroop leaders during the Battle of Algiers, died while leading his Legionnaires in a decisive counterattack that resealed the line. In another climactic action, waves of ALN fighters managed to breach the Morice Line only to be pinned down by the French mechanized and helicopter-delivered reaction forces. A total of 620 of the 820 men who penetrated the line were killed or captured. The series of efforts to breach the French fortified barriers cost the ALN upward of 6,000 men, a devastating setback that compelled the FLN to cease trying to breach the French fortifications.

While the French navy prevented the guerrillas from smuggling arms and men into Algeria, the Morice Line and the Moroccan barrier effectively blocked infiltration by land and thereby "established a kind of closed hunting preserve" where the French security forces could relentlessly conduct a battle of attrition.[1] Only some 8,000 ALN fighters remained inside Algeria. With the veterans gone, most of the remnants were young, inexperienced recruits who predictably suffered heavily whenever drawn into combat with the French.

Because the ALN dispersed and went into hiding, increasing numbers of Algerian civilians withdrew support for the rebels. In June 1960 an FLN political leader reported to his government in exile, "It becomes increasingly impossible to penetrate the barriers in order to nurture the revolution in the interior ... unless directed, supplied with fresh troops, effective weaponry, and money in great amounts, the underground forces will not be able to live for a long time let alone achieve victory ... The organic infrastructure has been dismantled in the urban centers, and it is increasingly nonexistent in the countryside."[2]

The Return of Charles de Gaulle

Just when it appeared that the FLN was on the verge of defeat the entire political climate in France changed. In Algeria, the *pieds-noirs* had greeted various proposals for reform as betrayal. On April 26, 1958, some 8,000 Europeans marched through Algiers and made a public oath: "Against whatever odds, on our tombs and on our cradles, taking our dead on the field of honor as our witnesses, we swear to live and die as Frenchmen in the land of Algiers, forever French."[3] In France, press investigations of

abuses in the resettlement program and new revelations about the practice of torture demoralized the public. The war's unpopularity combined
with numerous economic and social gripes to reduce domestic support
for the French government. A cabinet crisis fractured the weakened government and presented an opportunity for right-wing activists to strike.

On the day a new cabinet was scheduled to present its program to the
National Assembly, *pied-noir* activist groups in Algiers began widespread
demonstrations in an effort to influence the vote. They feared that the new
French government would abandon them and denounced the government for plotting "a diplomatic Dien Bien Phu." By the evening of May 13,
1958, they controlled Algiers and had established an emergency government. The French army in Algeria realized that it held enormous political
clout and supported this new government. France teetered on the edge of
revolution.

Into the ensuing leadership void stepped Charles de Gaulle. The settlers' revolt found the sixty-seven-year-old war hero in rural retirement
working on his war memoirs. But he had been closely following political
developments and was far from displeased when a new opportunity presented itself. In a memorable speech on May 19, 1958, de Gaulle deployed his brilliant rhetoric to reassure the nation. Alluding to events in
Algeria, de Gaulle said that France confronted "an extremely grave national crisis." But he also told the nation that it could "prove to be the beginning of a kind of resurrection."[4] The National Assembly voted de
Gaulle full powers for six months, thereby ending the Fourth Republic.

De Gaulle, in turn, judged Algeria a "millstone round France's neck."[5]
In his view the era of European colonialism was coming to an end and
there was no longer any alternative for Algeria except self-determination.
But it was of crucial importance that France grant Algeria this right. It
could not be forced upon any self-respecting French government at the
point of a gun or the detonation a terrorist bomb. As the new leader
phrased it, prior to negotiations the insurgents had to check "the knives in
the cloakroom."[6]

De Gaulle knew that to arrive at an acceptable solution he had to appeal to diverse political constituents and consequently had to handle the
situation with extreme circumspection. Thus, he moved slowly and cautiously, and with calculated vagueness. By so doing he failed to capitalize
on the opportunity created by military success in Algeria.

FLN leaders would later say that the weeks following de Gaulle's rise to power marked a low ebb for their cause. Their military forces had hurled themselves against the Morice Line and been badly defeated. Their troops were demoralized and when de Gaulle spoke about true equality for all Algerians within the French republic the great mass of Algerians appeared receptive to compromise. FLN leaders knew that they had to do something before de Gaulle's government could consolidate power. They responded brilliantly with a diplomatic offensive designed to take advantage of Cold War rivalry between the East and West by proclaiming a revolutionary Provisional Government of the Republic of Algeria. Arab nations hastened to recognize the new government. The Communist bloc, except for the USSR, followed. FLN spokesmen hinted at a new flexibility regarding a negotiated settlement and the international press enthusiastically endorsed this notion. Yet even as they won an important victory on the international front, military events in Algeria again threatened to defeat the FLN.

The Challe Plan

When de Gaulle assumed power he began to replace the command team in Algeria with his own loyalists. He chose General Maurice Challe to command the military. It proved an inspired choice. Still vigorous at age fifty-three, Challe had served with distinction in the Resistance during World War II. He had provided the British with valuable intelligence on the eve of the Normandy Invasion and earned both a British medal and a personal citation from Winston Churchill. Although trained as an airman, Challe possessed a keen appreciation for land tactics. Unlike his predecessor, he did not dabble in politics but rather was an open and honest leader with a surpassing ability to forge an interservice, team approach to problem solving. De Gaulle ordered Challe to deliver a crushing blow to the already reeling insurgent cause by a series of offensives designed to reduce the rebel pockets one after another. In de Gaulle's mind this offensive was like a preassault strategic bombardment designed to create a receptive environment for whatever he decided to do next.

Challe, in turn, believed that too many French soldiers, about 380,000 by his count, had been assigned passive roles guarding the Morice Line, securing the country's infrastructure, and protecting its villages. Only 15,000 remained in the General Reserve to conduct active operations. The result was that the French military had designated vast swaths of Algeria as "no-go zones," which effectively ceded these areas to the FLN. Indeed, the French had ruefully labeled one such zone the "FLN republic." Unwilling to remain passive and reactive, Challe planned to concentrate overwhelming force against each traditional insurgent stronghold. After eliminating the rebels and inserting pacification teams to take control of the population and prevent the insurgents from re-forming, Challe intended to move against another stronghold. He introduced his strategy to the army in Algeria with a simple catch phrase that everyone could understand: "Neither the *djebel* [hill] nor the night must be left to the FLN." He made sure that he had the right sort of tactical commanders to realize his vision by sacking nearly half the sector commanders and replacing them with more aggressive colonels.

The first offensive took place in the rolling country southeast of Oran. Although this area had long been controlled by the FLN, it presented less daunting terrain than the traditional insurgent strongholds in the Aurès mountains and the Kabylie. The elite paratroopers spearheaded the ensuing Operation Oranie, followed by mechanized columns issuing out of Oran to flood the countryside. It was essentially a giant search-and-destroy operation conducted with more technical sophistication than ever before. Using an integrated communications net that permitted command coordination between ground and air units, officers in airborne command posts managed a fast-paced series of moves for which the insurgent foot soldiers had no answer. American-supplied giant helicopters, the famous Piasecki H-21 "flying bananas," provided the capacity to land two entire battalions in five minutes. Three hundred slow, propeller-driven training aircraft were converted to ground attack roles. At first, pilots who had trained to fly modern supersonic jets complained bitterly. The former airman Challe ignored them and the complaints ceased when the pilots discovered, as would a future general of American airmen flying A-10s in Iraq, that slow was good for ground support missions. French mechanized columns cornered the guerrillas and the converted trainers allowed pilots to deliver bombs and rockets with pinpoint lethality.

During Operation Oranie, Challe also inserted into action numerous newly recruited *harki* units. The expansion had required de Gaulle's authorization. During a face-to-face encounter, Challe had insisted and de Gaulle had replied with characteristic haughtiness, "One does not impose conditions on de Gaulle!"[7] Challe refused to be overmastered and told de Gaulle to either give him the men or he would resign. Thereafter Challe

had select *harki* units form specially trained "hunter-killer" teams complete
with experienced trackers to search the interior for enemy presence. They
marched light, living off the land, and tracked small guerrilla bands
through remote regions that heretofore had been inaccessible to the
French. They carried radios, so if they contacted a large insurgent band
they could summon reinforcements. Helicopters rapidly delivered elite
fighters from Challe's General Reserve to surround and trap the enemy.
Moreover, the French benefited from accurate intelligence, much of it ex-
tracted by torture, but also numerous useful windfalls obtained from a
very successful radio-interception service.

The two-month-long Operation Oranie proved an outstanding success. The French claimed to have killed more than 1,600 guerrillas while
capturing another 460 along with large quantities of weapons and ammunition. Challe estimated that the campaign had eliminated fully half
the ALN manpower in the area. While the casualty claims may have been
inflated, there was no doubt that the French had delivered a staggering
blow.

Proof of success came when pacification teams, left behind after the
mobile forces departed, were able to work without significant interference
from the insurgents. Army engineers built roads to link formerly isolated
villages with the outside economy and the insurgents seldom were able to
thwart them by laying mines or blowing up culverts and bridges. SAS
teams moved into villages, raised self-defense forces, built more schools
and clinics than at any time since 1954, and worked hard to show the people the benefits of remaining French.

Encouraged by these results, and having built up his mobile reserve to
35,000 crack troops, in mid-April Challe shifted his forces east to the
mountains behind Algiers to begin a new offensive. Here the terrain was
more rugged and results less outstanding. The ALN fighters dispersed
quickly when the French appeared and thereafter successfully evaded contact. Challe tinkered with his tactics and pressed on through November
1959. The climactic offensive of the so-called Challe Plan was Operation
Jumelles, directed against the Kabylie, where the FLN had first raised the
banner of rebellion. From his command helicopter, Challe personally directed 25,000 men in a multiprong assault against the guerrilla stronghold. Marines conducted amphibious attacks along the coast, mechanized
columns penetrated remote valleys, *harki* hunter-killer teams searched the
forests while the paratrooper reaction forces waited on the airfields to

board their helicopters when called. Overhead, the ground attack aircraft loitered, waiting to swoop down against any target.

Even in Challe's opinion the results were disappointing. The ALN had learned from Challe's first campaign and again dispersed rapidly and gone to ground. Although the French claimed to have killed, wounded, or captured 3,746 Kabyle insurgents, how many of these people were merely civilians caught in the war's crossfire is unknowable. On the positive side of the ledger, the FLN acknowledged heavy losses. The French had lost several hundred killed, but compared to the insurgents the ratio was a very impressive one to ten. Particularly encouraging from a French standpoint was the fact that more insurgents surrendered than ever before and many of them volunteered to serve in *harki* units. To the French soldiers on the ground it appeared that the insurgency was in its death throes.

An experienced war correspondent toured Algeria and wrote, "From a purely military point of view, it could be said that the FLN has been beaten. Its last hundred-man *katybas* [organized combat companies] have taken refuge in the impregnable rocky highlands where they are contained. In other places . . . local *fellagha* [guerrillas] stay in the brush and the *katybas*, broken up into little groups of a dozen fighters each . . . change their hideouts every night. The only purpose of their operations is to maintain a feeling of insecurity."[8] Along the fortified frontier barriers, all the larger ALN units were reduced to harassing the barrier guards from their sanctuaries in Tunisia and Morocco. They could neither breach nor outflank the high-tension wires, barbed-wire entanglements, and floodlit minefields. Citing his campaign maxim to deny the guerrillas sanctuary in the hills, Challe proclaimed, "The rebel is no longer king of the *djebel*, he is trapped there . . . The military phase of the rebellion is terminated in the interior."[9]

How true was this assertion? If statistics cited by Challe were accurate, namely that half the FLN fighters in the operational areas had been eliminated, obviously the other half remained. If Challe's claim that the insurgents' logistical base had shrunk by 20 percent in the past year was correct, a substantial base was still present. Challe's assessment also overlooked the fact that by this time a new ALN chief of staff, Houari Boumedienne, had made the decision to cease supporting the *katybas* inside Algeria and instead rest, refit, and recruit a powerful new force in

Tunisia. There they would be in a position to return to Algeria when the time was favorable.

Moreover, Challe's large-scale search and destroy operations did not occur in a political vacuum. The question remained: to what extent had these "victories" persuaded the Muslim population to support the French and turn against the insurgents?

TEN

The Sense of Betrayal

Victory and Defeat

A FRENCH WAR REPORTER AND World War II hero, Jules Roy had been born in Algeria. As a *pied-noir*, he had special credibility. Roy visited a Kabyle village after a search-and-destroy operation had passed through. In some ways, apart from the tremendous number of battle-scarred or completely ruined structures, normality seemed to have returned. A French garrison provided sufficient security for there to be bus service to the distant city three times a week. The reporter saw fig and olive trees. The villagers harvested a potato crop four times a year. But as Roy probed deeper he uncovered the costs of pacification. One sixth of the population was dead or had disappeared, and most of them were men. Virtually every family had lost a male member to the French repression.

Military might had not converted these people to the side of the French. Most peasant families simply wanted to be left alone. They knew that if they chose to be "faithful servants of France" they faced insurgent denunciation as traitors to the Algerian homeland. Obligated to deal with the French and the insurgents, the peasants tried to take a stance straddling both sides. Roy discovered that many families had one man in the FLN and one serving with the French. The mayor's father had been assassinated by the FLN. The mayor's brother had been an officer in the French army but had deserted to the FLN. The mayor's uncle was a local FLN leader. Sixty women in the village had husbands serving with the FLN. Another sixty had relocated to live closer to their menfolk who served in the resistance. There were four women for every one man in the village. Too few able-bodied men remained to prune the fruit trees, so nearly 90 percent of the fig trees were neglected and no longer bore fruit. Likewise, the villagers had abandoned cork cultivation. In sum, the village's agricultural staples were gone.

In July 1959 the conservative French newspaper Le Figaro exposed to the French public a heretofore ignored aspect of pacification: population regroupment on a massive scale with associated abuse and neglect. Back in 1957, when military engineers had constructed the frontier barriers, the French initiated a population regroupment program that moved people away from the borders into new villages and towns. In the interior, near insurgent strongholds, there were other regroupments designed to isolate the people from the guerrillas. Thereafter, the French razed the abandoned villages and entire regions became free-fire zones. Lastly, as part of the Challe Plan, there were more large regroupments away from remote areas, again in order to move people outside the range of the insurgents. The population shifts eventually relocated at least 1 million people, or 11 percent of the Muslim population.[1] An approving French colonel observed, with unconscious irony, "In effect, we are reestablishing the old system of medieval fortified villages, designed to protect the inhabitants against marauding bands."[2]

Supposedly, the French army provided medical care, education, and employment for the relocated people. Le Figaro reported anything but. At a camp near Philippeville, for two years families had crowded into exposed tent cities where summer temperatures reached 110 degrees Fahrenheit. Children were emaciated stick figures dressed in torn rags. And the Philippeville tent city was not an isolated example. Roy wrote for L'Express about shantytowns near Algiers where refugees lived in "shacks in which even animals wouldn't live in France." Roy continued his inspections and encountered tens of thousands of wretched refugees living in squalid urban slums: "They have fled relocation and war, out of terror, and have become beggars and public charges . . . Without water, without sewage or sanitation of any kind, without land to cultivate and for the most part without work."[3] Even the paratroop general Massu found the scene at a regroupment camp outside of Algiers deplorable, with people living in miserable squalor below levels he had seen in the most destitute parts of sub-Saharan Africa.

The Figaro report and subsequent similar accounts in other newspapers shocked the French public. The depictions of the regroupment

camps were too close to well-remembered scenes of German concentration camps. Such accounts, along with continuing and disquieting reports of torture, demoralized the French public.

Yet from a strictly military perspective, Algeria looked entirely different. By the end of 1959 the combination of fortified barriers and the
Challe Plan had dramatically shifted the war's military momentum in the
French favor. Urban terror attacks had diminished to a tolerable level,
with an average of only four incidents a month occurring in Algiers. In
the hinterland, Challe's offensive had inflicted irreplaceable losses. The
offensive had also driven the ALN out of many of their traditional strongholds. Like wild African animals forced during the dry season to congre-
gate around water holes, the ALN concentrated in their remaining
sanctuaries, where they presented the French hunters a more vulnerable
target.

For one last agonizing time, French soldiers believed that the army's
blood sacrifices had brought victory. This belief would heighten their
sense of betrayal when de Gaulle concluded that the war was being lost
because of waning domestic support and international opposition to
colonialism.

IN SPITE OF all military successes, the French could not devise a political
formula to end the conflict. De Gaulle dreamed that historically close
cultural, commercial, and sentimental ties would preserve a union of Algeria and France. Toward that union he crafted new policies granting
Algerians the full rights of French citizens. De Gaulle went to Algeria to
announce plans to provide better education and medical services, to create
jobs for Muslims, and to admit them into the highest ranks of public service. These were variants of the reforms that had been promised in the
past. By now, the spirit of nationalism was too strongly entrenched among
the Muslim population to admit any compromise. When de Gaulle visited
a model resettlement town in the traditional insurgent stronghold of
Kabylie, villagers greeted him with cheers while schoolchildren chanted
"La Marseillaise." Just before he departed, a Muslim town clerk stopped
him to murmur, "*Mon général*, don't be taken in! Everyone here wants independence." Such encounters confirmed de Gaulle's belief that "in spite
of our crushing superiority in military means, it would be a futile waste of
men and money" to try to retain the status quo.[4]

On September 16, 1959, in anticipation of the opening of the UN General Assembly, de Gaulle appeared on television to address the nation. In a twenty-minute speech he directly mentioned the possibility of Algerian "self-determination" to be decided by referendum. It was the first time a French leader had publicly suggested this possibility. It marked a watershed. Every French proposal before this time was now irrelevant. There was no longer any chance of retaining Algeria within metropolitan France. Although de Gaulle himself did not yet perceive it, everything that followed was no more than issues of procedure and method.

This was a strategic victory for the insurgency and the leadership knew it. The FLN minister of defense, Belkacem Krim, the only living member of the original nine revolutionary leaders who had plotted the rebellion, broadcast to his hard-pressed fighters the news that "your struggle has obliged the enemy to talk of self-determination, thus renouncing the oft-repeated myth of *Algérie française*. His retreat is the fruit of your efforts."[5] Henceforth, all the FLN had to do was survive until France yielded to its demands. To ensure its survival, the FLN abandoned conventional military operations and substituted hit-and-run raids and acts of terrorism. These acts had the psychological and political purpose of showing the world that the FLN remained an unconquered force.

On the international stage, FLN cadres operating outside of Algeria garnered the reward for years of diplomatic labor. Their propaganda machine continually publicized accounts of French brutality. They contrasted international support for self-determination with the French repression of this right in Algeria. FLN propaganda undermined France's claim to represent Western civilization and France's historic revolutionary roots based on the Declaration of the Rights of Man. By skilled and relentless manipulation of the international media, FLN propagandists convinced the Non-Aligned Movement, as well as liberal factions in Great Britain and particularly the United States, to condemn French conduct. They used the United Nations as a stage to tarnish France and sow discord between France and her allies.

De Gaulle's last attempt to find compromise featured a policy of "association" by which an autonomous Algeria would remain loosely linked with France. He hoped to find a way to allow the *pieds-noirs* to remain and for Muslims loyal to France to assimilate peacefully into a new Algeria. This policy failed on all fronts. Muslim demonstrations in Algiers showed that anything short of total independence was unacceptable. In keeping with the emerging international consensus, on December 19, 1960, the UN General Assembly rejected de Gaulle's policy and instead recognized Algeria's right to independence. The French army grew demoralized. Addressing mourners at the funeral of ten paratroopers killed in Algeria, an army chaplain spoke for many when he said, "You have fallen at a time when, if we are to believe the speeches, we no longer know why we are dying."[6] Officers who had worked to protect Algerians from FLN reprisals, particularly the SAS officers who had developed close relationships with villagers in their areas, felt dishonored that de Gaulle would betray people who had trusted France. The extreme loyalists of French Algeria formed the Organisation Armée Secrète (OAS), a secretive terror group dedicated to retaining *pied-noir* control of Algeria. A revolt of French generals in Algeria, including General Challe, against de Gaulle's government, the so-called Generals' Putsch of April 1961, demonstrated a powerful French military faction's attitude toward compromise. With his own rule in jeopardy, de Gaulle concluded that he had no alternative but to enter negotiations with the FLN in May 1961.

This decision violated repeated French pledges never to negotiate with the terrorists. The FLN leadership correctly perceived that France needed a negotiated settlement more than the insurgents did. They stonewalled on every issue discussed at the conference table and within one year France had capitulated on every major point it had once asserted represented a vital national interest. On July 3, 1962, France officially recognized Algerian independence.

The Algerian settlement ended a sixteen-year French military effort to retain its colonies in Indochina and North Africa. The terms of the settlement guaranteed the safety and property of French colonists for three years. Unpersuaded, at least three quarters of the *pieds-noirs*, some 750,000 people, left the country they called home, the place where they and their families had been born and raised, to flee to France. The summer of 1962 witnessed terrible scenes as a desperate, uprooted European population pushed and shoved to secure a berth on a plane or boat bound for Marseilles. In a haunting echo of the FLN slogan "The suitcase or the coffin," they had to leave all property behind except for their allotment of two suitcases each. Another 50,000 moved to Spain, while 10,000 Sephardic Jews emigrated to Israel. In total, their exodus was the most massive population relocation to Europe since World War II.

Tragically left behind were those Algerians who had supported the

French. They included career soldiers, militiamen, elite members of the "hunt commandos," police, and government bureaucrats. At first SAS officers had arranged transportation to France for the men who were certain to face death if they remained in Algeria, namely the most devoted members of their units. But the French government halted this effort and forbade all "illegal" emigration from Algeria. By this act of surpassing dishonor, the French government thereby condemned several hundred thousand Algerian men and their families to reprisals at the ungentle hands of the FLN. As the weeks passed, horrific stories leaked from Algeria of former French loyalists dying by the hundreds while being compelled to clear the minefields of the Morice Line; of veterans forced to dig their own graves, swallow their French medals, and then face execution; of burnings, castrations, and the elimination of entire families, including young children. How many were killed is unknown, with estimates ranging from 30,000 to 150,000.

Why the French Lost

The war in Algeria lasted almost eight years. Two million French soldiers had crossed the Mediterranean to fight in Algeria. The official French tabulation of casualties reported 12,000 French combat deaths with another 6,000 killed by "accidents." The Algerian militia including the *harki* hunter units suffered 2,500 killed. The number of combat wounded totaled 25,000, with the astonishing figure of 28,700 enduring "accidental woundings."[7]

Over the duration of the war, the French estimated that 141,000 Muslim male combatants had been killed by security forces and another 78,000 Muslim civilians had been killed by terrorist action, 12,000 of whom were killed in internal political purges. On the other hand, in 1962 the FLN estimated that 300,000 Algerians had died from war-related causes. Later, the Algerian government raised this estimate to one million. No one ever counted the number of civilians "accidentally" killed during French search-and-destroy operations, losses from malnutrition and disease among the 1.8 million Muslims who either were regrouped by the French or became refugees, or the number of reprisal killings conducted by the FLN after the French departed. While the French totals surely are an undercount and the Algerian government's count may be exaggerated, the true number is unknowable. Taken as a whole, the war probably caused about a half million deaths, most of which were Algerian.

Coming in the wake of the national humiliation against the Germans in 1940 and against the Viet Minh in Indochina, the Algerian debacle was too much to acknowledge, so France tried to ignore it. Until 1999, France formally refused to call it a war, leaving others to label it the "War with No Name." Some of the long-suppressed secrets from the conflict emerged in the late 1990s. The start of the new century witnessed dramatic confrontations in the French press among senior French veterans, culminating in the 2001 publication of General Paul Aussaresses' memoirs. Aussaresses candidly admitted torture and summary executions and claimed that the French national leadership covertly authorized this conduct. His shocking assertions, in conjunction with other revelations, provide overwhelming documentation of the routine practice of torture and murder by French military and security forces during the Algerian War.

THE MILITARY INEPTITUDE of Algerian guerrillas surprised French veterans of Indochina. They remarked, "Thank God we are not dealing with Viets here!"[8] By virtually all military measures the armed wing of the Front de Libération Nationale failed. Likewise, inside Algeria the political wing did not enjoy much success. Unlike nationalist movements elsewhere, it failed to organize effective labor strikes or stimulate a widespread popular uprising. The year 1958 witnessed the armed wing at its peak strength. Yet when the FLN called for a Muslim boycott of the September 1958 referendum on de Gaulle's assumption of power, large numbers of Muslims voted in defiance of FLN pleas and threats. Nonetheless, in spite of military and political failure inside Algeria the FLN decisively achieved victory.

That victory came even though the French military waged a comprehensive counterinsurgency featuring all the classic ingredients, including fortified barriers to isolate the insurgents and eliminate outside support, light-infantry/hunter-killer tactics, extensive recruitment of local militia, and population "regrouping." The military effort created several opportunities for a political compromise leading to peace, but the requisite political resolution was lacking. About the time French military leaders believed themselves on the verge of victory, the corrosive impact of torture on French and Algerian public opinion became manifest. Political support for the war collapsed, resulting in a French withdrawal from Algeria.

The French counterinsurgency had the presumed benefit of featuring veterans with very recent experience in counterinsurgency warfare. For all their talk about understanding revolutionary war, French political and military leaders were unable to devise a consistent political-military counterinsurgency strategy. Broadly speaking, leaders divided into two camps, one promoting "soft" war and one insisting on "hard" war. The schism between the two camps was wide and affected almost everything. A representative of the "soft" war camp, David Galula, believed that it was vitally important for the military and the police to conduct arrests and detentions with great care in an effort to avoid alienating the civilian population. In contrast, embittered Indochina veterans such as Roger Trinquier and Paul Aussaresses thought that France had failed in that war because it had been too gentle and the way to end the insurgency was through a brutal policy that relied on torture and summary execution.

French counterterrorism as performed by Aussaresses and likeminded officers shows how readily security forces confronting terrorists become brutal. Aussaresses justified his conduct in pragmatic terms. Terrorist bombs were killing innocent people. The judicial system was incapable of addressing the situation. If a terrorist entered the legal system there would be a long delay before his trial and the chances were good that he would be freed and thus given the opportunity to launch new attacks. Aussaresses concluded that "summary executions were therefore an inseparable part of the tasks associated with keeping law and order."[9] Aussaresses and his ilk were not sadists. Rather they believed that they were performing the nation's necessary dirty work and took comfort in the familiar dodge that they were simply following orders. Indeed, it is almost certain that French military and political leadership all the way up to the top tacitly authorized torture and summary executions.

Having accepted the logical necessity for extralegal conduct, the next step inevitably extended the boundaries where such conduct was appropriate. In Aussaresses' mind there was no moral difference between the terrorist who placed the bomb and the members of his support network. The chemist who made the explosive, the bomb maker, the driver, and the lookout were equally guilty. Indeed, if Aussaresses had had his way he would have carried his counterterror operations back to France to kill the "suitcase men," the couriers and tax collectors who gathered funds among Algerian immigrants in France and carried the money to Algeria to support the insurgency.

Aussaresses was not the only one who held this opinion. Without regard to national borders, French assassination teams targeted arms merchants who supplied the insurgency. Inside France, the police killed an unknown number of insurgents and their supporters.

Algeria was a notable example of the perils of fixating on the military defeat of an armed insurgency. By most conventional measures, the French defeated the insurgents' military arm. However, the political and subversive struggle continued and the insurgents ultimately won out. In the words of historian Alistair Horne, "From the French army's point of view, their tragedy was that at various points they could see with agonising clarity (and not without reason) that they were winning the war militarily. But (not unlike the American commanders in Vietnam) it was not given to them to perceive that, at the same time, their chances of winning the war politically and on the wider world stage were growing ever slimmer."[10]

Given that the French objective was to retain colonial control over Algeria—the domination of 1 million settlers of European origin over 9 million natives—in the absence of radical political change the French in Algeria were doomed to fail. Even the most enlightened practitioners of pacification could offer nothing more than social and economic reforms within the existing political framework. What the masses wanted was self-rule.

Then and thereafter, the Algerian war attracted interest among British and American officers who contemplated how to confront the spread worldwide of Communism. French veterans of the conflict gave lectures attended by NATO officers and wrote articles in American and European military journals. American interest increased as the United States found itself becoming increasingly involved in Vietnam. However, that interest focused on counterinsurgency techniques—for example, the use of helicopters against guerrillas—rather than on the political implications of fighting a nationalist movement. When they looked at Algeria, American strategists were more interested in how to acquire the most efficient operational payoff than in performing a painstaking analysis of the underlying nature of the insurgency. Because of this typically American focus, American planners failed to derive vital conclusions regarding the political underpinnings of revolutionary warfare.

In France, the consequences of the war in Algeria continue to play out. The terms of the war-ending Evian peace agreement gave Algerian immigrant workers coming to France certain preferential treatment. Thereafter they lived as marginalized citizens in urban slums beyond the sight of most French people. Periodically there have been outbreaks of civil un-rest, but until 2005 France successfully managed to ignore most of the grievances of its Muslim population. The riots that began on the evening of October 27, 2005, in Clichy-sous-Bois, a working-class commune lo-cated in the eastern suburbs of Paris, have been another demonstration that the historic tension between France and its former Algerian citizens is not yet resolved.

PART THREE

The Malayan Emergency

ELEVEN

Crisis in Malaya

*The answer lies not in pouring more troops into the jungle, but in
the hearts and minds of the people.*

—General Gerard Templer, 1952[1]

The Empire's Setting Sun

MALAYA IS A PENINSULA STRETCHING 450 miles southeast from a border with Thailand to the island of Singapore. A spine of jungle-covered
mountains extends along the middle of the peninsula. At the time of the
Malayan Emergency, four fifths of the land was jungle, with the balance
consisting of rice paddies, rubber plantations, villages, and towns.

The British began establishing trading posts and naval bases on the
Straits of Malacca in 1786. During the 1820s the British imported Chinese
immigrants to work the rubber plantations and tin mines. Mining camps
at Kuala Lumpur, Ipoh, and Taiping grew to become the country's three
main urban centers. The presence of a large Chinese population caused
ethnic strife. Economics played a role, since the Chinese acted as middle-
men between producers and Malayan consumers and thereby dominated
retail and commercial life in Malaya. Differences in religion—the Malays
were Muslims, the Chinese were not—exacerbated tensions. Although accepting of British hegemony, the Chinese considered themselves superior

to the Malays and refused to be ruled by them. Consequently, the Chinese retained their own way of life and did not mix with the Malayan people.

In 1946, the British completed the unification of a country that heretofore had been a loose collection of sultanates. The new Federation of Malaya numbered 5.3 million people divided among three major ethnic groups: 49 percent Malay, 38 percent Chinese, and 11 percent Indian. By 1948, the year the Emergency began, about 12,000 Europeans, almost all of whom were British, lived in Malaya. British civil servants filled the upper echelon of government. British citizens managed the country's rich tin mines and rubber plantations. Although the sun had already begun to set elsewhere in the British Empire, Europeans living in Malaya continued to enjoy a life of colonial ease. At their places of employment they managed a biddable, low-cost labor force. Outside of work innumerable servants dealt with life's chores while their masters rotated from posh polo and tennis clubs to mountain resorts where they sought refuge from Malaya's hot, humid climate. Life was good, it had long been like this, and they saw no reason it should change.

The Communist Party

The Malayan Communist Party (MCP) formed in 1930. With some 15,000 members and 10,000 active sympathizers, almost all of whom were Chinese, the party was not particularly effective. It hosted a regional meeting in its foundation year, a meeting most notable for the attendance of a young Vietnamese Communist named Ho Chi Minh, and for the comprehensive surveillance by the British Special Branch of the Singapore Police Force. Subsequent mass arrests decimated the MCP.

Shortly after midnight on December 8, 1941, Japanese soldiers landed in northeast Malaya. During the subsequent fifty-four-day campaign, a combination of Japanese skill, air superiority, and British ineptitude caused the worst loss in the history of the British Empire. When Singapore surrendered, the British had lost over 138,000 men, most of them prisoners, while inflicting fewer than 10,000 casualties on the Japanese. Before the fall of Singapore, British officers managed to organize a small band of some 200 Chinese guerrillas led by the secretary general of the MCP. The guerrillas grandiloquently named their armed wing the Malayan People's Anti-Japanese Army. The British intended the guerrillas to fight against the Japanese occupation. Instead, guerrilla leaders mostly ignored the Japanese and concentrated on preparing for a postwar battle against the British.

Toward this goal, they cultivated relationships with a class of poor, marginalized Chinese who lived along the fringes of the Malaya jungle.

Before the Japanese invasion, Malaya's rural population was almost entirely Malay. Rural Malays lived in villages where they cultivated rice, fruit crops, and small rubber plantations. The Chinese lived in towns or worked in the mines and rubber plantations. During the war years, urban unemployment, the closure of many mines and plantations, and Japanese brutality forced thousands of Chinese to move to undeveloped land along the jungle edge. Because they subsisted on land owned by Malay sultans, they were called squatters. However, they were not squatters in the Western sense in that they were not migrants. Rather the Chinese remained on the land for years, with individual families erecting simple bamboo and palm leaf shelters, clearing small plots of land, and eking out an existence by growing vegetables. They did not form hamlets or villages; rather their homes were scattered along the jungle fringe. About a half million Chinese, 10 percent of the country's population, lived in this way and they became the principal pillar supporting the anti-British insurgency.

During the war years, while the Malayan People's Anti-Japanese Army opposed Japanese occupation, most Malays cooperated with the Japanese. While their level of collaboration annoyed the British, it was in fact little different from Malay conduct toward the British before the war. In 1945 the British returned to Malaya and found themselves much diminished in the eyes of the inhabitants. Having been badly trounced by one Asian people at the start of the war, the British no longer had an aura of invincibility. Still, the reopening of the mines and plantations brought some return to normality. However, although many Chinese men resumed their work in the mines and on the plantations, their families remained on their jungle clearings. Meanwhile, the Chinese-controlled Malayan People's Anti-Japanese Army established the Old Comrades Association, which ostensibly provided welfare for war veterans. In fact, it was a front organization whose real goal was to preserve a military framework so the guerrillas could be rapidly mobilized when the leaders called them to fight.

WORLD WAR II almost brought Great Britain to her knees. Postwar British politicians understood their nation's weakness and resolved to cede selected colonial possessions back to the native people. In Malay this initially took the form of the Malayan Union. Nearly the entire Malay population disagreed with the British decision to create the Malayan Union. The Malay majority opposed granting the Chinese and Indian minorities equal rights, particularly equal voting opportunities. Consequently, when the British celebrated the inauguration of a new Malay constitution in April 1946, no Malay political leaders or government officials attended. In response to Malay protests, the British wisely abandoned the constitution.

The year 1948 witnessed the signing of the Federation of Malaya Agreement. Its terms provided for a strong central government headed by a British high commissioner. He, in turn, appointed executive and legislative councils. Each of the federation's nine states retained its sovereignty, with each Malay sultan, or state ruler, accepting a British protectorate. This agreement was an acceptable arrangement for the Malay majority since it provided for considerable power at the state level and effectively disenfranchised the Chinese minority.

Consequently, the Chinese community in Malaya had little reason to support the Malay-dominated government. They held a contemptuous attitude toward all things Malayan and squirmed under the humiliating knowledge that these Malays and their British masters treated them as second-class citizens. Indeed, the government denied the Chinese full citizenship rights, Malays received preferential treatment in selection for government posts, and the Chinese rural squatters did not own the land they lived on even though no one before them had done anything to make their small plots productive. At the same time, an active minority of the Chinese living in Malaya considered Communism a political system devised by Chinese people working for the betterment of the Chinese. These ethnic and political tensions provided fertile soil for the Chinese-run Malayan Communist Party to plant the seeds of insurrection.

Back in 1946 and 1947, Malayan Communists had tried to implement the classic Russian pattern of revolution by seeding popular discontent through propaganda and economic disruption. The Communists exploited popular grievances by openly and legally spreading their message in schools, clubs, and youth groups. They had a particularly strong presence in the country's labor unions, so they tried to cause civil strife with strikes and similar nonviolent actions. Only a minority of union workers ever wholeheartedly supported these efforts. Indeed, when the British responded with restrictive labor laws that thwarted these efforts, most people approved. They were tired of conflict and disruption. All they wanted was a return to normality. By 1948 it was clear to the Communist leaders that the Russian revolutionary model was not working, so they converted to Mao's model. In June 1948 the new secretary general of the Malayan Communist Party, Chin Peng, mobilized the former anti-Japanese guerrilla army and committed it to a Maoist-inspired guerrilla war.

Terror Comes to Malaya

Born of immigrant parents in Malaya in 1924, Chin Peng had risen to prominence during World War II when he joined other Chinese Malayans who took to the jungle to fight the Japanese. His particular duty was as liaison officer to British commandos who arrived by submarine and parachute during the Japanese occupation. Although Chin Peng saw limited combat service, he displayed enough energy and drive to receive two British campaign medals as well as the prestigious Order of the British Empire, an award an embarrassed British government later withdrew. Chin Peng's particular skills lay in the art of political infighting. For military decisions, he relied on the much more competent former chairman of the party's Central Military Committee, Lau Yew.

Like Chin Peng, Lau Yew had at one time been viewed favorably by the British. He had led the Malayan contingent in the grand Victory Parade in London just after the war. Then and thereafter, Lau Yew closely studied Mao Tse-tung's dictates. The party's decision to wage a guerrilla war against the British meant that it was his responsibility to devise a victory plan. Lau Yew's plan followed the four-phase formula for revolutionary warfare. During phase one guerrillas would attack isolated, British-managed rubber plantations and tin mines as well as rural police and government officials in order to gain control of the rural population and to undermine the governments' prestige and authority. Undoubtedly the British and their "running dogs," the Malay officials and police, would flee for the safety of larger cities, leaving behind a void. Phase two called for filling this void, the so-called Liberated Areas, with a Communist presence. Here the guerrillas would gather and train recruits and prepare for phase three. In phase three, the strengthened guerrillas would fan out from the Liberated Areas to attack towns and villages and sever lines of communication. Then the guerrillas would form into regular units and enter phase four, a climactic conventional struggle leading to ultimate victory.

Party leaders circulated among the 7,000 retired members of the old wartime Malayan People's Anti-Japanese Army—soon to be renamed the Malayan Races Liberation Army although in fact some 90 percent were ethnic Chinese—and summoned them to battle. Many of these former guerrillas were now middle aged, enjoying a life of modest prosperity where at least they had a roof over their heads and ate regular meals. They had had their fill of living on the run in the jungle and were most reluctant recruits. Reluctant or not, some 3,000 heeded the call to mobilize, retrieved hidden weapons—many of them supplied by the British during the war—and traveled to their assigned jungle camps.

Supporting the combat elements was the Min Yuen, or "Masses Movement." They were indistinguishable from the majority of the Chinese population. They wore no uniforms and looked and acted no different from innocent farmers and rubber tappers. In rural areas the Min Yuen organized clandestine cells within the squatter villages. These cells formed the crucial link between the people and the guerrillas. Motivated by a combination of extortion, coercion, and genuine support for Communist goals, the rural Min Yuen provided the guerrillas with food, intelligence, money, and recruits. To gain urban support, the Min Yuen behaved ostensibly as normal civilians going about their daily business as waiters in British clubs, clerks in the government, and teachers in the schools. In fact, while buried in the fabric of normal society these urban Communist sympathizers spread propaganda, provided intelligence, collected taxes, and informed on those who collaborated with the government.

Because of feelings of racial solidarity, many Chinese sympathized with the goals of the Malayan Communist Party. Many more were nervous fence-sitters, uncertain who was eventually going to win and therefore unwilling to support either side except under compulsion. They recalled the startling British collapse in 1942. They saw an ascendant Communist force spreading across their ancestral homeland in China and pondered the possibility that Mao's victorious legions might flow south into Malaya. Given such musings—and the knowledge that they and their families would be defenseless against Communist reprisal in the event the British abandoned Malaya—there was little reason to support the government until that government clearly proved that it was going to win.

Although Lau Yew planned to follow the four stages of revolutionary warfare, he did not give the Min Yuen much time to promote revolutionary spirit. He expected his forces to pass rapidly through the four stages of revolution. Based on what he had seen at the start of World War II, Lau Yew expected the British who managed mines and rubber plantations to flee as soon as phase one operations began. He and his fellow leaders reasoned that in the absence of income from these holdings, the British would have no reason to remain in Malaya. In the absence of the British, it would be simplicity itself to take over the country from the "running dogs." The Communists' military tactic of choice was terror.

ARTHUR WALKER MANAGED an isolated rubber plantation in the state of Perak. His small office lay at the end of one of Malaya's loneliest roads but this did not alarm Walker. He had spent twenty of his fifty years in Malaya and was comfortable with the country's daily rhythms. He had just returned from his morning inspection of the estate when three young Chinese rode up to his office on bicycles. They entered Walker's office. His dog started barking and Walker tried to quiet him. The young men greeted Walker in Malay: "Salutations, sir!" The affable Walker cheerfully returned their greetings. Two shots rang out and Walker fell dead.

Thirty minutes later, ten miles away, twelve armed Chinese surrounded the office of the Sungei Siput estate. Inside, manager John Allison and his twenty-one-year-old assistant, Ian Christian, were discussing business with their Chinese clerks. Revolver-wielding Chinese entered the office and compelled the white men to march to a nearby bungalow. They wanted Allison's gun. Having secured the manager's revolver, they marched their victims back to the office. A gunman reassured a frightened Malay clerk, "Don't be afraid. We're only out for Europeans and the running dogs"[2] They bound Allison and Christian to chairs and executed them.

Eighteen miles away, a phone rang in the upper floor of a two-story building. The building housed the headquarters of the Perak State Police. On the ground floor, thirty-two-year-old Robert Thompson worked as a Chinese-affairs officer. Fluent in Cantonese, he was listening to an elderly Chinese woman detail her grievance when a police officer descended the stairs and came running toward Thompson's desk. For Thompson, the moment forever remained indelibly imprinted in his brain: the slowly rotating blades of the ceiling fans barely stirring the ovenlike air; native clerks dressed in white duck suits diligently laboring at their desks; the alternating bands of light and dark on the wood floor caused by sunlight filtering through the rattan curtains; a white man running when no one ever ran in Malaya's enervating climate. Flushed with excitement and exertion, the officer stopped at Thompson's desk: "Bob—it's started!"[3]

Indeed, the murder of three European planters on June 16, 1948, marked the beginning of war in Malaya.

FOR THE FIRST six months of the insurgency, the Communists registered an average of more than two hundred incidents per month. Special assassination teams composed of professional revolutionaries targeted government officials in order to disrupt government operation. Their ability to strike throughout the country surprised and shocked both the Europeans living in Malaya and British authorities. However, like many strategic plans, the Communist strategy to liberate Malaya collapsed when their enemies refused to follow the Communist script. Instead, the government appealed to the targets of terror, its officials and the European elite, to remain steadfast in the face of danger.

In turn, planters and mine managers armed themselves, fortified their bungalows, and carried on with business. Peter Lucy and his wife, Tommy, lived on a rubber plantation eight miles from Kuala Lumpur. In spite of its proximity to a major city, the plantation was the target of frequent attacks. The couple built a sandbagged stronghold (and later put sandbag walls around the nursery where Tommy delivered twin infants), ordered the construction of watchtowers and laying of barbed wire to protect the workers, installed armor plating on their Ford truck, and resolved to carry on. Tommy wrote, "We have to make up our minds that guns, ammunition, and guards are the order of the day." She put her words into practice by manning a light machine gun whenever the Communists attacked. Many British expats agreed with Tommy when she asserted, "Our biggest value is from the point of view of morale. I'm quite sure it makes a great difference to the labourers and the other people in the district so see that we're carrying on normal lives."[4]

The government helped the rural plantation and mine managers by quickly creating a force of Special Constables, nearly all of whom were Malays. At first they were woefully armed and indifferently trained. But even so, they helped provide a modicum of protection both for government officials who continued to work in rural areas and for the rural European population. Because of the government's initial responses and the resolve of the expat community, and contrary to Communist expectations, there was no mass, panic-stricken flight out of the remote interior.

The terrorists found it easier to kill civilians who were reluctant to provide support for the revolution than to kill government officials or armed and wary planters. In a typical incident, guerrillas appeared one night at the homes of three squatters who had refused to pay their requisitions. The guerillas assembled the three families, selected one child from each, and hacked the children to death before their parents' eyes. They departed with the warning "Pay or we will kill another of your children." During the first outbreak of the insurgency, guerrillas killed 223 civilians, only 17 of whom were Europeans; almost all the rest were Chinese.

Terror came easy to the guerrillas. However, Communist leaders quickly realized that when guerrillas sabotaged mine equipment, slashed rubber trees, and murdered the managers who operated the mines and plantations, they destroyed the means of production and thus ruined the ability of Chinese peasants to support themselves. Moreover, their failure to direct their forces to carve out a "liberated zone" that could serve as a base area to nurture the insurgency ultimately proved disastrous. In sum, phase one operations neither produced popular uprisings, fatally disrupted the economy, nor built a secure sanctuary. The faltering campaign of sabotage and terrorism persuaded the Communist leadership to follow Mao's Chinese example and gird for a long guerrilla war designed to break British will.

TWELVE

Personality and Vision

The British Army

ON JUNE 18, 1948, JUST TWO DAYS after the killing began, British authorities made a federationwide declaration of emergency. The first set of emergency regulations gave the police—a force almost exclusively composed of Malays officered by Britons—sweeping extra powers to search, detain, and enforce curfews. On July 23, the government declared the Malayan Communist Party an unlawful society. To impose its will, the government initially had a regular military force of ten understrength infantry battalions (two British, six Gurkha, and two Malay), a 10,000-man Federation Police force (supplemented over the next three months by 24,000 Malay Special Constables), and a Royal Air Force contingent of some 100 planes.[1] The squadron of aging but still versatile Spitfires could attack ground targets. The squadron of Sunderland flying boats had no direct value against the guerrillas. It fell to the army to play the leading role in the initial counterinsurgency campaign.

Throughout its history the British army had taken a supporting role behind the Royal Navy as the lead actor in national defense. By the middle of the 1800s about 80 percent of the regular British army was stationed abroad, where it policed imperial territory. The army evolved as a disparate collection of individual battalions accustomed to long service in isolated locations. British leaders used the small decentralized army to achieve limited goals at limited cost. This background shaped the army's philosophy toward counterinsurgency operations in Malaya. Three principles prevailed: minimum force, civil-military cooperation, and flexible small-unit tactics. In many ways, the British Army was institutionally well-suited to wage an effective counterinsurgency. But the strategic capabilities of the senior leadership also influences outcomes. The commander of British forces in Malaya, Major General Charles Boucher, began his military service in a Gurkha unit and ascended to command of the Tenth Indian Brigade in World War II. Captured by Rommel's troops in the western desert in June 1942, Boucher was held as a prisoner of war in Italy until 1943, when the armistice with Italy allowed him to escape his Italian guards and make his way to Allied lines in southern Italy. Thereafter, he again led Indian troops in combat, this time in bitter mountain fighting at Cassino and against the Gothic Line. Boucher described his strategy on July 27, 1948: "My object is to break the insurgent concentrations, to bring them to battle . . . to drive them underground or into the jungle, and then to follow them there . . . I intend to keep them constantly moving and deprive them of food and recruits, because if they are constantly moving they cannot terrorize an area properly so that they can get their commodities from it; and then ferret them out of their holes, wherever these holes may be."[2]

Boucher's conventional formulation received favorable local press coverage—"Boucher Promises More Toughness" was a typical headline—but it was not a practical solution to the insurgency. It worked only as long as the guerrillas stood and fought, which was not long at all. Thereafter, security forces conducted large-scale, multibattalion sweeps through the jungle that proved futile. The guerrillas' bases were invisible from the air and almost impossible to find by ground search. A British patrol entering the overgrown jungle fringe could easily consume four hours to trek one mile. Soldiers passed within five yards of a concealed guerrilla without seeing him. Likewise, searchers could be within fifty yards of a 100-man guerrilla camp and never know that they were so close to their elusive objective. As early as the fall of 1948 an operational analysis suggested that elaborate sweeps were of dubious value. Later analysis would show that it took about 1,000 man-hours of patrolling to eliminate one guerrilla.

Undeterred, conventionally minded officers persisted. In spite of their code names evoking historic heroism, Operations Ramillies, Blenheim, Spitfire, and the like failed. It was more the pity because at the war's start the British held a priceless opportunity to defeat rapidly an insurgency unexpectedly deprived of its most able military commander.

Paths Not Taken

When Lau Yew perceived that acts of terror had failed so far to drive off the British or to create Liberated Areas where the guerrilla force could expand and gain strength, he ordered increased attacks. Isolated police stations were a special target. Lau Yew thought that a massed force of several hundred guerrillas could easily overrun a station defended by a sergeant and his ten constables. Most of these attacks were humiliating repulses. With hindsight it could be seen that Lau Yew was guilty of strategic impatience. He had thought that the insurrection would achieve decisive results by the end of August 1948, but in fact the Communists had come nowhere close.

In mid-July 1948 an informer told a British police superintendent, the legendary Bill "Two-Gun" Stafford—a veteran of fifteen parachute jumps behind Japanese lines in Burma who earned his moniker by always carrying a revolver under each armpit—when and where some important Communist officials were to attend a jungle meeting. Stafford and some of his loyal Chinese detectives surrounded the meeting place. During the ensuing firefight Stafford shot and killed an armed insurgent who turned out to be Lau Yew. Lau Yew's death threw the insurgency into disarray and left its military operations in the hands of inexperienced and not particularly able leaders. Here was opportunity for the British if they had the wit to perceive it.

One officer who possessed the combination of experience and insight was Lieutenant Colonel Walter Walker. Like Two-Gun Stafford, Walker had fought in the Burmese jungle against the Japanese. The unique skill set required to survive in jungle combat informed his decision to create a "Ferret Force" in July 1948. It consisted of small teams each composed of twelve British Empire volunteers, soldiers from the Malay Regiment, a signals detachment, highly skilled Dyak trackers recruited in Borneo, and a Chinese liaison officer. A British volunteer with local knowledge led each Ferret Force group. The Ferret Forces were thus perfectly tailored for the task of hunting insurgents in their jungle bases. Unfortunately they disbanded within five months, a casualty of bureaucratic infighting over policy, administration, and methods. Still, the abortive experiment demonstrated the value of its innovative core concept, namely, small patrols guided by native trackers and accompanied by interpreters and local troops.

Walker was also convinced that many hard-learned lessons in World War II–era jungle warfare had been forgotten because of the army's focus on conventional warfare. This amnesia was particularly apparent when regular army units conducted large-scale sweeps. They called it "jungle bashing" and in Walker's mind this connoted exactly what was wrong. An officer described a jungle-bashing operation: "We had now been in the jungle for five continuous weeks, taking part in one of those big operations . . . During the whole period we had neither seen nor heard any sign of the enemy."[3] To help rectify this problem Walker established a training center dedicated to "studying, teaching and perfecting methods of jungle fighting."[4] This Jungle Warfare Training Centre contributed useful tactical innovations but in the absence of a coherent strategic plan to defeat the insurgents such innovations were not enough.

Instead Boucher continued with his map-perfect search-and-destroy missions that were heavy on the searching but did little useful destroying. Typical was the experience of a newly arrived regular British infantry regiment, the Green Howards. The Green Howards arrived in Malaya early in the conflict at a time when the guerrillas still operated in large units of 100 men or more. The battalion zealously searched the jungle over a four-month period, saw guerrillas just five times, and killed one of them. The regiment's altogether typical experience amply revealed Boucher's strategy to be a virtual guarantee that the fight against the insurgents would be a long, drawn-out affair.

THE SENIOR BRITISH official on the ground when the Emergency began was Sir Edward Gent. His brief time in command suggests that Gent would have been unequal to the challenge. Before such a judgment could be conclusively made, Gent died in an airplane accident. In September 1948 Whitehall appointed his successor, Sir Henry Gurney. If central casting had selected a man to play a British proconsul, Gurney would have received first call. An Oxford graduate, avid sportsman, and immaculate dresser—he insisted on wearing a tie, jacket, and felt hat in spite of Malaya's heat and humidity—Gurney's celebrated panache achieved legendary status during his tenure as chief secretary in Palestine. There he had insisted on his daily round of golf regardless of the disruptions around him, finishing his last round the day before he ended British administration and theatrically departed Palestine on the last plane out of the country.

However, beneath this image was a man of unusual perception who made two key contributions to the fight against the Malayan Communists. Gurney asserted that the conflict was a competition between political ideologies. If the military was left to follow its instincts, the result would be an escalation that would inevitably use all available military might. Civilian casualties would ensue, which would turn more people to the Communist side. Instead, Gurney insisted that in this war of ideas, the army should provide military support for a political war rather than the civil administration providing political cover for a purely military effort. Over the objections of the military—it was ridiculous that "a bunch of coppers should start telling the generals what to do," complained General Boucher—Gurney insisted on civilian control of the counterinsurgency.[5]

Robert Thompson, now installed in the government secretariat in Kuala Lumpur, where he coordinated intelligence reports, enthusiastically endorsed Gurney's philosophy. A single misguided bomb created countless enemies. Even if accurately delivered, all the bombs and shells in the world would not touch a Communist cell operating in a high school where it produced new recruits for the insurgency.

Gurney's second insight was to understand the insurgents' dependency on the Chinese squatters. His solution was breathtaking: to relocate them into villages where they would be isolated from the guerrillas and protected from insurgent terror. No one expected the squatters to uproot their lives willingly. The incentive was land grants. Gurney reasoned that by becoming legal stakeholders, the squatters would possess a strong motive to support the government. Relocating one tenth of the country's population was an expensive and challenging logistical feat. Moreover, the Malay sultans who owned the land had to be persuaded to cede it to the squatters. Gurney reckoned it would take eighteen months to get the program well and truly launched. Meanwhile, the Malayan Communist Party strengthened its hold on the squatter population.

The irreducible minimum of logistical support the guerrillas required was rice, weapons, and ammunition. The jungle provided none of these. Consequently, the guerrillas operated from jungle bases no more than a few hours away from populated areas and relied on the Chinese squatters who lived along the jungle edge for money, food, medicine, clothes, intelligence, and recruits. Most jungle bases had only one access trail. This path typically extended up from a jungle valley past a small lean-to. This shed served as a supply point to where carrying parties deposited their forty-pound rice sacks and the guerrillas picked them up. The guerrillas hauled the rice up a rugged, nearly perpendicular ascent overlooked by the first of at least two well-concealed guard posts. The camp itself lay on cleared ground but the upper story of primary-growth jungle was always left undisturbed to conceal the camp from aerial observation. Likewise, the camp's approach was always screened from the trail so that "no part of it could be seen from more than five yards away."[6] Every camp had a secure escape route in case security forces found it.

Because of this meticulous attention to camouflage and concealment, military patrols seldom found a guerrilla camp unless they had a defector willing to guide them to it. When the security forces did approach a camp, the guards usually delayed them long enough for the camp inhabitants to flee. A British officer described accompanying his patrol toward a camp and encountering a single rifle shot. What to do? He could not accurately judge from where the shot came. Should he move his men to the left or right or simply charge blindly straight forward? Meanwhile, the guard had accomplished his task. His warning shot alerted his comrades. The fleeing insurgents always outpaced their pursuers since the latter did not know the terrain and had to fear ambush and booby trap.

So it was that the contest against the insurgents featured all the usual frustrations of guerrilla warfare: the absence of fixed lines, the lack of decisive geographical objectives, the illusion that there might be a decisive battle, and the inability to separate enemy fighters from the civilian population.

The Rise of General Briggs

In Great Britain, war in Malaya began at a time when a new Labor government headed by Clement Attlee was in control. Attlee believed that eventually Malaya should achieve independence, but he and his party also thought that the British government should never negotiate while terrorists had guns pointed at British heads. Attlee's government signaled its determination to defeat the insurgency by sending reinforcements to Malaya in the summer of 1948, including the Second Guards Brigade. This marked the first time in British history that any soldiers serving in the Household Brigade had ever been deployed outside of the British Isles during what was notionally a time of peace. In spite of the fact that the British people had not yet recovered from the tremendous effort spent in World War II, a vast majority supported the fight in Malaya. Over time, the confidence of the British government and the British people in victory rose and fell according to progress and setbacks. However, their basic determination ultimately to win would prove to be a hallmark of the Malayan Emergency.

However, by 1950 there was a growing disconnect between perceptions of progress and the reality on the ground. Slowly the realization that the situation was getting worse gained ascendancy among British leaders and politicians. Simultaneously, Communist successes on the mainland of China emboldened the insurgents. They were better armed and organized than ever before. They held the initiative and were conducting regular ambushes along roads and railways and attacking police stations to obtain arms and reassert control of the villages. Each month the guerrillas killed or abducted scores of civilians. The police had lost confidence and appeared powerless to stop the terror.

After two ineffectual years of counterinsurgency, Attlee's government summoned from retirement Lieutenant General Sir Harold Briggs to coordinate all antiterrorist activities conducted by the security forces. Briggs was a World War II veteran who had commanded with distinction the Fifth Indian Division in Burma. His experience in jungle warfare was the prime reason the government chose him. Briggs wanted to decline the appointment but his former chief, Field Marshal Sir William Slim, overcame his reluctance. Briggs's task in Malaya was daunting: he was a former soldier acting in a civilian capacity as director of operations, in charge of military operations in support of a civil government.

Briggs arrived in Kuala Lumpur during the first week of April 1950. On the basis of his prior briefings and quick in-country tour, he reported his impressions to High Commissioner Gurney. Insurgent morale and strength were increasing. They drew support from the country's Chinese population, particularly the squatters. Active propaganda and terror squads were embedded in the Chinese population and those cells were "undetected and unscathed" because of lack of useful intelligence. Government counterinsurgency efforts were badly hampered by the lack of Chinese-speaking officials. In a startling departure from his predecessor, Briggs concluded that military successes against the "bandits" had little capacity to degrade the insurgency. Instead he agreed with Gurney that the proper focus was to win over the Chinese population. Only then could the initiative be wrested from the insurgents.[7]

However, Briggs related that the Chinese population lacked confidence in the government's ability to protect them against Communist terrorists and particularly the Traitor Killing Squads. The Malayan Chinese Association, a government-promoted effort to offer Chinese civilians an alternative to Communism, remained inert due to fear of Communist reprisal. Briggs recognized that this could not be changed everywhere all at once and thus avoided the temptation to operate simultaneously throughout the country. Instead, he proposed a gradual program, methodically securing the country in phases from south to north. The ultimate objective was the elimination of the whole Communist organization in Malaya.

Briggs began by recasting the tools needed to carry out his strategic intentions. He created the Federal Joint Intelligence Advisory Committee in May 1950. Prior to this time, intelligence came from the military, civil government, or police. With each entity pulling in a different direction, there was redundancy and omission. The new committee coordinated the collection, analysis, and distribution of all intelligence. Its success inspired the formation of the Federal War Council to coordinate all military, civil, and police counterinsurgency efforts. With Briggs serving as chairman, this small group was designed to be a flexible tool to devise policy and allocate resources. Meanwhile, the Special Branch continued as the sole internal security department in charge of dealing with internal subversion and counterespionage.

Having forged the necessary tools, Briggs addressed strategy. Heretofore few planners had understood the political dimensions of the conflict and the salient role played by the local people. The Malays already appreciated that however much they wanted independence from Britain as a long-term goal, they did not want to live in a nation where the Chinese merely replaced the British as overlords. Briggs clearly saw that the people who mattered were the Chinese. He resolved to implement programs to convince the Chinese, particularly the rural squatters, that an independent Malaya offered them a more attractive future than a Malaya dominated by Communist Chinese rulers. Toward this goal Briggs wanted to avoid indiscriminate punitive measures and focus on providing security for the squatters against the terrorists.

Because of the ongoing Korean War and a host of other imperial commitments, Briggs could not request a large military presence. To compensate for the manpower shortage, he proposed to recruit Chinese into an Auxiliary Police so they could participate in defending their homes against the insurgents. This provocative idea contained the obvious risk that a recruit could be disloyal to the government. He could desert to the Communists, provide them with inside information about military operations, or even lead a British patrol into an ambush. Accordingly, Briggs was willing to move slowly on this initiative to give time for the new recruits to prove their reliability. But overall, in Briggs's view, the potential gain outweighed the risk. Quite simply, without the cooperation of the rural Chinese the British could not defeat the insurgents.

New Villages

The centerpiece of what became known as the Briggs Plan was wholehearted implementation of Gurney's population-resettlement program. Gurney's original program had been "conceived in uncertainty, carried [out] in indifference and born in haste . . . bitterness, recrimination and hostility."[8] Under General Briggs the program operated much more efficiently. The government designed dormitory villages for the rubber and tin wage earners and agricultural villages for rural farmers. A well-protected truck convoy appeared at dawn in the old village, British soldiers helped the inhabitants load their possessions, and the trucks whisked the people away to a new life. Each relocated family received building materials to erect a house and a $100 cash payment. The impressive logistical feat impressed Gurney: "The machine now works so quickly that a piece of virgin jungle becomes a settlement of 200 houses complete with roads, water and police posts and fencing in ten days."[9]

Gurney did not see that the speed of the resettlement came at the sacrifice of careful preparation. Some of the new agricultural villages were on unproductive soils and had been chosen merely because no one else wanted the land. The village infrastructure was often poorly built with contaminated water and sewage systems that spread disease. Regardless, from a British standpoint the mandate was to move the squatters as fast as possible behind barbed wire in order to isolate them from the insurgents. By the end of 1951 authorities could report the mission almost accomplished, with the relocation plan 80 percent complete: about 400,000 squatters had been moved into more than 400 "New Villages."

Formerly, the inhabitants of the New Villages had lived in self-sufficient isolation. They were unaccustomed to community life. The role of the Chinese-speaking British resettlement officer was crucial for their adaptation. Finding willing and capable candidates to serve as resettlement officers was difficult. While many British spoke Malay, few spoke Chinese. Briggs scoured the corners of his administration to locate suitable resettlement officers. He insisted that all government departments release their most able Chinese-speaking officials for this duty. From outside came more recruits including former missionaries who had fled China in the face of Communist pressure. By dint of language skills, hard work, and tactful cultural sensitivity, the resettlement officers eased the transition from rural squatter to village dweller.

However, there were not enough to go around. Consequently, after a resettlement officer established a New Village's basic administrative structure, he moved on to create the next village. He left behind a Malayan Chinese administrator who assumed resettlement duties. These brave men had to live in the New Village, where they were prime targets for assassination. In addition, they faced tremendous temptation in the form of bribes from families seeking special favors or kickbacks from merchants dealing with scarce goods. Although some died at the hands of the Traitor Killing Squads and some succumbed to corruption, the remarkable fact is that most performed an exceedingly difficult job with courage and integrity.

They could not have survived in the absence of the village police post. A typical police post numbered ten or a dozen men, all Malays, who found themselves trying to secure a village that was home for 500 to 2,000 Chinese. They received no help from the inhabitants and were commonly betrayed. Every hour a phone call came from district headquarters. If a policeman failed to answer, headquarters had standing orders to dispatch immediately a patrol to assist the isolated post, which presumably was under attack. Because the guerrillas had great difficulty with command and control due to the inability of their detachments to communicate quickly with one another, they usually fled when the reaction team arrived. A determined police post could defend itself against most attacks even in the face of surprising odds. Nonetheless, as long as the Communists had the capacity to form combat teams of 100 men or more, every police post was under deadly threat.

Death of a High Commissioner

The Briggs Plan, with its notable emphasis on winning popular support over killing insurgents, eventually produced decisive long-term results. However, this was not immediately apparent. In April 1950 the commander in chief of the Far East land forces, General Sir John Harding, declared, "Our greatest weakness is the lack of early and accurate information of the enemy's strength, dispositions and intentions."[10] Harding well understood the reluctance of rural Chinese to denounce the Communists: "The Chinese population is generally content to get on with its business even if it entails subsidizing the Communists; nor is it willing generally to give any information to the Police Force for fear of reprisals until it is given full and continuous security by our Forces."[11]

More than a year later, in June 1951, the British high commissioner, Sir Henry Gurney, and Briggs issued a combined assessment of the situation. For public dissemination they confidently claimed that the campaign had reached a turning point. They knew that the reality was something else. A police report in September 1951 stated, "Thousands of Chinese of all walks of life are now living behind barbed wire and are expected to be policed by a handful of untrained men who are tied down by gate and perimeter patrol duties. Proper police work is well nigh impossible and duties in resettlement areas result in corruption, boredom and ill discipline."[12] In addition, many squatters remained outside the New Villages, where they were subjected to insurgent coercion.

In October 1951 Gurney complained that after three years of British efforts to protect the rural Chinese by organizing a massive population shift into the New Villages, Chinese Communists had infiltrated these villages, were active in schools and labor unions, and were not being denounced by the Chinese inhabitants of the New Villages. Gurney bleakly concluded that if things continued on their present course the Chinese rural population would soon fall under Communist control.

Two days after this gloomy prediction Gurney and his wife departed the capital to spend a weekend at a rural resort. While his Rolls-Royce climbed a steep, narrow road, a guerrilla platoon opened fire with Bren guns and rifles from concealed positions in the jungle undergrowth. Thirty-five bullets riddled Gurney's Rolls and flattened its tires. Gurney managed to open the door and stagger to a roadside ditch, where he died, having apparently sacrificed his life to draw fire so that his wife, who remained crouching on the floor of the Rolls, could live. The high commissioner's escort vehicle arrived on the scene and engaged the guerrillas with Bren gun fire. A bugle call from the jungle overlooking the road sounded the retreat and the shooting stopped as the guerrillas withdrew along a previously cleared line of retreat.

The guerrillas had no idea whom they had killed. Rather, they had set their ambush on a portion of road frequented by security force traffic and waited to see who drove by. British intelligence did not know that Gurney's death came from a band of opportunistic guerrillas shooting at a careless target. They suspected that the Communists had deeply infiltrated the security forces. A desperate frenzy of military action ensued. Royal Air Force bombers dropped tons of ordnance onto possible jungle escape routes. Twenty-five-pound medium batteries of the Royal Artillery bombarded the jungle. Infantry units near and far bashed through the undergrowth looking for the men who had killed the high commissioner. When these efforts proved futile the British resorted to removing the entire population of the nearest Chinese town and leveling it. However satisfying the revenge, it could not hide the fact that the autumn of 1951 marked the nadir of British efforts to counter the insurgents. Three weeks after Gurney's death, another ambush in the same area killed sixteen and wounded seventeen. During the ensuing month, security forces suffered their heaviest weekly casualties ever.

The rise in combat casualties suggested to the public that Great Britain was involved in a never-ending conflict with victory nowhere in sight. Public confidence both in Malaya and in the United Kingdom waned. The public was skeptical about official pronouncements having heard ever since 1949 frequent predictions that the Emergency would soon be over. The response was reminiscent of the experience when the American public had wondered why it took more men to keep the Philippines "pacified" than to win the war in the first place. Malay politicians began to question openly the wisdom of British strategy.

The Malay majority wavered. They resented how the British government directed resources and granted privileges to the Chinese, almost as if it was rewarding the lack of Chinese commitment to the government. One Malay politician suggested that the country was approaching chaos because of the slow progress in defeating the insurgents and the likelihood that worse fighting lay ahead. In overly polite and understated language he warned, "The number of [Commonwealth] troops pouring into this country has been creating a feeling of suspicion on the part of the masses." The Malay public worried that an even more "bloodthirsty war" was about to begin.[13]

In December the brilliant Briggs fell ill with what proved a fatal sickness and retired. Efforts to name his successor stumbled when several prominent candidates declined the appointment, thus causing civilian morale to plummet further. The British commissioner of police proved unequal to his task and was relieved. Racial antagonism between Malay and Chinese intensified. Government policy makers appeared to have lost all direction, and defeat loomed.

THIRTEEN

A Modern Cromwell

A Plan and a Man

By October 1951, the Malayan Communist Party Central Executive Committee met to review the war to date. Over the past year guerrillas had staged some 6,100 incidents while inflicting the highest record of losses on civilians and security forces. The Central Executive Committee did not have precise figures. What they did know was that they had massed their fighters to the greatest possible extent in an effort to obtain important results. Company-sized units of 100 to 300 men had attacked remote police stations, European business offices, and mining installations. The goal was to overpower the regular and irregular police guards, capture weapons and ammunition, and demoralize the native constabulary. These assaults had been costly and seldom succeeded. The Central Executive Committee did not realize that its fighters had become demoralized, with many shying away from contact with the British.

The second major Communist objective was the New Villages. Communist agents had infiltrated squatter communities to persuade the people to resist relocation. Guerrillas ambushed truck convoys conveying the squatters to the New Villages. They fired into newly settled villages in hopes of stampeding the inhabitants. In spite of making the strongest possible effort, the Communists had failed to prevent the expansion of the New Villages.

During its October 1951 review, the leadership concluded that while it could foment terror, depredations against the people—slashing rubber trees, burning workers' huts, sabotaging public utilities, ambushing Red

Cross convoys, derailing trains, shooting up New Villages, killing for identity cards—merely increased the general population's misery. The committee decided that these tactics had been a mistake since they alienated
the very people they most needed to support the insurgency. The MCP
leadership decreed that henceforth the masses were to be courted. The
sole legitimate targets for terrorist operations were the British and their
"running dogs."

The Executive Committee resolved that in order to wage a protracted
struggle, the formed guerrilla units had to break contact with the security forces and withdraw deeper into the jungle to rest and refit. Couriers
set out on foot to disseminate this decision to all guerrilla units. The jungle was no longer a completely safe haven. Fear of ambush and the need
to dodge British patrols caused the couriers to move cautiously from one
jungle post office to the next. Consequently, months passed before many
guerrilla leaders received the new orders.

At the time no one realized the enormous significance of the committee's decision. The British had no knowledge of this strategic shift for almost a year. Only then were intelligence officers able to link prisoner
interrogations with captured documents to discover that there had been a
fundamental shift and that the insurgents had lost their revolutionary momentum. The shift most dramatically changed the status of the village
police posts. For the previous three and a half years, policemen had confronted a mortal threat of massed attack by overwhelming numbers.
Henceforth, attacks came from small bands of twenty to thirty and were
typically only nuisance raids. Relieved of their fear of annihilation, the village police could focus on providing security and restoring law and order.

Yet it was the inherent nature of a counterinsurgency that the British
were unable to assess accurately its progress until after the fact. The British
did not perceive that the tide was turning. They did not know Communist
strength had declined to perhaps 500 hard-core guerrillas supported by another 4,000 fighters of indifferent morale. They did not know that the year
1951 would prove the high-water mark of the insurgency.

The Return of Winston Churchill

Great Britain's October election of 1951 brought a new Conservative government led by a revived Winston Churchill. Churchill returned to office
to find his country still struggling from its exertions during World War
II. Food stocks were as depleted as they had been at the height of the

U-boat menace in 1941. Strict food rationing remained in place. Prosperity seemed a distant mirage. The Malayan Emergency was costing the nation's pinched economy half a million dollars per day. In Asia, some 800,000 United Nations soldiers including a Commonwealth Division were challenging Communism in Korea. More than 100,000 French troops were fighting the Viet Minh in Indochina. Although Churchill supported both fights, he believed that the fate of the entire Far East truly depended on Malaya. The prime minister requested a complete report on Malaya, and its contents depressed him. Committees charged with winning the war were spending most of their time bickering. The police force was riven with factions. Worst of all, in Churchill's view, no one seemed to sense the urgency of the problem. He issued orders to Secretary of State Oliver Lyttelton—"The rot has got to be stopped"—and sent him to Singapore.[1]

Lyttelton arrived in Malaya before Christmas 1951. His initial survey convinced him that the British were on the verge of losing Malaya. On his last night at King's House he found the regular staff absent, replaced by police officers. They sheepishly reported that the Chinese butler who heretofore had served the secretary his after-dinner coffee had been removed from his position because he was a Communist agent.

Lyttelton described the essential conundrum facing a counterinsurgency: "You cannot win the war without the help of the population, and you cannot get the support of the population without at least beginning to win the war."[2] The antagonism between the Malay majority and the Chinese minority seemed overwhelming. A Malay political delegation met with Lyttelton to propose a compromise solution: accept the existing situation and let Malaya be granted independence forthwith under British administration.

This proposal was immensely attractive. It addressed the prime Malay concern about power sharing with the Malayan Chinese by acknowledging that the Malays would remain politically dominant. If the British accepted it would motivate Malays to put forth far more effort in the war. It meant the war would come to an end soon and Commonwealth troops could escape what appeared to be a jungle quagmire. But in the minds of Lyttelton and Churchill the proposal violated basic British values, not the least of which was the preservation of a disintegrating empire, and smacked of declaring victory and going home. Consequently they rejected it.

Instead Lyttelton recommended a colossal organizational change: the installation of a supreme warlord in charge of both military and civil affairs. As Lyttelton pondered candidates he briefly considered Britain's most famous warrior, Field Marshal Bernard Montgomery. He correctly suspected that the immensely proud Montgomery would not want to risk his reputation in Malaya's jungles. However, Montgomery did send a Lyttelton a brief note of advice: "Dear Lyttelton, Malaya. We must have a plan. Secondly, we must have a man. When we have a plan and a man, we shall succeed; not otherwise." If the field marshal's advice was rather obvious—Lyttelton later wrote with British understatement that "this had occurred to me"—it still made the solid point that heretofore British efforts had yet to marry leadership and strategic execution.[3] That was about to change.

The Rise of Sir Gerald Templer

Lyttelton's choice for warlord was General Sir Gerald Templer. Templer arrived in Malaya in February 1952 to assume an exceptional posting as both the high commissioner and operational commander of the military. Not since Oliver Cromwell had Britain invested a soldier with this combination of military and political power. But Templer was an exceptional man. He had served in the trenches of France during World War I, competed on the 1924 British Olympic hurdles team, won the army's bayonet fighting championship, earned the prestigious Distinguished Service Order in Palestine, and risen to corps command during World War II's Anzio campaign. During the Allied occupation of Germany he was director of military government and later became the director of intelligence at the War Office. His combination of combat and civil leadership coupled with an intelligence background well prepared Templer to meet a novel challenge.

Templer coined the phrase "winning hearts and minds" to describe the foundation of a counterinsurgency strategy.[4] He tackled the difficult problem of constructing a political system that would unite Malaya's many ethnic groups into a stable structure. He was very much a man of action, disdaining all theoretical constructs. He saw that the existing bureaucracy, with its numerous committees and duplication of authority on the state and district levels, was failing because the civilians, policemen, and soldiers could not agree. He told one such committee, "My advice is for you to thrash out your problems over a bottle of whiskey in the evenings. If you can't agree I don't want to know why. I'll sack the lot of you and bring in three new chaps."[5]

Templer's political goal was a united nation of Malaya with "a common form of citizenship for all who regard the Federation or any part of it as their real home and the object of their loyalty."[6] With Templer's encouragement, in January 1952 the United Malay National Organization and the Malayan Chinese Association cooperated to form the Alliance Party. The Alliance Party contested the capital's municipal elections and won nine of eleven seats, thereby vaulting itself into national prominence. Templer pledged that legislative elections would be the first step toward independence.

The issue of what would happen after independence haunted some Europeans and many Malayans. One experienced reporter warned, "Unless a united Malayan nation is achieved before the British government hands self-government to the country a much more terrible Emergency of racial strife may break out."[7] Templer addressed this problem head-on. In September 1952 all aliens born in Malaya, including most notably 1.2 million Chinese, received full citizenship. Later Templer signed a decree requiring every New Village to have a school where the language of instruction was Malayan. Newly constructed primary schools in other towns and villages had the same requirement. The ability to speak Malayan was intended to cement future generations to a united Malaya while reassuring the current majority Malay population. Templer also explicitly addressed the question of land tenure when he said that the inhabitants of the New Villages needed to own the land where they lived. By deft political manipulation, Templer cleverly changed the calculus of battle. By hitching the forces of nationalism to an emerging democratic Malay state, the British undercut an insurgency against colonial oppressors and replaced it with a competition for the future of an independent nation.

Encased in this velvet glove was an iron hand. Ten days after describing his vision for a united Malaya, a particularly bloody guerrilla ambush brought Templer to the town of Tanjong Malim, fifty-five miles north of Kuala Lumpur. The town had a bad reputation for violence, with almost forty incidents in the past three months. Recently seven Gordon Highlanders had died in an ambush and fifteen civilians and policemen had been murdered. Now for the sixth time guerrillas had cut a water pipeline outside of town. This time they remained on the scene to lure the repair crew and its police escort into a carefully prepared killing zone. Among the killed were a highly respected district administrator— the celebrated Michael Codner, who had earned a Military Cross for his role in the famous "Wooden Horse" escape from a German prison camp during World War II—the area executive engineer of public works, and seven policemen. Once again no townsperson admitted hearing, seeing, or knowing anything about the ambush.

Templer ordered community leaders to assemble and then during an hour-long rant charged them with "cowardly silence." He said that he would install a new town administration backed with more troops. When some nearby listeners nodded approval, Templer lashed out: "Don't nod your heads, I haven't started yet."[8] He proceeded to impose a twenty-two-hour-a-day curfew, during which time no one was to leave their homes. No one was to leave town at any time. Templer closed the schools and bus service and reduced the rice ration by 40 percent.

How long these measures remained in place would depend upon the townspeople. Ten days later each household received a confidential questionnaire in which they were supposed to denounce any known Communists. With a fine sense of the theatrical, Templer had the completed questionnaires deposited in a sealed box, brought to the capital by selected community leaders, and then opened the letters himself. He read them, made notes, and then destroyed the originals to preserve confidentiality. He sent the village notables home with instructions to tell the people how the letters had been handled. After processing the questionnaires, authorities made some minor arrests and Templer gradually lifted the restrictions. From a tactical standpoint, Templer's angry retaliation failed; the people arrested were Communist supporters or sympathizers, not members of the guerrilla band who actually had ambushed the repair crew. Moreover, given the limited extent of literacy in the town, the use of written questionnaires was not the best way to obtain responses. But strategically Templer had made his point: a new authority was on the scene and was prepared for stern action when called for.

Because of Codner's hero status, the incident received widespread publicity. Templer's notion of collective punishment produced a storm of protest from British and international media. Among many, the *Manchester Guardian* labeled his behavior "odious." Templer cared not. His first months in Malaya had an electric political and morale-boosting impact: "he was not only there, but was most certainly seen to be there."[9]

A Winning Strategy

By British standards, Templer commanded a sizable force including half of the line regiments in the entire British army, all its Gurkha battalions, and a variety of regiments from the remnants of the far-flung empire, including the King's African Rifles and the Fijian Regiment. He intended to wield them differently, moving away from large sweeps and instead concentrating on keeping units in one area long enough so they could learn the local terrain. Templer also thought that various British units had acquired valuable experience in jungle fighting and that this knowledge needed to be collected and disseminated in a systematic way. The result was a booklet entitled "The Conduct of Anti-Terrorist Operations in Malaya." Based on the syllabus of the Jungle Warfare Training Centre, it was written in just two weeks. It was a practical how-to compendium describing techniques for patrolling, conducting searches, setting ambushes, and acquiring intelligence. Printed in a size that fit into a jungle uniform pocket, "The Conduct of Anti-Terrorist Operations in Malaya," inevitably given the acronym ATOM, served as a soldier's bible. Templer inscribed his own copy with this notation: "It is largely as a result of the publication of this handbook ... that we got militant communism in Malaya by the throat."[10]

The improvement in jungle tactics coincided with the insight that the vast, apparently impenetrable jungle actually held a limited network of trails and that the enemy had no choice but to use them. Communist couriers, food requisition parties, and organized units carrying out operations had to traverse these trails some time or another. Rather than noisily bashing about the jungle on useless large-scale sweeps, the British tactic of choice became the setting of an ambush overlooking a trail, followed by a patient waiting period. Platoons operated along the jungle edge for ten to twenty days at a time. They spent most of their time watching and listening.

For a superior officer, the notion of passively waiting for the enemy to appear flew in the face of conventional training. For the soldiers waiting silently hour after hour trying to ignore the leeches, mosquitoes, sleep-inducing heat and humidity, and fatigue, it was not pleasant. A British officer wrote, "I had grown used to the jungle during the war in Burma, but there we were always in large parties and in touch either by sound or wireless with the units to our left and right. Also we always had some idea of where the enemy was. Here we were just a little party of ten men, completely isolated, and the enemy was God knows where. He might be behind the next bush, or the one beyond that, or he might be a hundred miles away. We never knew."[11]

Most of the time no one passed the ambush site. Yet statistics revealed that on average a soldier on patrol encountered an insurgent once every 1,000 hours. The same soldier waiting patiently in ambush saw an insurgent once every 300 hours. Typically, a contact did not occur until after the ambushers had been in position for more than twenty-four hours. An officer tabulated his accomplishments at the end of his tour. He had spent 115 days in the jungle: "I was with my company when we shot and killed a terrorist. I set an ambush with a section of my platoon which shot and killed a terrorist. My platoon shot and killed a terrorist in an ambush while I was on leave. A company operation in which I took part resulted in four terrorists surrendering. I fired at, but missed, a terrorist who was running away from a camp which we were attacking."[12] Based on conversations with fellow officers, he concluded that he had experienced a fairly active tour of duty.

Jungle ambush was not comfortable, it was not glorious, but in this war it was the most effective purely military tactic.

Food Denial

The Malayan jungle did not produce enough food to sustain the guerrillas. They needed to obtain sustenance from sympathizers living outside the jungle to survive. The British knew this and conceived a strict food denial program (what became known as Operation Starvation) to starve the guerrillas. Weakened by hunger, they would become vulnerable to military operations or surrender. The food denial strategy proved a devastating measure that eventually defeated the insurgents.

The British carefully followed a three-phase approach to implement the food denial strategy. A months-long intelligence-gathering operation inaugurated the program. Special Branch officers infiltrated the Min Yuen support organization inside a designated village. During this time, military patrols deliberately avoided this village. Instead, they operated in adjacent areas in the hope that their presence would push the terrorists toward the apparent sanctuary of the designated village.

The second phase began the day the strict food rationing began and lasted three to five months. It included house-to-house searches to seize food stores and the arrest of known Communist agents who had been identified by the Special Branch undercover agents. Thereafter, security forces tightly guarded the supply convoys that delivered rice to the village. The rice was cooked centrally by government cooks while armed guards looked on. Within the village, authorities controlled the sale and distribution of all other food. Meanwhile, the military patrolled the nearby jungle to provide security against insurgent attacks.

The people were told that the restrictions would end as soon as the terrorists had been killed or captured. If all proceeded as planned, the villagers would tire of this intrusive disruption and denounce the Communist infrastructure. Then, in the final phase, Communist turncoats would lead Special Branch operational teams, masquerading as Communist terrorists, against higher-level formations.

THE FOOD DENIAL effort was not airtight. At first many of the village perimeters lacked illumination, making it easy for Communist sympathizers to throw food and medicine to the waiting guerrillas outside the wire. As perimeter security improved, the sympathizers turned to other tactics. Villagers smuggled rice by hiding it inside bicycle frames, cigarette tins, or false-bottomed buckets of pig swill on the supposition that a Malay policeman, because of his Muslim religion, would be unwilling to touch anything to do with swine. When security forces detected these dodges, the insurgents increasingly turned to using children to smuggle food.

The soldiers and the police usually harnessed their efforts in tandem. An infantry officer wrote, "The police could not take on the fighting against the bandits in the jungle, whereas we could not undertake the normal process of maintaining law and order in the villages and towns and protected areas."[13] Another infantry officer inspected his men while they were on gate duty at a New Village. Long lines of pedestrians, cyclists, and vehicles impatiently waited to leave the village while hour after hour the men of the South Wales Borderers performed meticulous vehicle and body searches. He wrote, "It is not easy to turn one's battalion into a cross between a body of high-class customs officials and police detectives, but what I saw that morning confirmed everything that has been said about the adaptability of the British soldiers."[14]

As the security forces became ever more serious about enforcing food regulations, which meant time-consuming personal body searches each morning, villagers became understandably more angry about the long lines as they went outside the wire to work in the fields and jungle. Communist propagandists tried to magnify village grievances, claiming security forces were taking indecent advantage of females during searches. Although the international press published some of this propaganda, it failed to deter the British from intensifying their food denial efforts.

The mere possession of food outside the wire risked a penalty of up to five years in prison. The government reduced the number of stores authorized to sell food, banned tinned Quaker Oats because it was an insurgent emergency ration, restricted the sale of high-energy foods and medicines, and ordered shopkeepers to puncture tins of food in the presence of the buyer so tropical heat could begin its spoiling process and prevent the food from being stockpiled for the insurgents. Other draconian measures severely restricted the quantities of tinned meat, fish, and cooking oil permitted in individual households.

While the New Villages were subjected to the methodical imposition of food denial measures, military search-and-destroy operations in adjacent areas proceeded. Often during these operations the security forces imposed a severe rice ration on the local inhabitants. Government spokesmen claimed that this ration was "just enough to keep a person in good health." According to the Chinese Chamber of Commerce this was not true. The rice ration created "fifty thousand half-starved people, many of whom were too ill or to weak to work."[15]

Templer and his subordinates were not blind to the human suffering caused by the food denial program. They also considered other adverse consequences such as the real risk of spawning a repressive governmental bureaucracy and the impact of international opprobrium. They weighed the operational effect of the food denial policies versus the impact on civilian morale and pressed ahead. At the same time, the British offered the people an enormous incentive to cooperate. The British called this inducement the "White Area," a symbolic cleansing of the red taint of Communism.

White Areas were almost literally the carrot to the stick of Emergency regulations. When a region demonstrated loyalty to the government and a corresponding dramatic reduction in Communist activity, authorities suspended Emergency regulations including most especially food restrictions, curfews, limited business hours, and controls over the movement of people and goods. The inhabitants of the New Villages still had to live within their assigned villages and maintain their defenses. But compared to their onerous life under Emergency regulations, this was freedom. The government declared the first White Area in September 1953 and during the next two and a half years extended this designation to include almost half the country's population.

AS TIME PASSED, the operational effects of the food denial program were dramatic. The guerrillas literally began to starve. They could hardly lean on sympathizers to provide for them since those sympathizers could honestly say that strict rationing, central cooking, thorough gate searches, and swarming security patrols prevented them from smuggling food to the guerrillas.

When British intelligence pinpointed a guerrilla band on the verge of starvation, security forces flooded the area and food denial operations intensified. At such times civil life came to a standstill as the security forces imposed curfews of up to thirty-six hours along with very strict rice rationing. Knowing that the guerrillas would have to move or die, military forces flooded the area to set ambushes along every possible trail. One such operation in Johore featured three infantry battalions, five Area Security Units, two Police Special Service Groups, and a "volunteer" force of ex-guerrillas. For five weeks these forces operated in conjunction with strict local food denial and pervasive psychological warfare efforts. They never killed a single guerrilla, yet their presence led to the collapse of guerrilla morale. Hobbled by hunger, compelled to keep on the move while dodging patrols and ambushes, the guerrillas initially survived only by operating in ever-smaller groups. This dispersal led to the breakdown of command authority. In the absence of officers, individuals found it easier to surrender. As unit disintegration continued, the leaders concluded that further resistance was futile and they too surrendered.

This type of operation could only work in compact, carefully targeted areas where the security forces could completely dominate the terrain. The Johore operation required an enormous expenditure of effort to capture one guerrilla and receive the surrender of eleven more. However, it was an operational approach to which the guerrillas had no answer.

FOURTEEN

Victory in Malaya

The Battle for Intelligence

THROUGHOUT HIS TENURE IN command Templer emphasized the paramount importance of intelligence. "Malaya is an Intelligence war," he repeatedly asserted.[1] In the absence of good intelligence, jungle patrolling, no matter how professionally carried out, failed to produce results. As one officer noted, "No intelligence meant no contacts and no contacts meant no intelligence."[2]

In theory, the police were in the best position to provide useful intelligence. However, until Templer set in train comprehensive reforms, both police and military intelligence were often inaccurate or useless. A British officer, John Chynoweth, served with the Malay Regiment. He received a top-secret debriefing of an informer and used the information to plan a patrol. The result was "the most colossal mess-up of an operation ever."[3] Only a last-second instinct for restraint prevented Chynoweth from accidentally killing innocent villagers. He pondered what had gone wrong and speculated that the informer might have deliberately denounced the villagers as part of an ongoing personal feud, might have made a genuine mistake, or might have simply hoped that the patrol would somehow encounter a terrorist and then he would "earn" his reward. After another eight-day sweep that failed to find the enemy, Chynoweth wrote in June 1953, "I'm sure this is not the way to get them. We are not fighting an army, but small groups who do not fight pitched battles . . . Bandits can move many times faster than any of our platoons, are clever and desperate and elusive. The best way is to get information from villages or surrendered bandits who lead one to a definite camp."[4]

In a conflict where intelligence was king, very little useful intelligence came from the Chinese villages until the government established secure police posts within the villages. These police stations then became the hub for security and intelligence. The local police knew who should and who should not be present in a village. Their ability to distinguish residents from outsiders severely curtailed Communist movement. When the police arrested a Communist sympathizer, or better still an agent or courier, he or she might divulge useful information allowing the security forces to roll up an entire Communist cell.

As part of their counterinsurgency philosophy that emphasized acting within legal boundaries, the British worked hard to improve the police. Great Britain had considerable experience in handing over colonial authority to the native people. Part of this process was to train the police. To help in Malaya, the British summoned experienced trainers from around the Empire including hundreds of former police sergeants who had served in Palestine. In January 1952 Colonel Arthur Long, commissioner of the City of London Police, came to Malaya to reorganize the Federation Police and Special Constables. Within a year the Federation Police had compiled comprehensive lists of Malayan Races Liberation Army personnel and documented the local areas where they operated. Armed with this specific and precise intelligence, small hunter-killer platoons went after the guerrillas.

In contrast to the regular army units who had bashed through the jungle, the hunter-killer platoons were well-trained units composed of soldiers who had learned how to operate in the jungle. They were superbly fit in order to operate in the enervating environment, and first-class marksmen. Their sharpshooting skill was important because shoulder-fired weapons remained the weapon that inflicted almost all casualties on the enemy. The combination of jungle stamina, fire discipline, knowledge of the country, and high morale made the men of the hunter-killer platoons implacable foes of the guerrillas. Yet even when nourished with good intelligence, these platoons still spent hundreds of hours of fruitless searching in order to locate the insurgents. Then, when contact came, it was fleeting, and "bags" seldom exceeded two or three guerrillas killed.

Another tool in the war for intelligence was a national registration program. Introduced early in the Emergency, it required every person over

the age of twelve to register at the police station to obtain an identity card complete with photo and thumbprint. Thereafter, they always had to carry this card with them while the police retained a copy. To make the system work the government had to provide a strong incentive. It chose coercion. People needed to show their cards to obtain a food ration, to build a home in a resettlement village, to expand their garden plot, and for a host of other daily activities tied to economic survival. Naturally the civilian population resented all of this but they quickly appreciated that life was easier with rather than without their cards.

From a security viewpoint, the program was a great success. Registration hampered all Communist movement and activity. But it was particularly effective in the New Villages, where it helped separate the insurgents from the local populace. In the New Villages, police established cordons early each morning to screen people as they embarked on their daily routines. The police detained anyone without a card or whose card showed that they were not local. People who did not appear for work that day immediately attracted police attention and became the subjects of closer investigation.

Chin Peng and the Communist leadership correctly saw that the registration program was a serious threat and ordered the Traitor Killing Squads into action. They assassinated the village photographers and registration officials who worked in the program. The also targeted the rural rubber tappers and rice farmers. Guerrillas seized their registration cards and threatened to kill them if they reregistered. The police responded with a simple policy change. Each morning they collected workers' cards and issued tallies when they left the village. Upon returning, workers exchanged the tallies for the cards. If the guerrillas had stolen the tally, the worker merely had to reregister. Guerrilla leaders eventually concluded that their efforts to disrupt the program were counterproductive and abandoned this campaign as part of their strategic reappraisal conducted in October 1951.

Early in the conflict, the British had also begun a reward program whereby they paid set sums for weapons and munitions surrendered to the security forces and offered a higher inducement for leading a patrol to a guerrilla base. Under Templer's leadership the British raised the bounty for killing or capturing Communist insurgents. The largest bounty was placed on the head of Chin Ping: 250,000 Malayan dollars (£30,000, approximately $83,700) if delivered alive, half that amount if killed. Either sum was a staggering figure for Malaya. At the time the offer of oversized rewards caused some criticism. Police and government officials wondered about the justice system's essential fairness whereby a known murderer, a man who had targeted policemen and rural administrators, could receive a sum for a few minutes of work betraying his comrades that far exceeded what a loyal man could ever earn during a lifetime of faithful service.

The commander of the Malayan Races Liberation Army in southern Malaya, Ah Koek, known as "Shorty," had a price tag of 150,000 Malayan dollars if taken alive or 75,000 if killed. In October 1952 his bodyguard murdered him and delivered his head to obtain the reward. A newspaper reporter gleefully observed that since Ah Koek was only four feet nine inches tall, this came to almost $3,000 an inch, probably the most expensive "head price" ever paid. The elimination of a well-known insurgent leader boosted British morale but had little collateral benefit since most of these men could be readily replaced. More useful than the bounty was the reward system for actionable intelligence.

Security force officers were constantly surprised at the willingness of Communist turncoats to guide them to their old positions to kill or capture their former comrades. In part this was a monetary calculation on the turncoat's part: he received a bounty to surrender and could collect more by leading productive raids. In part it was a calculus of survival: a turncoat had to fear the notorious Traitor Killing Squads, which would target the turncoat's family if they could not eliminate the betrayer himself. The turncoat judged the best way to preempt retaliation was to kill his comrades before they could pass on information to these death squads.

End Game

In late spring 1954 Templer left Malaya. In his mind much remained to accomplish. As he departed he famously warned against complacency, saying, "I'll shoot the bastard who says that this Emergency is over."[5] Then and thereafter, Templer was a controversial figure. His brusque, even rude personality did not win him many friends. Detractors claimed that he merely happened to be the man in charge when the tide turned. Indeed, he did benefit greatly from decisions made by his predecessors. Still, by any objective measure his success had been extraordinary. In 1951, the year prior to his arrival, insurgents had staged 2,333 major incidents while inflicting more than 1,000 casualties among the security forces and another 1,000 against civilians. In 1954 there were 293 major incidents causing 241 security force and 185 civilian casualties. Guerrilla strength had declined by two thirds from its peak.

Templer had also promoted the expansion of the popular militia called the Home Guard. It was an ambitious effort fraught with risk, the fruits of which were not apparent until after Templer had left Malaya. Trained by British and Commonwealth officers, the Home Guard grew from 79,000 in July 1951 to 250,000 by the end of 1953, at which time they defended seventy-two New Villages. A typical village had thirty-five Home Guards. Assignments rotated among them on a daily basis, so on any one night only five were on guard duty. At nightfall, the guards drew weapons from the police armory and patrolled the perimeter wire. Their tasks were threefold: to detect and resist guerrilla attack, to thwart the internal activity of the Traitor Killing Squads, and to prevent the villagers from smuggling food outside the wire. Although subjected to terrorist intimidation and murder, the Home Guard maintained a surprising resilience. By the end of 1954 they had received 89,000 weapons and lost only 103. In 1955 they lost 138 weapons out of a holding of 15,000. Still, even this record was unsatisfactory to some Europeans in Malaya who loudly demanded the Home Guard be disbanded.

Authorities ignored the complaints. It became clear that the degree of loyalty to the government exhibited by the Home Guard mirrored the attitudes of the villagers. If Communist terror had cowed the villagers, the Home Guard was passive for fear of Communist reprisal against themselves and their families. When later there was a major guerrilla attack against two New Villages in Johore in 1956, the Home Guard defended the villages tenaciously—in spite of the fact that many villagers had assisted the guerrillas—and repulsed the attacks. This was enormously heartening for both the Home Guards and their advocates.

TEMPLER'S DEPARTURE MARKED the end of the Cromwell-like era of one man having both civil and military powers. Templer's deputy high commissioner ascended to take over state finances and high policy. Lieutenant General Sir Geoffrey Bourne took command of the soldiers and police. Under their leadership, the next three years witnessed tremendous progress on both the political and military fronts.

By the end of 1955, British intelligence estimated that Communist strength had shrunk from a peak of 8,000 armed guerrillas to around 3,000. Every metric indicated that the food denial policy was working. The local population was increasingly cooperating with security forces. Their assistance led to the elimination of virtually all Communist forces in South Selango. Likewise, in the state of Pahang security forces eliminated an estimated 80 percent of enemy forces, thereby creating the largest White Area in the country. The trend toward victory continued. In 1956 the security forces lost forty-seven killed. By the next year this total fell to eleven; the year after, ten. In 1959 and 1960 only one policeman died due to insurgent activity.

While losses among the security forces declined, the army and police continued to whittle away at the remaining insurgents. During 1957 the rate of guerrilla elimination averaged one per day. During the last years of the Emergency this steady rate of attrition reduced insurgent numbers to some 500 hard-core guerrillas operating in small groups of five to twenty men. They lived like hunted animals, incapable of meaningful military operations, intent only on survival. They had entirely lost the initiative. Only two hopes for insurgent victory remained: popular discontent with the Emergency regulations, particularly the food denial policies, would spawn some kind of popular rebellion, or the government would make a new, colossal blunder.

Back in 1953, a large-scale British sweep to locate the MCP Politburo had failed. Nonetheless, Chin Peng and the senior Communist leadership made the decision to follow Mao's dictate to retreat when the enemy pressed too hard. They slipped over the Thai border. This border described a very irregular line some 370 miles long. Most of it ran through thick jungle. A substantial Chinese population lived along the Thai side of the border and provided succor for the MCP Politburo for the remainder of the war. However, from this remote sanctuary they could not coordinate strategy with the armed detachments to the south. Thereafter insurgent remnants trekked north to join the headquarters inside the Thai sanctuary, and security forces found it almost impossible to locate them.

A break came when the third-ranking member of the politburo, Hor Lung, decided that further resistance was futile and surrendered at a remote police post. The British head of the provincial Special Branch took Hor Lung and his two bodyguards to a secure place while the British pondered how to proceed. The temptation to trumpet this important capture was almost irresistible. Instead, with the defector's consent, the Special Branch returned Hor Lung to the jungle with instructions to persuade his comrades to surrender. To avoid the real possibility that security forces might encounter and kill him, the military considered suspending local operations. Upon further reflection they decided this would arouse suspicions, so instead they deliberately routed patrols to adjacent areas near enough to preserve the appearance of normality but not so close as to threaten Hor Lung. Most impressively, the British managed to keep the entire thing a secret. The reward for this restrained, well-conceived effort came over the next four months as 160 Communists surrendered, including 28 whom the government ranked as "hard-core."

By the end of 1958 only four known guerrillas remained in all of Johore and just two in Negri Sambilan. Major guerrilla actions averaged a mere one per month. By October 1959 the British estimated total insurgent strength at 700, most of whom were in Thailand. The handful of holdouts still in Malaya lived in the most inaccessible parts of the jungle, where they found conditions changed and survival even harder because the jungle-dwelling aborigines had concluded that there was no future in supporting the guerrillas. In the last two years of the Emergency, one 300-man aboriginal force killed more guerrillas than all the other security forces combined, apparently using their traditional blowpipes to deadly effect.

On July 31, 1960, the government declared an end to the twelve-year-long State of Emergency.

Why the British Won

The final human reckoning showed that the security forces lost 519 soldiers and 1,346 police killed. Official government statistics showed that the Communist terrorists murdered 2,473 civilians and abducted another 810 during the Emergency. The insurgents lost 6,711 killed, 1,289 captured, and 2,704 surrendered. In other words, during the entire Emergency, security forces killed or captured about six guerrillas for every soldier or policeman lost. As had been the case during the Philippine Insurrection, the security forces enjoyed a tremendous tactical edge whenever combat occurred. The problem in Malaya, as in the Philippines, was finding the insurgents so they could be engaged.

Certain special circumstances contributed immensely to the British victory. The Malaya Communist Party almost exclusively comprised ethnic Chinese who were alien in creed and race to the majority Malay population. Historically, the Chinese and Malays had been at odds with one another. Had the Communists been able to use the rallying cry of nationalism they might have partially overcome this divide. However, the British explicitly promised independence and could point to the examples of India, Pakistan, and Burma as proof of their ability to fulfill their promise.

Party leaders proved inept strategists. They ignored basic precepts of revolutionary warfare by failing to mobilize the masses and neglecting to establish secure base areas. Instead of relying on patient propaganda efforts and sympathetic treatment to persuade the people to conform to their goals, the impatient insurgent leaders took shortcuts. They notably failed to heed Mao's cautionary dictum that indiscriminate terror against the masses was counterproductive.

The British, on the other hand, did many things right. Although the military's initial emphasis on conventional operations was misguided, the government's first set of political decisions had enormous, positive influence on the war's outcome. Crucially, at no time did the government concede its authority to the insurgents by abandoning inhabited areas. Consequently, the insurgents were unable to rest, refit, and build inside Malaya.

The decision to maintain a civil government presence in the face of terror derived from the insight of a handful of enlightened British officials who understood that political stability was a major component of victory. The symbol of this stability was the presence of a normal, workaday government that both performed its routine tasks and, of critical importance, was seen by the public to be doing this. Thus, the government urged its officials, the police, and the European elite to remain steadfast and continue with their routines even in their isolated outposts. Not only was there no mass exodus of panic-stricken people fleeing from the terror, but local government officials, virtually 100 percent Malay outside of the New Villages, maintained routine administration in spite of Communist terror. They recorded births, deaths, and marriages, and this atmosphere of apparent normality informed people that the government had the will to endure.

The government was able to function throughout the country because of the security provided by local police posts. The police, in turn, survived because British military forces compelled the Malayan Communists to abandon large-unit operations. This meant they lacked the strength to overrun the police posts.

THE BRITISH RESISTED the temptation to respond to acts of terror by extralegal means. Instead, the government functioned within the boundaries of the law. It enacted some very tough laws including the imposition of strict curfews, a mandatory death sentence for carrying arms, and life imprisonment for those caught supporting the terrorists. But legislators passed these laws in a transparent, legal manner, and they were subject to the concurrence of the courts and applied even-handedly to all citizens.

For example, the police could detain a suspect for up to two years without trial. However, the suspect enjoyed a right of review by a High Court judge and a panel of local assessors. This helped mitigate the impact of holding some 10,000 suspects in detention. There was very little local protest. Undoubtedly the efforts to maintain legal and fair administrative approaches contributed to the muted response. However, it must be noted that the Malay majority thoroughly approved the mass roundup of Chinese.

The British appreciated and benefitted from the antipathy most Malays felt toward the Chinese. It would have been easy for the British to ram through whatever measures the high commissioner and his staff desired. It would also have been strictly legal, since the treaties between the Malay sultans and the British Crown stipulated that British advice had to be accepted. Instead, the British used persuasion. They treated the Malay sultans as equal partners in the struggle against the insurgents. Because of this treatment, they enjoyed excellent cooperation both during the Emergency and afterward.

The British also benefitted from a robust demand for tin and natural rubber created by the Korean War. This demand both created jobs and filled government coffers, allowing the British to pay for social programs that ameliorated the impact of Emergency regulations. A daily reality of full employment at a decent wage looked more appealing than the Communist promise of struggle leading to a better life at some indefinite future time.

The leadership of some very able officers, most notably Briggs and Templer, contributed to victory. The British counterinsurgency expert Robert Thompson called the adroit Templer "the last of the great British proconsuls," and he lived up to this claim.[6] Within one year of arriving in country, Templer reached a crucial insight that influenced all that came after: "the shooting side of the business is only twenty-five percent of the trouble and the other seventy-five percent lies in getting the people of this country behind us."[7] Regardless of the ebb and flow on the battlefield, the British successfully convinced the people of Malaya that they intended to remain until they won. Next they provided security from the terrorists. Then they provided social and economic benefits that gave all the people regardless of race a promise of future progress and prosperity. Templer particularly showed a keen appreciation of the need for racial reconciliation. He encouraged the formation of the Alliance Party and promised early elections leading to independence.

On the military front, the British rejected large unit sweeps and indiscriminate use of firepower. The security forces had official sanction to kill anyone found in the jungle on the basis that they were terrorists or terrorist sympathizers. Yet there were few systematic abuses of this mandate. Instead, the emphasis was on capturing terrorists rather than killing them. Key to success was coordinating military, police, and civil activities. Unlike in Indochina, where the Viet Minh conducted devastating large ambushes against battalion-sized and bigger targets, the Malay Communists lacked the numbers and firepower to fight such actions. Consequently, except for the most remote police posts, security forces did not have to fear being overrun. Although the British could call upon artillery and bombers, they accepted that the war would be a struggle of small arms. By limiting the use of heavy weapons the British limited the harm done to civilians. To fight effectively a war with small arms the British emphasized individual marksmanship and jungle craft as taught in the handbook "The Conduct of Anti-Terrorist Operations in Malaya."

Another component of victory was the fact that security forces did not commit routine outrages against the people. There were always instances of corruption when soldiers or officials accepted bribes to ignore Emergency regulations. There were incidents of police brutality, particularly during the early years of the Emergency. Police recruits, especially those who had worked in Palestine, were used to conducting interrogations with the butt end of a rifle. In the field, army patrols that could not find the insurgents and could not communicate with a sullen, Chinese-speaking population vented their frustrations by indiscriminately burning Chinese homes. Since a rubber tapper working in the jungle and a guerrilla looked exactly the same, soldiers shot and killed innocent people. The practice of dropping a few rounds of ammunition or a weapon around the body of a civilian to avoid having to explain why the person was killed was not unknown. Nonetheless, in contrast to behavior in so many other counterinsurgencies such as Algeria, Cyprus, and Palestine, security forces did not systematically brutalize the civilian population.

Lastly, British leaders understood that winning the war in Malaya would take time and they fully committed to what one general called "the long, long war."[8] In turn, a solid majority of the British public patiently supported the war. Such strategic patience was necessary, particularly in the effort to dismantle the Communist infrastructure that undergirded the insurgency. One combat officer likened the difficultly of contending

with this infrastructure to a skin disease that causes a face rash: "Temporary relief for the rash can be obtained by local treatment. For a time it
may even disappear, but unless the cause of it is found and removed the
rash will assuredly break out again." The British understood that if they
eased up, the Communist leaders would recruit replacements and within
six months "be back in the same dominant position."⁹ Consequently, instead of making a show of force and then moving on, instead of sporadic
efforts that condemned them to capturing the same objective repeatedly,
the British employed a methodical but ultimately relentless approach to
pacification.

Superficially, the British experience in Malaya resembled the situation
in Vietnam in the 1960s. Both the physical environment (a seemingly all-
concealing tropical jungle) and the nature of the opponents (a Western
conventional army versus a Communist, Asian guerrilla army) suggested
that the Malayan experience was highly relevant to Vietnam. However,
the American military studied the Emergency with the same narrow focus that it applied to Algeria, confining itself to specific military subjects.
Consequently, according to Sir Robert Thompson, their conclusions were
"largely superficial" and most notably the Americans "never compre-
hended" the social and political dimensions of the conflict.¹⁰

Nonetheless, the successful campaign in Malaya, as interpreted by
Thompson, influenced both South Vietnamese and American strategy in
Vietnam. When trying to transfer the lessons of Malaya to Vietnam, counterinsurgency experts overlooked several factors. First and foremost, in
Malaya, Great Britain had complete control of the police, civil service, and
military services. Instead of these entities resisting reform, they could
spearhead reform. As opposed to South Vietnam, Malaya had no common
border with another Communist country. Also, the insurgent movement
was concentrated within the Chinese population. Popular grievances
among the Malay majority were insufficient to make a Chinese Communist guerrilla look like a liberator to a Malayan peasant.

Moreover, even among the Chinese population of Malaya the insurgent
cause enjoyed only halfhearted support. Dedicated support only came
from squatters who had nothing to lose except their illegally acquired
homesteads. The squatters lived in defined areas along the jungle edge,
which greatly eased the problem of bringing them under tight control.
They did not have a long-standing connection with the land from which
they were moved. Consequently, when the British introduced the New Vil-

lage program, the squatters complained but there was no extreme reaction associated with a people experiencing change to their traditional way of life.

Lastly, the British who lived in Malaya enjoyed established ties with the local community while those in the colonial service had deep understanding of the Malayan political and social system. Their counsel and advice helped inexperienced officers and men contend with an alien environment.

In contrast to Vietnam, the insurgents in Malaya never became militarily formidable. By the time American ground troops intervened in Vietnam, Communist units of up to battalion size were conducting ambushes and assaults. As a Malaya veteran, General Richard Clutterbuck, observed, "If we had lost the battles of 1950 and 1951, this is what our war would have been like; but we did not lose them."[11]

All of these essential differences disguised the difficulties of applying the British strategy in Malaya to the American counterinsurgency in Vietnam.

THE FEDERATION OF Malaya merged with Singapore and the colonies of British North Borneo to form Malaysia in 1963. Three years later, the hardcore remnants of the Malaya Liberation Army, numbering fewer than 500 men, showed they still had teeth. A guerrilla band, unimpressed by the British 1960 announcement that the Emergency was over, ambushed and annihilated a fifteen-man Thai-Malay motorized patrol near the border. They continued sporadic operations until 1989. Twenty-nine years after the official end of the Emergency, they signed a peace accord with the Thai and Malaysian governments and ended military activities.

In 2004, after three years of escalating violence that the Thai government tried to pin on "bandits," Thailand declared martial law in its provinces bordering Malaysia. The former enemy, Communist "bandits" from Malaya, were no longer the culprits. Rather the government blamed a Muslim separatist movement dedicated to evicting its "colonial oppressors" and regaining control of lands it claimed had been "illegally incorporated" by Bangkok some 100 years ago.

PART FOUR

The Vietnam War

FIFTEEN

In Search of a New Enemy

In default of knowing what should be done, they do what they know.

—Eighteenth-century German general Maurice de Saxe on
conventional leadership[1]

A Nation of Villages

THE SOUTH VIETNAM OF THE 1960s was a nation of villages. The original written Vietnamese character for "village" came from a Chinese character that signified "land," "people," and "sacred." Ninety percent of the population of 16 million lived in one of the nation's 2,500 rural villages. Most were poor peasants who supported themselves by working nearby rice fields or fishing in adjacent waters. They spent their lives within a few miles of their birthplaces, insulated from the outside world by the structure of family and village life. The village was the heart of Vietnamese social and economic relationships.

An ancient Vietnamese edict said, "The emperor's rule ends at the village wall." Rural people greeted outsiders, which meant anyone not from the village, and particularly foreigners, with deep suspicion. During a century of colonial rule, villagers learned to think of the government as a remote body that collected taxes, demanded unpaid labor, and conscripted young men for the military. They cherished a tradition of resistance against distant authority and memories of successful war against foreign invaders. For as long as most villagers could recall, there had been fighting—against the Japanese in the 1940s, against the French in the 1950s, and now against a government based in Saigon.

The Communist leaders of this current conflict possessed the esteem, or at least the grudging respect, of many Vietnamese because they held claim to the great victory over the French imperialists in 1954. In contrast, the anti-Communists in the Saigon government possessed little popular support because of their association with the French imperialists. The fact that the government's strongest support came from 850,000 northerners who had moved south in 1954 to escape Communist rule further alienated South Vietnam's villagers.

Roots of Insurgency

On May 7, 1954, the climatic battle of the First Indochina War ended when Communist Viet Minh soldiers captured the last French strongholds at Dien Bien Phu. Later that summer diplomats in Geneva negotiated the terms of the French withdrawal along with a cease-fire and a provisional military demarcation line at the seventeenth parallel. The so-called partition was supposed to be a temporary measure, a compromise leading to elections and a unified Vietnam. Meanwhile, the Communists in the north and the anti-Communists in the south organized separate states. The United States, in turn, viewed Indochina through the lens of the Cold War. American political leaders and the Eisenhower administration regretted what the French had lost and thought that they could do better. However, according to the terms of the Geneva agreement, Vietnamese representatives from the north and south were to meet in July 1955 to arrange the mechanics for a general election. The voting would follow one year later. From the American perspective, the problem with any general election was that the wrong side would probably win. Eisenhower's secretary of state, John Foster Dulles, began casting about for means to thwart the election. Simultaneously, South Vietnamese president Ngo Dinh Diem spoke out against any election on the ground that fair elections in Communist-dominated areas were impossible. Diem's public utterances interfered with a variety of more devious American plans. An American diplomat in Saigon cabled the U.S. State Department, "Vietnam Government must agree [to] play the game at least in appearance and cease repudiating [the Geneva] Agreement."[2]

While most everyone in the U.S. government endorsed the strategy of

checking Communist expansion by supporting anti-Communist governments in South Vietnam, the Joint Chiefs of Staff warned that any political maneuvering that prevented the victory the Viet Minh had earned on
the battlefield risked a strong Communist military reaction. Indeed, in
1956 Diem declined to hold the elections called for in the Geneva declaration. The Communist political underground in South Vietnam understood that Diem's decision denied them a path to victory via the ballot
box. Their response came in 1957 when a terror campaign began against
local officials of the Diem regime. Assassination squads chose their victims carefully, targeting men "who enjoyed the people's sympathy" while
leaving "bad officials unharmed in order to . . . sow hatred against the
government."[3] Three years later, Communist leaders formed the National
Front for the Liberation of South Vietnam (NLF). It was a classic Communist front organization designed to disguise its true roots in order to
acquire support from non-Communist South Vietnamese nationalists.
At the vanguard of the NLF were southern Communist guerrillas who
would be labeled by the South Vietnamese government with the deroga-
tory term Viet Cong.

   To conquer the south, the NLF followed a policy that closely integrated
tactics and strategy into a unified whole—a whole that in contrast to Western military strategy recognized the interplay of military, political, and social dimensions. Unlike most military forces, the Viet Cong emphasized
organizational learning and adaptation. Candid self-criticism sessions occurred at all command levels. Meaningful after-action reviews led to new
tactics. They were also willing to learn from foreign experience. The Viet
Cong experimented with tactics and doctrine, latched on to what worked,
and then rapidly spread the lessons. Adaptation and change were hallmarks of the Communist Vietnamese way of war.

   Long before 1960 and long before the South Vietnamese government
understood that it faced a significant insurgency, Communist propaganda teams had laid the foundation for the NLF campaign. Many of the
personnel were recruited from the most gifted village youth. Some had
traveled north for training and then returned to join like-minded people
and speak about the corruption of Saigon government officials, the in-
equity of land ownership, and the promise of a brighter future under
Communist rule. The propaganda teams explicitly set about changing
the way rural people viewed their lives and future prospects in order to
motivate village youth to fight and to inspire the balance of the village to

assist them. By convincing peasants that they were able to address peasant grievances, the Communists made impressive strides toward building a dedicated base of popular support. Then in 1960 the insurgency exploded into violence.

"If Freedom Is to Be Saved"

The insurgents held an enormous advantage: a powerful ally, North Vietnam, that had access to every inch of South Vietnam's land borders. The American ally, the South Vietnamese, was a weak reed dominated by an elite minority that was corrupt, inefficient, and badly frightened. During the years prior to the outbreak of violence, American advisers had trained the South Vietnamese army for conventional warfare to repel a direct, Korean War–style invasion across the demilitarized zone along the seventeenth parallel. When instead Communist insurgents committed to guerrilla warfare emerged as the prime threat, the American military mission in Saigon prepared a Counterinsurgency Plan. It called for expanding the South Vietnamese military and increasing American assistance. In return, President Diem was to broaden political support for his government.

On the eighteenth anniversary of D-Day, June 6, 1962, President John F. Kennedy spoke to the newly minted army lieutenants at West Point and described the special challenges posed by insurgents:

> This is another type of war, new in its intensity, ancient in its origin—war by guerrillas, subversives, insurgents, assassins, war by ambush instead of by combat; by infiltration, instead of aggression, seeking victory by eroding and exhausting the enemy instead of engaging him. It is a form of warfare uniquely adapted to what has been strangely called "wars of liberation," to undermine the efforts of new and poor countries to maintain the freedom that they have finally achieved. It preys on economic unrest and ethnic conflicts. It requires in those situations where we must counter it, and these are the kinds of challenges that will be before us in the next decade if freedom is to be saved, a whole new kind of strategy.[4]

The president's remarks were designed to underscore the administration's commitment to create an effective counterinsurgency strategy. However, in spite of the increased flow of American assistance, the erosion of

South Vietnamese government authority continued. Regardless, the U.S. Army resisted mightily all proposals for new doctrine, organization, and training aimed at combating insurgents. However, as trouble in Southeast Asia increased, numerous people in and out of government warned that the situation required measures well beyond a conventional military response. An American colonel serving as an adviser in the Mekong Delta echoed Templer's formulation in Malay in an essay for the prestigious service journal *Army*, entitled "Fighting the Viet Cong": "Most of us are sure that this problem is only fifteen per cent military and eighty-five per cent political." The solution was not just killing Viet Cong but instead "coupling security with welfare."[5]

The army brass wanted nothing to do with such notions. General Earle Wheeler, who would rise to serve as chairman of the Joint Chiefs of Staff under President Lyndon Johnson, represented the army's position in an address in late 1962: "It is fashionable in some quarters to say that the problems in Southeast Asia are primarily political and economic rather than military. I do not agree. The essence of the problem in Vietnam is military."[6] Before putting such conclusions to the test, the U.S. military had to endure a protracted, British-inspired experiment.

Strategic Hamlets, Strategic Lunacy
One man who had received great credit for implementing the successful British counterinsurgency campaign in Malaya was Robert Thompson. At Diem's invitation, Thompson arrived in South Vietnam in 1961 as head of the five-man British Advisory Mission. Thompson toured the countryside and concluded that Communist control of the rural population presented the gravest challenge to the South Vietnamese government. Thompson firmly believed that Diem's government could survive only if it protected the rural people and they in turn began to support his government. Based on his Malaya experience, Thompson's solution was to build a solid base of political support by protecting rural villages with local security forces.

In detail, Thompson advocated what was called the "oil spot" strategy. The South Vietnamese government would occupy and secure selected areas where Diem's regime already was strong in order to deprive the Communists of their ability to recruit, tax, gather supplies, and obtain intelligence. Over time, government control would expand, or seep outward like a pool of oil, ultimately merging with adjacent controlled areas to create a larger oil spot. Eventually the uncommitted segments of the population would align with the government, thereby facilitating the further spread of government control. At that point the insurgents would be faced with the impossible choice of either engaging superior government military force or withdrawing from populated areas. In the absence of protection from its military wing and confronted with a diminishing base of popular support, the insurgent political apparatus would erode leading to eventual victory.

The oil spot strategy was well grounded in the historical record. It received its first Vietnam test in 1962. The Diem government built fortified enclosures, called strategic hamlets, in order to deny the Communists access to the civilian population. In addition, these hamlets put the villagers within the reach of the government administrative structure, allowing the government to provide better social services such as schools and infirmaries. At the same time government propagandists tried to convince the people that not only were the Communists morally wrong but also they were losing. However, the Diem government ignored Thompson's recommendations about where to build the first strategic hamlets and insisted on locating them in remote, Viet Cong–dominated areas. Worse, Diem ignored the peasants' fierce attachment to their native villages and transgressed the custom of village autonomy by compelling them to relocate to the new hamlets regardless of their personal wishes. They then had to perform "voluntary" labor to build the hamlets. They could depart to tend their fields only with permission and while accompanied by security forces whose job was to protect them from the guerrillas. In sum, the government was forcing rural people to abandon their traditional way of life in exchange for security and asking them to think well of the government for demanding this upheaval.

The Strategic Hamlet Program began in March 1962 under the optimistic code name Operation Sunrise. An army detachment drove the Viet Cong into the nearby jungle while a security force entered the village of Ben Tuong. About a third of the families agreed voluntarily to relocate but the other two thirds accepted relocation only at gunpoint. Government forces then razed the village to the ground. The "new" Ben Tuong consisted of a concrete infirmary and administration post and freshly cleared ground. The families had to build their own homes while also constructing fortifications. Notably, there were very few men of military age present in the "new" village. Most of them were serving with the Viet Cong.

Three months later, the Viet Cong conducted a near-perfect ambush in broad daylight near the model strategic hamlet. They killed twenty-six South Vietnamese soldiers, several public works officials, and two American military advisers. The ambush could not have been carried out without the help of the local villagers. Whether this help came from willing cooperation or intimidation hardly mattered. The Diem government, the British Mission, and the U.S. Military Assistance Command, Vietnam (MACV) argued about what had been done and what to do. All three actors refused to acknowledge honestly what was taking place—namely, that a nationalist-inspired insurgency was winning a war against an unpopular, corrupt government—and instead, in the predictable fashion of a bureaucracy under stress, all three continued to promote an unchanged policy featuring more of the same. Unsurprisingly, the Viet Cong also continued with more of the same. A little over a year later, in August 1963, they overran Ben Tuong.

And so it went throughout the country. Whereas in Malaya the Communists had too few fighters—at most 8,000 armed men against 300,000 men in the security forces—to attack the New Villages, this was not the case in Vietnam. The South Vietnamese militia who defended the strategic hamlets proved woefully inept. The hamlets were not mutually supporting. The Viet Cong took advantage of their isolation by staging assaults to compel relief columns composed of regular South Vietnamese units to be dispatched from distant bases. Then the Viet Cong ambushed the relief columns with deadly effect. Also unlike the British in Malaya, the Strategic Hamlet Program lacked adequate local police and government forces living in the hamlet. In sum, the program proved counterproductive by alienating the people it was supposed to convert to the government side and chewing up valuable military units that were sent to save the hamlets from being overrun.

Moreover, it soon became apparent that Diem and his brother, who was in charge of the program, were more interested in using the program to expand their influence rather than to protect and inspire peasants to fight the Viet Cong. The construction of each new hamlet gave Diem an opportunity to install a party loyalist. The creation of a new government bureaucracy allowed him to hand out even more lavish rewards while consolidating his family's power. Numbers told a tale of strategic lunacy: whereas the British in Malaya spent three years to establish 500

New Villages, the South Vietnamese created more than 8,000 strategic hamlets in under two years, with most of the construction and relocation taking place in the first nine months of 1963.

John H. Cushman, a future lieutenant general, received the assignment of visiting the southern tip of the country to assess progress. Cushman ordered the American advisers and their South Vietnamese counterparts to make a simple, color-coded map with red marking areas of Communist control, yellow showing contested areas, and blue indicating government-controlled areas. There were only two criteria for government control: officials could move around at night without an escort and there was no open Viet Cong taxation. South Vietnamese officers dutifully created the map. It appeared encouraging until an American adviser pointed out a blue area and asked to visit. The South Vietnamese officer protested vehemently, explaining that it was far too dangerous. In Saigon, a senior American staff officer complained that the program "is a disaster. They're doing it too fast. They're coming in here with grandiose schemes and massive enterprises, and nothing's happening. They don't even do a good whitewash job."[7]

By 1964, after the Viet Cong had overrun all of the first four "showcase" strategic hamlets, the failure became manifest to all. The debacle had been costly. It gave the Viet Cong priceless propaganda material. It revealed Diem's government to be inefficient or, what was worse, aloof and out of touch with Vietnamese rural reality. It also discredited Thompson and the British Mission, which was just fine with the American military mission in Saigon. They had never welcomed British interference and had chafed at the defensive nature of Thompson's approach to counterinsurgency. In their minds, tying down combat troops in static garrisons while pursuing civic action programs was not the way to defeat a Communist insurgency. Some American planners believed that they had a better idea and set out to prove it.

In the Central Highlands

Some twenty-nine tribes numbering more than 200,000 people lived in the central highlands along South Vietnam's western border. Collectively labeled "Montagnards" in the same way that native Americans were called "Indians," they were a village-centered tribal society practicing subsistence slash-and-burn agriculture. The fact that they occupied strategic ground that potentially blocked Communist infiltration routes made them pawns in the war. The Communists exploited Montagnard dissatisfaction with the Saigon government and made them prime targets for propaganda and recruitment. Diem's government treated them as second-class citizens and tended to ignore them as primitive, remote, and insignificant. The American mission in Saigon wanted to enlist minority groups in the counterinsurgency fight. The U.S. Special Forces received the assignment of recruiting the Montagnards.

From Rogers' Rangers in the French and Indian War to Darby's Rangers in World War II, the American military had employed special units for special duties. But the Special Forces were a unique departure. In response to Communist wars of national liberation, the U.S. Army had created the Special Forces for the purpose of waging unconventional war within a conventional war environment. Boosted by President Kennedy's personal interest, the Special Forces enjoyed an elite status reflected by the jaunty green berets that became their signature. Twenty-four Green Berets entered Vietnam in November 1961. At first they operated under the CIA's direction, and therein lay the basis for bureaucratic strife that eventually thwarted a very promising beginning.

The original mission was to organize and train a paramilitary Montagnard force to provide village security and a select "strike force" to conduct offensive actions and border surveillance. Like the American regular forces that were to follow, the Special Forces initially lacked an appropriate counterinsurgency doctrine. Regardless, team members were intelligent and flexible. They worked hand in hand with the Montagnards to dig bunkers and fortify their village and provided training and weapons for a volunteer militia. They built a dispensary where the team medic healed and cured that which answered to modern medicine, and slowly forged bonds of trust with the tribesmen.

The Montagnard units were called Civilian Irregular Defense Groups, or, in this war that granted virtually every unit and program a ponderous acronym, CIDGs. After the pilot program showed progress, more Special Forces teams arrived to expand the CIDG program by first building a cluster of fortified villages and then moving the secure perimeters outward. This was, of course, exactly the approach recommended by Robert Thompson. It was a process of trial and error, which an official army historian later argued was "one of the most successful programs for using

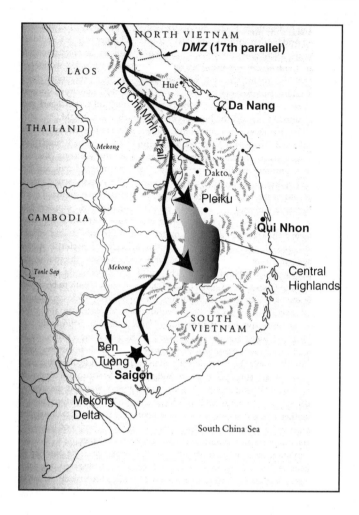

civilian forces ever devised by a military force."⁸ At the time the CIA
agreed. By the end of 1962, all statistical measures indicated that the
CIDG program had achieved startling progress.

Yet many senior army leaders had never liked the Special Forces, with
their unorthodox conduct and culture, and consequently had never been
supportive of the CIDG program. But what really stuck in their craws was
having army personnel controlled by anyone but army brass. An army
evaluation team arrived and grudgingly acknowledged the accomplishments of the CIDG program but complained about the improper use of
the Special Forces. Eventually the army replaced the CIA and took charge
of the program. Thereafter, the CIDG program continued its rapid growth

but completely changed in focus. Instead of gradually building mutually supporting, village-based security networks, American planners in Saigon either converted the Montagnard militia into Territorial Forces or upgraded them into mobile strike forces. In either case, the change meant the abandonment of local security in the Montagnard communities since the former militia no longer lived and operated in their home villages.

The senior American commanders at the Military Assistance Command, Vietnam, particularly wanted to use the Montagnards to block infiltration from Cambodia. So, repeating the mistake of the Strategic Hamlet Program, they assigned the Special Forces the task of building new CIDG camps in remote border regions. These camps were far from all support and thus painfully exposed to enemy attack. The ensuing Communist assaults overran two camps. These debacles highlighted endemic problems that were to haunt all pacification efforts in Vietnam. The camps were vulnerable during the hours of darkness, when reinforcements were unable or unwilling to come to the rescue. In areas where the Viet Cong dominated the villagers, the attackers were able to complete their approach march and assemble without detection. The Viet Cong were also often able to infiltrate into the ranks of the defenders before the attack and thus obtain detailed intelligence about the garrison. By the time the defenders knew that they were under attack the Viet Cong were already at or inside the camp's protective barbed wire.

Another festering problem was relations with the South Vietnamese military. South Vietnamese Special Forces held nominal command authority over the CIDG camps. But they were often reluctant to perform their duties. Moreover, they typically detested the Montagnards, who heartily reciprocated. In this unpromising environment, the U.S. Special Forces were supposed to defend their bases, conduct offensive actions into Communist base areas, improve the Montagnards' living standards through civic action programs, and develop Montagnard support for the central government. In spite of all obstacles, the Special Forces made remarkable progress.

THE EVOLUTION OF the Special Forces program from local defense to offensive combat operations was another recurring theme of American counterinsurgency efforts. American officers, particularly senior officers who had learned their trade in World War II, were imbued with an aggressive military philosophy summarized in the phrase "find 'em, fix 'em, destroy 'em." In their experience American mobility and firepower reigned supreme. They deemed the slow business of pacification unpalatable and did not think that it should tie down American fighting men.

They were about to get the opportunity to impose their vision of how the war should be fought, because American political leadership had come to the realization that the Communists were winning the war. The Viet Cong main-force fighters were routinely defeating Saigon's regular soldiers, thereby opening the way for the guerrillas to return to the villages and undo whatever progress the South Vietnamese government had made. Equally alarming, while the South Vietnamese military was losing control of the countryside, Vietnamese politicians in Saigon engaged in a seemingly endless battle for power. The resultant political instability meant that America's ally could neither fight nor govern.

With defeat looming, President Lyndon B. Johnson and his advisers decided that the only way to stem the tide was to send regular American ground forces to Vietnam.

SIXTEEN

Pacification, Marine Corps Style

Enter the Marines

ON MARCH 8, 1965, TWO MARINE BATTALIONS began landing in South Vietnam, the first wave of an American commitment that surged to a peak strength of 549,500 men. The marines came to provide security for a key airfield and related installations, including a top-secret intelligence center. Airlifts brought one battalion directly onto the Da Nang airfield. The other battalion conducted an amphibious landing complete with tanks and artillery. As they waded ashore in full battle gear it appeared that they were restaging the Iwo Jima invasion. Instead of encountering blistering machine-gun fire, they met a throng of South Vietnamese dignitaries and a collection of attractive girls who presented colorful leis of tropical flowers. Before the marines landed, some 23,700 American advisers and support troops were on the ground in Vietnam. Two hundred and six had died the previous year. The arrival of the marines in Vietnam marked a watershed. In the sad words of General William C. Westmoreland, "The time when we could have withdrawn with some grace and honor had passed."[1]

The Marine Corps retained some institutional memory of how to conduct counterinsurgency operations. Between 1909 and 1926 the marines had intervened in Central America four times. During these "Banana Wars," they fought local guerrillas or bandits, established an armed constabulary, and became involved in various forms of civic action. By 1934 a marine major concluded that despite its successes the Marine Corps was making unnecessary errors. He issued a challenge: "We might well ask ourselves 'Have we fully profited by past experiences?' "[2]

In response, the Marine Corps published the *Small Wars Manual*, a distillation of lessons learned from previous interventions. It was a practical compendium of how to fight an insurgency. It explicitly recognized that pure military strength might be unable to overcome an insurgency whose basis lay in economic, political, or social causes. It promoted a blended approach to counterinsurgency with a heavy dose of psychology. It advocated the employment of as little violence as possible in order to avoid native bitterness that would obstruct the return to peace. However, with unfortunate ill-timing, the Corps issued its final version of the *Small Wars Manual* in 1940, which guaranteed its quick passage to apparent permanent irrelevancy. World War II saw the Marine Corps change focus from counterinsurgency to amphibious assault. The change was so thorough that the officer who wrote the 1960 training manual on fighting guerrillas did not even know that the *Small Wars Manual* had ever existed.

But the Marine Corps is a tight tribe, and even in 1965 some marines still remembered their counterinsurgency history.[3] Senior marines, including the commandant of the Corps, had been commissioned in the early 1930s when the experiences and stories of fighting Sandino in Nicaragua and Charlemagne in Haiti were still fresh. Lewis Walt, commander of the marine expeditionary force that landed in Vietnam, had been a young cadet in 1936 whose company commander was the renowned Lewis "Chesty" Puller. Walt recalled that Puller "told us tales about fighting in Haiti and Nicaragua" and "every story had some point."[4]

However, when trying to apply historical experience to Vietnam the marines confronted two fundamental differences. The Guardia Nacional in Nicaragua and the Haitian Gendarmerie were local constabulary forces commanded by marine officers. In Vietnam, all Americans had a strictly advisory relationship with the South Vietnamese forces. Second, during the Banana Wars the marines had been their own boss. In Vietnam, the U.S. Army was boss.

Moreover, in 1965 the marines labored under two flawed doctrines. Their own doctrine had been revised only three years earlier. In an astonishing understatement of both the lessons of history and the Corps' own experience, the 1962 field manual *Operations Against Guerrilla Forces* paid lip service to the *Small Wars Manual* by observing that success against guerrillas was affected by the attitude of the civilian population instead of emphasizing that the battle for popular support was the key conflict in fighting an insurgency.[5]

In addition, the marines operated under the Military Assistance Command, Vietnam, headed by General Westmoreland. Westmoreland was an army general whose views had been formed by his conventional war experience. He followed the army doctrine that focused on achieving victory by destroying the enemy's army in open combat. General Walt quickly found the army doctrine unhelpful at best. Walt later recalled that shortly after arriving in Vietnam he realized that he personally "had neither a real understanding of the nature of the war nor any clear idea as to how to win it."[6] But he and his men had to learn fast because like it or not, the mission to provide airfield security plunged the marines into the pacification business.

A "Good Start" in Le My

The airfields were located in northern South Vietnam, a five-province region designated by allied commanders as I Corps. The vast majority of the residents of I Corps lived along the fertile coastal strip where they grew rice and fished. Along a 100-mile sector of the coast the marines established three huge enclaves—from north to south, Hue/Phu Bai, Da Nang, and Chu Lai—and set to work preparing to defend the airbases and their associated infrastructure.

The Viet Cong dominated the hamlets surrounding the middle of the three enclaves, Da Nang. When marine commanders pondered how to accomplish their mission they realized that about 150,000 civilians lived within 81 mm mortar range of the airfield. Since hit-and-run mortar bombardment was a Viet Cong tactic of choice, this was a problem. They decided to conduct an experiment based on the Corps' heritage of small-wars operations. The first target was the village of Le My, located on strategic ground eight miles northwest of Da Nang. A marine battalion commander surveyed the neighborhood on May 8, 1965. A Viet Cong sniper killed one of the marine scouts, thus providing persuasive evidence that the enemy was present. Three days later, two marine companies swept through Le My, easily evicting the two Viet Cong platoons based in the village. The marines made the male villagers destroy punji traps (concealed pits full of sharpened bamboo stakes), fill in trenches, and dismantle bunkers. Meanwhile, South Vietnamese government officials verified the identifications of the 700 village inhabitants and sent fifty-odd to

Da Nang for further questioning. Three days later a mixed force of militia, including recently recruited local villagers, relieved the marines.

While the militia purportedly worked to eliminate any remaining Viet Cong, marine patrols saturated the area to provide security for the village. The marines also initiated a comprehensive civil affairs program much like what had been done during the "benign assimilation" phase of the Philippine insurgency. They built a schoolhouse and medical dispensary, established a central market, and trained local nurses. In sum, the marine pacification effort in Le My followed the approach advocated in the *Small Wars Manual*. Lieutenant General Victor Krulak, widely regarded as the Corps' leading theoretical counterinsurgency expert, visited Le My and pronounced it a good start: "The people are beginning to get the idea that U.S. generated security is a long term affair."[7] Le My became a model for future marine pacification efforts. It also did not work.

In the absence of locals willing to denounce Viet Cong military and political operatives embedded inside Le My, the so-called Viet Cong infrastructure, marines remained clueless about their presence. The Viet Cong infrastructure were the people who provided political and military direction to the Communist war effort. They recruited youth who fought in the Viet Cong regular forces. They collected food and taxes to support the fighting units. Most important, as a Viet Cong defector related, was the fact "that the people were willing to cover for us at all times. They would not report our activities or locations to the government forces."[8] The Viet Cong infrastructure formed a highly structured bureaucracy that presented the South Vietnamese government with a deadly political and military challenge. Quite simply, the war could not be won unless this infrastructure was destroyed.

The task of identifying the insurgent infrastructure should have fallen to the Vietnamese National Police. But most police were too inefficient, corrupt, or frightened to perform this job. Consequently, within months of the marines entering Le My, the Viet Cong were back in place, their operatives secure through a combination of genuine popular support and the threat of terror. In December 1965, some seven months after the marines had first entered Le My, the Viet Cong gave the villagers a chilling lesson by capturing and torturing a prominent South Vietnamese pacification official and then burying him alive.

The Le My experience was only too common. That same December, near the southern enclave of Chu Lai, marines participated in a banquet with the village elders of Tri Binh. The next day, with the enthusiastic participation of the hamlet's chief, marine and South Vietnamese officials staged a flag-raising ceremony. On December 24, a marine Civil Affairs Team held a Christmas party for the villagers. On Christmas Day the marines invited the children to attend a celebration at battalion headquarters. On the last day of December, a Viet Cong assassin killed Tri Binh's chief.

The failure to provide real security and the failure to follow up on the first village clearing operation at Le My were reminiscent of the Philippine Insurrection experience. In Vietnam, a handful of insightful people understood the importance of civilian confidence in American fortitude. One such person was a Vietnamese official in Le My. He asked General Krulak, who was inspecting a newly "pacified" village, "All of this has meaning only if you are going to stay. Are you going to stay?"[9] Vietnamese peasants had seen first the French and then the Saigon government commit and then withdraw forces, leaving the villagers to cope with the consequences. These villagers may have wanted relief from the Viet Cong and their forced requisitions and military draft. But before they aligned with the Americans or the central government, they needed to know that the counterinsurgents were going to be there to protect them for the long term.

The Combined Action Program

In the summer of 1965, the northernmost marine enclave centered around the airfield of Phu Bai. Because the marines here were stretched thin, the battalion civic affairs officer suggested utilizing an overlooked resource, the local militia, called the Popular Forces (PF). The battalion developed a plan to integrate a PF platoon with a marine rifle squad. An accommodating Vietnamese divisional commander concurred, and so was born the war's most innovative pacification approach, the Combined Action Program. A young lieutenant named Paul R. Ek received the assignment of implementing this vision through the establishment of the first Combined Action Platoon (CAP).

Ek had prior experience as an adviser in Vietnam. More important, he had taken an intensive two-month course in Vietnamese and could understand and speak well enough to communicate in most situations.

From a pool of volunteers Ek picked the best men to form four rifle squads. He gave them a one-week primer on Vietnamese language and culture so they could know their place in this rural society—"who to call 'sir' and whom to call 'you,' " as Ek phrased it—and the marines entered four villages to live and work with four militia platoons.[10]

Ek's mission was to "run counterinsurgency operations" to defend the military installations at the nearby Phu Bai airfield.[11] Foremost in Ek's mind was the need to handle things differently than the French. Although the marines would be occupying villages, they were not to behave as an occupying force. Ek thought that by assisting the people and training the militia the marines could build an infrastructure to compete with and eventually replace Viet Cong influence.

The terrain consisted of densely grouped homes surrounded by open rice paddies. The Viet Cong dominated the area but did not maintain a regular military presence. Instead, several times a week Viet Cong tax collectors or propaganda teams made nocturnal visits. The propaganda teams held meetings and distributed leaflets to spread the message that the Vietnamese had successfully resisted powerful foreign armies in the past and they could do so again. With slogans such as "Unite the People, Oppose the Americans, Save the Nation," they kept patriotic and revolutionary fires burning. They also warned against cooperating with the Americans and issued threats against those who served as American "puppets." Although the CAP soldiers seemingly controlled the villages, such visits sought to remind the villagers who was truly in charge.

Ek figured that the Viet Cong would react to the marines in one of two ways: by immediately attacking to wipe out his platoon or by leaving them alone to make blunders that would alienate the villagers. The Viet Cong chose the latter but failed to reckon with the resolution of Ek and his marines to avoid such blunders. Unlike the French, they did not try to impose their own methods but rather adopted and used local approaches. The PFs, many of whom were seasoned anti-Communist fighters, particularly appreciated this attitude. Ek's marines also adopted a special policy that whenever there was firefight they made sure the militia participated. That way, if a mistake or a stray round injured a noncombatant, the blame would come to the combined PF-marine team instead of falling solely on the Americans.

In the Phu Bai area, as elsewhere, each village consisted of multiple smaller hamlets. At first the marines visited the hamlets only during the

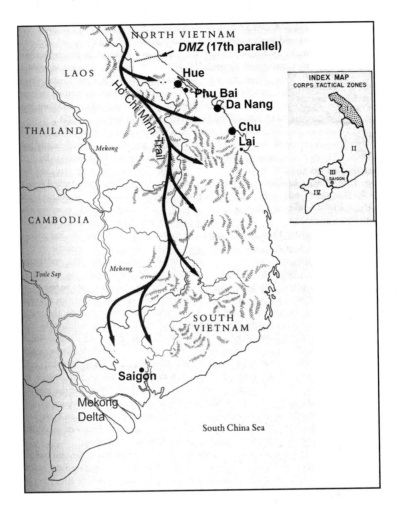

day and while accompanied by the militia. They avoided direct contact with the inhabitants. Instead, each marine kept a notebook to record his observations about the people's daily habits. By learning what was routine, the marines learned what was extraordinary. They acquired a special sense, "an attitude you feel," that indicated the extent of Viet Cong control.[12] Then, having grown confident in their new environment, the marines and Popular Forces saturated the area with nocturnal patrols and ambushes.

Contact with armed enemy was infrequent. Alarmed by the unexpected marine tactics, the Viet Cong avoided the four CAP villages. However, it became apparent that the Communists and the villagers had arrived at a tacit agreement whereby the Viet Cong would leave them alone as long as the villagers contributed money and rice to the NLF. But the rice harvest of 1965 was poor and the Communists needed food, so they sent women and children to the market to purchase rice. Villagers began tipping off the militia, thereby allowing CAP patrols to intercept the rice agents. Ek came to learn that the armed enemy "were the easy ones" to find and eliminate; it was the unarmed rice or tax collector or the woman who showed a torch from her home to betray an ambush site who were the more difficult foe.[13]

Ek and his superiors judged the Phu Bai experiment with Combined Action Platoons a success. With hindsight it can be seen that several special circumstances contributed to this outcome. The first set of CAP marines were highly motivated, experienced volunteers who were quick-thinking and socially aware. Two thirds of this first cohort volunteered to extend their tour with the Combined Action Program rather than depart Vietnam. Backing them were some especially competent Provincial Forces and an unusually efficient national police unit. The four trial villages lay in open rice paddies with no easy route for Viet Cong infiltration. Lastly, the Viet Cong responded to the marine presence with a wait-and-see attitude. Later CAPs would have none of these advantages.

SEVENTEEN

Progress and Setback

Life in the Village

THE SUCCESS AT PHU BAI PERSUADED the marine leadership to expand the Combined Action Program. Officially, the program emphasized destroying the insurgent infrastructure embedded within each village while protecting the people and government officials from insurgent reprisal. As it formally evolved, a fourteen-man marine rifle squad plus a navy corpsman operated with a 38-man local militia, or Popular Forces (PF) platoon. Because the marine rifle squads were dispersed around different CAP villages, young marine sergeants or corporals held independent command positions. Their counterparts back in Central America during the Banana Wars, as well as British noncommissioned officers (NCOs) in Malaya, had served in the same way. While not unprecedented, it was still a heavy responsibility. The NCOs and their men received a short primer on Vietnamese language (although the language barrier remained the cause of frequent and sometimes fatal misunderstandings), culture, and history before being permanently assigned to a hamlet or village where they lived twenty-four hours a day, seven days a week.

For the villagers, the most popular American was the navy corpsman. Hundreds attended his sick call. As one marine rifleman recalled, "You won't find too many Marines that'll dispute the fact that Doc won more hearts and minds than all of us combined."[1] Far more difficult was the challenge of forging an effective command relationship between the marine NCO and the Vietnamese platoon leader. It was one thing to establish the principle that they shared responsibility for the well-being of their troops and operated on the basis of mutually agreed courses of action. It was something else to adhere to this principle.

If the men meshed, it proved a good blend, with the marines instructing the PFs in basic small-unit tactics and discipline while the Vietnamese taught the marines the terrain and informed them about the local population. In the absence of harmony, a PF platoon commander exercised his power by refusing to cooperate. Many of the problems with the militia stemmed from sources beyond the control of the marines. The Popular Forces troops sat on the bottom of the pecking order in the allied order of battle. They were nominally volunteers recruited within their native villages to protect their own families. In reality they served at the discretion of the Vietnamese district chiefs. Sometimes they remained in their home villages but too often they were sent elsewhere for ancillary duties such as guarding fixed installations or acting as bodyguards for well-connected politicians. Even worse, the PFs often received assignments outside their home villages, where the inhabitants viewed them with the deep suspicion directed at all outsiders and foreigners. At all events, until much later in the war, the PFs received last call on weapons and equipment. The Viet Cong outgunned them and they keenly felt their inferiority. Lastly, service in the Popular Forces did not provide draft exemption. Consequently, most able-bodied men were in the regular forces, leaving the ranks of the militia filled with the very young, the too old, or the physically or mentally infirm. Out of such unpromising material, marine NCOs set to work to forge motivated anti-Communist fighters.

Special Men in a Strange Place

Like the original volunteers who served with Lieutenant Ek around Phu Bai, the nineteen- and twenty-year-old marines who volunteered for service in the initial CAP cohort were special. They had at least four months' combat experience and personal records free of disciplinary blemishes. They had to receive favorable endorsements from their commanding officers and had to be without discernible racial prejudice against the Vietnamese. This last qualification eliminated many candidates, since more than half of all marines candidly acknowledged that they did not like any Vietnamese.

For those who made the grade, CAP duty proved lonely and dangerous. The marines involved in the Combined Action Program confronted myriad difficulties, many of them unperceived by generals and civilian theorists. The program's success depended on establishing cooperation and trust with the militia and the villagers. The inability to speak the language and the difficulty of understanding an alien culture made these goals almost unattainable. Even had the CAP marines spoken Vietnamese, it would have been hard for them to penetrate the complexities of village life with their bewildering (at least to an outsider) network of inter- and intrafamilial relationships.

Among many cultural differences leading to tension was the attitude toward personal property. Whereas the marines believed in the sanctity of such property, the Vietnamese did not consider "borrowing" an unused object wrong, and in the marine view they had a very elastic notion of what constituted "unused." If a marine came in from patrol in a rainstorm and hung up his poncho to dry, a militiaman would borrow it to begin his patrol and perhaps return it three months later when the rainy season had ended. Nothing provoked the marines more than the frequent thefts by the militiamen, with cameras, watches, and other personal possessions disappearing with alarming regularity. Even items vital to security disappeared: "Every morning we would awake to find that a few more barbed wire stakes or another roll of barbed wire had walked out of the compound overnight."[2]

The marines conceived that they and the militia were "in it"—patrolling, guarding, repairing, and the welcome respite of actually fighting—fifty-fifty. But they saw the militia as not carrying their weight. Whereas the marines were on duty round the clock, the "lazy" militia routinely took breaks, including three-hour siestas at noontime. Worse, too often the PFs seemed unwilling to fight. The marines sarcastically labeled their behavior "search and avoid." They would accidentally-on-purpose cough loudly or discharge a weapon at a purported foe, thereby compromising a carefully set ambush. The marines knew that the village's sons and daughters served in the Communist ranks. They understood that a militiaman might be reluctant to fire at a potential relative. But given that they were putting their own lives on the line, the CAP marines still found it hard to tolerate such conduct.

In the absence of cooperative militia and living amidst an indifferent civilian population, the CAP marines could accomplish little more than any other American soldiers. One patrol leader recalled conducting more than sixty night ambush patrols and at least as many daytime patrols and never encountering the enemy. This led to the inevitable suspicion that the militia were in cahoots with the Viet Cong. (The marines also suspected that an unknown number of the militia were in fact either Viet Cong agents themselves or at least had made discreet accommodations with the enemy. So when a PF guide refused to advance any farther along a jungle trail, a marine had to consider: was it because the dangers were really too great or because the PFs had reached an accommodation that divided territory into "ours" and "yours"? Such suspicions led to enormous frustration, stress, and often alienation: many marines developed an attitude that while the militia would steal anything not nailed down and do whatever necessary to avoid danger, it didn't matter, because the marine would be leaving pretty soon. Marines with this attitude would not give their wholehearted effort to make the CAP program work.

WHEN THE CAP marines first moved through a typical hamlet the villagers avoided contact with them. They ducked quickly into their homes and quieted children who called out. They exuded a palpable atmosphere of fear, avoidance, and apathy. To the villagers, the marines were just another group of armed strangers come to plague them in a conflict without end. Indeed, throughout the war rural people seldom shared information with outsiders, whether Americans or South Vietnamese. But once the CAPs proved that they were present for the long haul, villagers overcame their fears and began using the militia or children to relay intelligence to the marines. Some of it was not useful, along the lines of "The VC will come here sometime next month." But some was: "A tax collector comes to Minh's house tonight at eleven." If the marines and the militia successfully acted on these tips by killing or capturing a Viet Cong tax collector or recruiting agent, by ambushing a Viet Cong propaganda team, or by repulsing a sapper attack, the flow of actionable intelligence increased.

The PFs, in turn, gained confidence and agreed to extend the range of their patrols. Meanwhile, a marine civic action noncom worked to obtain cement to repair hamlet wells. Other marines spent small sums in the hamlets and people began to benefit economically from their presence. As the months passed additional positive changes in village attitudes occurred and the quality of the intelligence improved. But progress could be undone so easily. To succeed on CAP duty, individual marines had to exhibit nearly flawless conduct. Bad behavior by one could and did reverse months of trust building. If a marine greeted a village girl with inappropriate familiarity or a man who never should have been assigned to CAP duty exploded in a racist rage, patient progress was lost. External factors over which the marines had no control also impeded progress: an American vehicle accidently injuring a hamlet child, an errant artillery round destroying a home, a passing convoy of front-line soldiers throwing objects at the hamlet's people out of dislike for all things Vietnamese.

Moreover, although the CAP might maintain a presence in a village for three or four years, the particular Americans involved rotated away to other duties, thereby severing personal relationships between the marines and the villagers. As a 1969 assessment reported, "Their replacements, fresh from the States, spoke no Vietnamese . . . and, arriving in an area that seemed to hold no threat from the enemy, they could see little reason behind the requirements for continual military efforts. As a result, some relaxation of discipline occurred."[3] And this was what the patient Viet Cong agent embedded somewhere in the village waited for, even if that wait went on for months or years.

The Viet Cong Adapt

Even when the CAP marines managed to cope with all the social problems caused by the inevitable friction between a foreign army based in the middle of deeply suspicious rural society, the adaptable enemy could nearly always cause a setback. The village of My Phu Thuong, located only five miles from the first marine CAP village in Phu Bai, demonstrated this adaptability. When the CAP started to make progress, the NLF leadership summoned the best half of its twenty-man standing village guerrilla force to a special training program. These chosen ten were to spearhead a counterattack at some future time. Meanwhile, in their absence, recruiters entered My Phu Thuong to enlist ten replacements, including two women, all of whom belonged to the American-armed local self-defense force.

Having dealt with its manpower problems, the Communists at My Phu Thuong also adjusted their operational methods. Because the CAP ambush teams had begun to interdict the local trails, the guerrillas extended their underground tunnel network. Because some villagers had begun to

support CAP activities, the Viet Cong intensified attacks against informers and collaborators.

A key to Communist adaptability was the possession of good intelligence. Guided by people intimately familiar with the local terrain, a Communist recon team would conduct a careful study. Briefing and rehearsal
followed, and then came the assault. In the seemingly pacified village of
Phuy Bong it came at 2:30 a.m. when all the marines and militia were
caught in the patrol base. A North Vietnamese assault force pinned them
in the base while enemy soldiers swarmed through the three hamlets that
composed the village. The Communists killed four PFs and then brazenly
set up a mortar next to the village market. The mortar fired against a
bridge, undoubtedly with the intent of provoking American return fire
that would damage the village. Although in this case the ploy failed, the attackers succeeded in their goal of reminding villagers that they still were
vulnerable to reprisal. Worse, the next morning the marines discovered
why their efforts to defend their base had been so difficult: wires controlling their Claymore mines—a vital component of their defensive
scheme—had been cut, rendering the mines useless. The obvious answer
was "an inside job," betrayal by one of the militia. During the subsequent
investigation matters grew so heated that a marine apparently beat a PF.
And so the precarious bonds of trust dissolved and the insurgents chalked
up another small victory.

All these factors made it hard for even dedicated CAP marines to provide village security. In the absence of security Viet Cong terrorists struck:
kidnapping the sister of a particularly effective militia officer, killing the
kindly old couple who ran a beverage stand frequented by the marines,
leaving a note with the message that this was the certain fate for all traitors
pinned to the breast of a mutilated civilian who had provided intelligence
to the marines. And always lurking was the fear that someday the marines
would leave and the Viet Cong would resurface.

Problems Emerge

A CAP marine had a 75 percent chance of being wounded once during
his tour and a 30 percent chance of being wounded a second time. Almost 12 percent died. High casualty rates occurred because as the program expanded the enemy recognized the threat and made CAP villages
high-priority targets. They were particularly vulnerable at night, when
most of the defenders were out on patrol and only four marines and six

or so Popular Forces remained. Thus a typical nocturnal attack by fifty or sixty Viet Cong enjoyed overwhelming numerical advantage and routinely inflicted serious losses. And, as had been the case with the CIDG camps established by the Special Forces, reaction forces—this time American, not South Vietnamese—were reluctant to come to the rescue because they feared night ambush.

Therein lay a flaw. Even in areas of heaviest concentration, the CAPs and their supporting reaction forces could not prevent the enemy from massing to attack a vulnerable garrison. In essence, like the garrisons of the larger strongpoints and firebases, the marines on CAP duty owned only the ground they occupied. Aided by thorough local intelligence, the Viet Cong usually navigated between the American and South Vietnamese positions to attack when and where they wanted. Thus the CAPs failed to provide the villagers with the security that was the necessary precursor to everything else the Americans hoped to achieve.

At its best, the CAP program attracted brave, dedicated men who over time took the goal of helping their village to heart. In spite of the manifest hardships and dangers, in 1967 60 percent of the 1,100 marines assigned to CAP duty volunteered to extend their tours. They knew that the progress they had achieved was precarious and that much depended on the personal relationships they had forged and the local knowledge they had acquired. They wanted to see the job through.

However, as the CAP program expanded, the quality of its marine participants declined. For some marines, the transition from regular combat duty to CAP duty proved too difficult: "We've been up in the mountains for months where it's been kill, kill, kill; now we come down here and are told we're supposed to love them all. It's too much to ask."[4] Combat officers were understandably reluctant to release their best men for CAP duty. Instead, they had every motive to send their misfits. As one colonel recalled, "Although the requirement states that they should be volunteers, it doesn't demand volunteers." So he followed a rule of thumb that "if a man doesn't object he is a volunteer."[5] Other participants came from combat service support units.

As time passed the selection process increasingly paid mere lip service to official requirements. One bored supply clerk who applied for CAP duty recalled his five-minute interview. It was clear to him that the clinching question was a hypothetical query about how he would respond if a militiaman stole his camera. "The right answer was self-evident, and I laid it on with a trowel."[6] By demonstrating his "cultural sensitivity," the clerk, who had no combat experience and spoke only a few words of pidgin Vietnamese, aced the entrance exam.

But passing the exam and actually being effective in the field were two different things. During indoctrination, instructors had told the CAP marines that the Vietnamese people would perceive that they were better than the French and would grow to like them. Arriving in his assigned village, one volunteer soon learned that this was not so: "We could read it in the studied indifference of the people as we passed, the way they ignored us even as we searched their homes and property."[7] It was plainly evident that the villagers considered the marines as just another species of foreign barbarian.

A marine colonel complained that the two teams in his tactical area lacked ground combat experience and skills as well as knowledge of Viet Cong tactics and "were unfamiliar with the social and religious customs of the people they were living with."[8] Equally distressing, the PFs with whom the two inexperienced teams worked were not local villagers. The local men were absent, having been drafted into either the South Vietnamese army or the Viet Cong, or having gone into hiding to evade service with either side. In a society where village identity was everything, these CAPs "kept themselves aloof from the villagers they were supposed to be helping."[9] Needless to say, neither team accomplished anything useful, failing to capture a single enemy combatant, let alone dismantle the embedded Viet Cong infrastructure.

The marine presence in Vietnam swelled from the initial two battalions to a peak strength of 85,000 men in 1968. However, the CAP never reached its benchmarks, although it expanded to 57 units in 1966 and 79 in 1967. In 1967 CAP employed a mere 1,249 marines and 2,129 militia. Even at its height, CAP operated in only some 20 percent of the villages in I Corps. A major obstacle was the reluctance of South Vietnamese leaders to commit manpower to the program. Marine planners had envisioned a ratio of one marine to three Popular Forces. This ideal was never met. By 1970 the actual ratio fell to one marine to one and a half PF.

Even at this diminished ratio, advocates pointed to some undeniable statistics indicating the effectiveness of the CAP approach. Consequently, senior marine commanders continued to promote the program. The officer who first supervised training for CAP duty, Lieutenant Colonel William R.

Corson, described it as "a specific and unique response to the challenge posed by the Communist doctrine of Wars of National Liberation."[10] Proponents cited the fact that in 1966 there were about 110 villages in the Marine Corps area of responsibility. Less than one quarter of them were considered government-controlled. Within this cohort, villages where a CAP operated for six months or more achieved a 60 percent secure rating or better, a rise of 20 points since the arrival of the teams and a rating judged to indicate that the government had established "firm influence" in the village. Notably, the performance of the Popular Forces in the CAP villages was far superior to militia elsewhere. In the entire I Corps, only 12 percent of all PFs participated in CAPs, but they accounted for almost 29 percent of all enemy killed by the Popular Forces. Overall, the kill ratio, a statistic much beloved by MACV, was fourteen Viet Cong to one marine or PF, as contrasted with a three-to-one ratio for Popular Force units not serving with CAP marines. Armed with such statistics, marine leaders tried to persuade MACV to adopt the Combined Action Program for all of Vietnam.

However, the North Vietnamese main-force threat, a threat of unique gravity in I Corps because of its shared border with North Vietnam, compelled the marines to trim their goals for expanding the rural pacification program. Then in January 1968 the Tet Offensive exploded on the ground in Vietnam and on the television sets of a stunned American nation.

BACK IN 1966, thunderous congressional applause had greeted President Lyndon Johnson's State of the Union address when he said, "I believe that we can continue the Great Society while we fight in Vietnam."[11] Johnson's decision to wage war in Vietnam with minimum disruption of domestic life remained both publicly and politically popular until the human and financial cost of the war rose. However, as the months passed, and in spite of a large and steady escalation of American troop strength and firepower, there seemed to be little progress. The beginning of the large search-and-destroy missions in 1967, with their attendant increase in American casualties, coincided with a large increase in racial and civil unrest in the United States. During the first nine months of 1967, public antiwar protests, ranging from minor demonstrations to full-scale riots, occurred in 150 cities. Public skepticism about the war's final outcome caused Johnson to worry privately, "This thing is assuming dangerous proportions, dividing the country and giving our enemies the wrong idea of the will of this country to fight."[12]

Two major factors fed this skepticism: a lack of candor about the American policy in Vietnam that extended throughout the Johnson administration from the president to the military spokesmen in Saigon, and immensely skillful North Vietnamese and Viet Cong manipulation of public opinion. Far better than anyone in the Johnson administration, the Vietnamese Communists understood the link among international opinion, American public opinion, and battlefield outcomes. This understanding informed the Communist conduct of what became known as the Tet Offensive, a surprise, nationwide offensive that coincided with the traditional Vietnamese celebration of the lunar new year.

On the night of January 30, 1968, as revelers swarmed Saigon's streets to celebrate the Year of the Monkey, the explosions of thousands of traditional firecrackers rocked the air. Slowly, as some of the 67,000 Viet Cong committed nationwide to the first assault moved from their safe houses into attack position, the sounds of combat replaced the sounds of festival. The ensuing synchronized ferocity brought fighting into previously untouched urban centers and surprised every allied commander in Vietnam and in Washington. To achieve this feat, the Communist leadership concentrated its forces. The act of concentration exposed the Communists to American firepower and they suffered terrible losses. By the time the offensive ended, the Communists had suffered 40,000 to 50,000 battlefield deaths while killing between 4,000 and 8,000 South Vietnamese soldiers and inflicting about 4,000 American casualties.

By any conventional calculation, Tet was an enormous Allied military success. Instead, the American public perceived it as a complete debacle. It shattered their confidence in official statements regarding the war's progress. The public's perception astonished many combat soldiers. Standing next to enemy corpses stacked like cordwood outside his headquarters, one American cavalry officer mused, "To our complete bewilderment in the weeks that followed, nobody ever publicized this feat of battlefield triumph. Instead, we read that we had been defeated."[13] Quite simply, the American public had witnessed on television an unprecedented scenes of bloodshed and concluded that the Communists remained much stronger than American political and military leaders had led them to believe.

That February, the voters of New Hampshire expressed their shock by giving dark-horse antiwar candidate Eugene McCarthy almost enough votes to defeat the incumbent president. McCarthy's vote total underscored public disapproval of Johnson's war management from both the right and left. For every two voters who wanted out of Vietnam, three anti-Johnson voters believed the president should unshackle the military and let them fight. Nationwide opinion polls showed that for the first time more than half the people considered involvement in Vietnam a mistake. Johnson tried to stop his slide in public esteem, telling the nation that Hanoi was trying to "win something in Washington that they can't win in Hué, in the I-Corps, or in Khe Sanh."[14] But it was too late for Johnson to save his presidency.

After Tet

In Malaya, the Communist capacity to attack isolated police posts dramatically declined as the war progressed. In Vietnam, the opposite occurred. Whereas prior to Tet a Viet Cong attack against a CAP compound typically involved 20 to 30 guerrillas, beginning with Tet they featured between 150 and 200 troops backed by powerful supporting weapons. One such attack against a compound defended by 48 marines and militia began with a mortar and recoilless rifle bombardment. Simultaneously, sappers detonated Bangalore torpedoes to blow gaps in the defensive wire. The attackers instantly surged through the breaches and rapidly fanned out to attack preselected objectives. They hurled grenades and satchel charges into the dispensary, command bunker, and ammunition bunker. Intense rifle fire covered their rapid withdrawal. Only seven minutes elapsed from the time the first mortar rounds exploded until the attackers withdrew. The assault happened so quickly that there was no time for a reaction force to intervene, and it was delivered with lethal precision, killing four marines and four militia while wounding nine marines and eight militia.

An assault against a CAP village in the northernmost province of Quang Tri pitted a reinforced North Vietnamese battalion against some fifty to seventy marines and militia. The PF performance was uneven. One Vietnamese lieutenant hid in a bunker until morning. Two PF privates fled to an ammo bunker, tossed out the ammunition to make room, and hunkered down in safety until the fighting ended. The situation grew so desperate that the marines called in close support artillery "to save our skins" without regard for the fact that the artillery fell on the homes of the villagers.[15]

Such assaults, duplicated throughout I Corps during Tet, inflicted such serious losses that the marines made a fundamental change. As one marine captain working in the Combined Action Program observed, "The complexion of the war has changed," with civic action "gone by the wayside."[16] As long as there was a menacing North Vietnamese presence, CAPs had to restrict where they sent patrols. In places where the enemy had either overrun or come close to overrunning the CAP compounds, the marines took a more draconian attitude toward the civilian population. Homes that interfered with fields of fire were leveled. People living in hamlets that had always been considered sympathetic to the enemy were relocated, their homes destroyed, and the area redesignated as a free-fire zone.

It seemed that fortified CAP patrol bases provided the enemy with too easy a target. A CAP marine noted, "It only takes about three seconds to overrun a small perimeter."[17] Henceforth, most CAP teams abandoned these bases and adopted a new approach, called a "mobile CAP." Rather than providing the enemy with a fixed target, during the day the marines and militia set up temporary command posts, or "day havens," where they rested and ate. They relocated before nightfall to set up new command posts that served as hubs from which they sent out patrols. They carried all their food and weapons with them and moved around in an almost random way, thereby avoiding a routine that might provide the enemy with a predictable target. The marines and PFs shared food, a few comforts, and a great deal of discomfort.

Then and thereafter, the mobile CAP was controversial. The absence of a fixed base imposed enormous physical and psychological strain. It was a complete departure from most of the principles underlying the original CAP strategy. The fact that the marines did not feel safe staying put in one place sent an unmistakable message to the villagers. No longer was there a permanent place for village officials and their people to go to seek help and security. The theory underlying a permanent CAP post held that it served as a center for pacification and an alternative to what the Communists offered. That theory was now abandoned.

However, mobility did please senior commanders because of the reduction in CAP marine casualties. Also, the mobile CAP posed a new challenge for the enemy. As one CAP leader explained, the marine mobility kept the Viet Cong "guessing"; they "don't like to come after you unless they've had a chance to get set and do some planning."[18] So as the war continued, the marines proceeded with a modified but still unique experiment in counterinsurgency. In 1967 one typical dedicated CAP marine responded to an interviewer's query about the effectiveness of the CAP: "We've got some real good PFs here and the CAP is what's going to help win this war."[19]

THEN AND THEREAFTER it was left to a handful of military specialists to assess the validity of the marine strategy. At the time, regardless of what the marines accomplished by pursuing their vision of pacification, the very fact that they were trying infuriated many among the army high command. General Harry W. O. Kinnard, the commander of the first army division to arrive in Vietnam, the famous First Cavalry Division, Airmobile, later pronounced himself "absolutely disgusted" with the marine approach. Major General William E. Depuy, Westmoreland's chief of operations and commander of the army's First Infantry Division, concurred: "The Marines came in and just sat down and didn't do anything. They were involved in counterinsurgency of the deliberate, mild sort."[20] Had Depuy read the 1940 edition of the *Small Wars Manual*, with its emphasis on applying the least force to achieve decisive results while exhibiting "tolerance, sympathy, and kindness" toward the civilian population, he might have understood better what the marines were about.[21]

Instead, MACV focused on the Communist main-force threat, and it was formidable. In 1966, an entire North Vietnamese division had invaded across the demilitarized zone separating North and South Vietnam. The invasion compelled Marine General Walt to reposition about half the marines who had been assigned to pacification duties. The statistical analysis so dearly loved by Pentagon planners highlighted the challenge. In the middle of 1966, in I Corps the enemy had 17,000 North Vietnamese regulars (NVA); 8,000 Viet Cong armed, equipped, and trained for conventional combat; and 27,500 guerrillas. Each month an estimated 2,600 regulars infiltrated across the demilitarized zone and the Viet Cong gained 2,000 recruits. Against such numbers, pacification could make little progress. Clearly, the solution had to start with curtailing the enemy's ability to reinforce and recruit. Only then could pacification make progress, and even then it would take an estimated fifty-one months to destroy the Communist infrastructure. The somewhat more optimistic marine assessment recognized that until the NVA threat was gone, the marine enclaves would be unable to link up, the oil spots unable to merge. Then another twenty months would be needed to establish effective government control and this presumed improved, increasingly effective South Vietnamese forces.

Herein lay another huge problem. Until the Tet Offensive, the marines and regular South Vietnamese forces had shielded, albeit imperfectly, the villages from the enemy main forces. But the government forces, both the militia and the civil officials, were unable to convert the villagers to the government side. According to decisions made in October 1966, the South Vietnamese were supposed to undertake the balance of the pacification effort throughout Vietnam. This effort faltered for numerous reasons, including corruption and ineptitude, with the results ranging from ineffective to counterproductive. Even had the existing South Vietnamese forces been effective, there were not enough of them. The village-based Popular Forces and National Police were keys to an effective pacification program. However, casualties and desertion, and a nationwide competition for qualified recruits, left both forces badly under strength and filled with marginal manpower. In I Corps, American planners estimated that another 18,000 militia were required along with twice the number of available National Police. The Rural Development effort was likewise weak, with only 13 operational teams when planning called for 111. At that rate, marine analysts estimated it would take twenty years to complete the government's planned Rural Development policy.

The British in Malaya had understood that pacification was a long, drawn-out process. They made an open-ended commitment to see the job through. If the Combined Action Program was to succeed, it required a similar commitment. As the Vietnamese official in Le My, the first village to experience the marine version of pacification, had said to General Krulak, "All of this has meaning only if you are going to stay. Are you going to stay?"[22]

EIGHTEEN

The Army's Other War

Westmoreland's Way of War

THE MARINE CORPS STRATEGY TO PACIFY I Corps confronted opposition both from senior South Vietnamese leaders and from the head of MACV, General William C. Westmoreland. For the South Vietnamese leaders, pride and politics played a role. They did not want the marines accomplishing something that they could not do. They also wanted their own fingers in what they sensed could become a very lucrative pacification pie. Somewhat oblivious to these underlying currents, Westmoreland had reached the plausible conclusion that because the South Vietnamese spoke the language and presumably understood the local culture they were better suited for pacification than Americans. The "Other War" was no doubt important, but Westmoreland's every instinct informed him that the path to victory lay in defeating the Communist regular units in a big-unit war of attrition.

The fifty-year-old Westmoreland had seemed marked for high command ever since his West Point days, when he was appointed first captain of cadets and won the coveted Pershing Trophy for leadership. In World War II he achieved a distinguished record as commander of an artillery battalion during the North African Campaign and later as chief of staff for the Ninth Infantry Division. His qualities impressed the paratroop general James Gavin, who invited Westmoreland to transfer to the airborne forces after the war. Westmoreland performed very well in a succession of prestigious postings, including commander of the elite 101st Airborne Division and superintendent of the U.S. Military Academy, where he introduced counterinsurgency into the West Point curriculum. In keeping with the military's burgeoning emphasis on scientific management, he also completed a course of study at the Harvard Business School.

Before assuming command in Vietnam, Westmoreland had traveled to Malaya to study how the British had dealt with their insurgency. Robert Thompson escorted him. Westmoreland found the trip interesting but not particularly relevant. He concluded that there were simply too many differences: the British had commanded both their own and the entire civilian military and government apparatus, the ethnic Chinese insurgents were easily distinguished from the population, and there were no cross-border sanctuaries for the Malayan insurgents. Westmoreland decided that "we could borrow little outright from the British experience."[1]

As he gazed across Vietnam's strategic chessboard, Westmoreland saw a valuable fighting asset, the marines, hunkered down within their enclaves. In Westmoreland's mind this represented waste. Indicative of his attitude was his reaction to a marine report regarding promising results from a civic action program called Country Fairs. Westmoreland responded that this was all well and good, but he did not want any dissipation of American strength "to the detriment of our primary responsibility for destroying mainforce enemy units."[2] He made it abundantly clear that he wanted the marines out searching for the main-force Communist units in order to bring them to battle. Henceforth the counterinsurgency effort took place against a background of conventional combat between American and Communist main-force units, most notably including North Vietnamese regulars.

As the dominant military partner in this effort, the U.S. army acted according to its limited-war doctrine, which called for rapid restoration of peace achieved by decisive combat with the enemy. This doctrine played to the army's strengths: its massive firepower and tremendous mobility conferred by a helicopter armada. The army would conduct a war of attrition utilizing the weapons and tactics designed to defeat the Soviet Union in a conventional conflict. It would grind down the Communists until they gave up. The "Other War," the counterinsurgency campaign, would always be subordinate to this war of attrition. When asked at a press conference what was the answer to insurgency, Westmoreland gave a one-word reply: "Firepower."[3]

———————

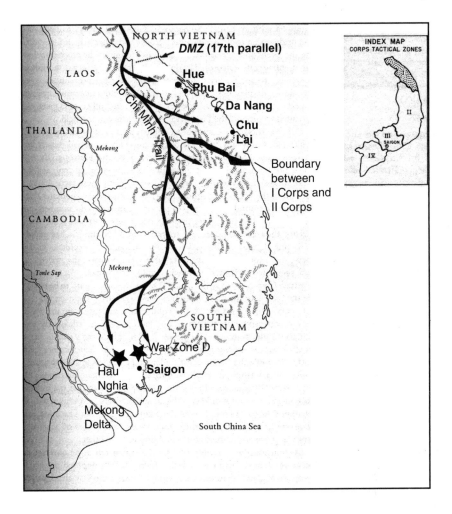

THE SO-CALLED BIG-UNIT war hugely complicated the counterinsurgency without changing some of its basic dynamics. While the U.S. military provided a security shield, U.S. civilian agencies continued working to implement social and economic reforms in order to win popular support for the Saigon government. This popular support would both legitimize the government, thus depriving the Communists of a crucial plank in their antigovernment rhetoric, and delegitimize the guerrillas.

At the same time, the U.S. Army participated in pacification. Its involvement included civil affairs, which were efforts to improve rural living conditions, and direct provision of village security, a task absorbing only a small portion of the army's combat strength. In spite of Westmoreland's initial skepticism, the army particularly touted its involvement in Country Fair operations that combined civic affairs projects with cordon-and-search operations. The intent was to tackle one village at a time, root out the Viet Cong infrastructure, and build popular support for the government.

Thirteen miles north of Saigon was the village of Tan Phuoc Khanh. Because of its strategic location in the notorious and Communist-dominated War Zone D, the region had been the focus of numerous allied military campaigns. In June 1966 they tried again when a joint force of South Vietnamese and American regulars entered Tan Phuoc Khanh to conduct a Country Fair. Over succeeding days the Americans provided security while Vietnamese teams organized local elections, conducted a census, and began small construction projects. Meanwhile, a joint task force spent three days trying to uncover Viet Cong agents. Given that the Viet Cong had spent years establishing themselves deep inside Tan Phuoc Khanh, this was far too little time. The regulars departed—the villagers missed the Americans, who had actually provided real albeit too-brief security, and were happy to see the backs of the South Vietnamese soldiers, who had preyed on them—and the local militia took over security duties.

Sensing weakness, the Communists began probing. In November 1967, some seventeen months after the Country Fair, a Viet Cong company overran Tan Phuoc Khanh's central watchtower. The next month a hamlet chief resigned for fear of his life. At year's end two American field evaluators visited the village and correctly concluded that the official rating that labeled Tan Phuoc Khanh "secure" was wrong.

The experience at Tan Phuoc Khanh was typical of the U.S. Army's attitude toward pacification. A Country Fair operation might attract good publicity with its army band entertaining the villagers and civil affairs personnel running a diverting lottery. A barbecue fed people for a day. A medical team could provide inoculations lasting much longer. None of these things harmed the war effort. But by the same token, none of them was anything more than a palliative that accomplished little toward establishing lasting security or forging stronger bonds between rural villagers and their remote government in Saigon.

The Rise of Robert Komer

For all the blame that American planners heaped upon the South Vietnamese for their faltering pacification efforts, a hard look in the mirror showed significant American failures as well. The inability of U.S. military and civilian agencies to pull in harness impeded significant progress. After years of fighting an insurgency, many American military and civilian strategists appreciated, albeit with varying degrees of clarity, the importance of pacification. Some also perceived that existing programs were truly inefficient. While the unwillingness of a rural villager to support the government involved a host of difficult, sometimes incomprehensible cultural issues, management and organizational issues were two things Americans understood. They could be tackled by improved efficiency, reorganization, and the application of more resources—in other words, by the application of sound management practices—or so an influential group of bureaucrats claimed.

An ex-CIA analyst named Robert Komer gained the ear of Secretary of Defense Robert McNamara and had himself appointed to Saigon to serve as chief of pacification. Komer was nothing if not energetic. His ability to force his solutions on an unresponsive bureaucracy earned the hot-tempered Komer the nickname "Blowtorch." In 1967, he oversaw the hatching of a centralized pacification program called Civil Operation and Revolutionary Development Support (CORDS). President Johnson invested high hopes in the program, knowing that CORDS had far more resources—funds, personnel, and equipment—than previous efforts. He recalled Komer's prediction that after one year of operation there would be decisive progress.

The Tet Offensive arrested progress on the pacification front. The American press described Tet as a terrible blow, particularly against the pacification program. A *Washington Post* columnist claimed that the Tet attacks had "killed dead the pacification program." The *Christian Science Monitor* agreed, saying that "pacification has been blown sky high."[4]

Indeed, the Tet attacks inflicted enormous damage. With the notable exception of the CAP villages around Da Nang, the shield erected by American ground forces had failed to deflect main-force Communist units from moving through and attacking the rural population. More than 40,000 civilians were killed or wounded with about 170,000 homes destroyed or damaged. Some 1 million civilians fled the carnage to seek safety in squalid refugee camps. Tet significantly weakened the government's standing in the countryside as officials abandoned rural projects and joined the exodus. A CAP militiaman described his dismay: "That attack scared everybody for years. From then, we could not be sure about the defenses of the army."[5]

However, Tet caused the Communists "agonizing and irreplaceable losses," particularly among the best Viet Cong fighters and most skilled members of the clandestine infrastructure who had emerged to assist and even participate in the attacks.[6] Because of these losses, the Tet Offensive created a vacuum of power in rural areas. It left the NLF hugely vulnerable to a counterstroke, if the United States and its allies could deliver it.

Pacification's High Water Mark

On the first day of July 1968, South Vietnamese president Nguyen Van Thieu announced a strategic response to the Tet Offensive. After years of trial and error, American and South Vietnamese planners had finally adopted an integrated pacification program that made population security the primary goal. On the same day, General Creighton Abrams replaced Westmoreland as MACV commander. Under Abrams's direction, a purportedly new strategy, the so-called one-war plan, emerged. It explicitly recognized the dual need to keep the Communist main-force elements away from the populated areas and to root out the Viet Cong infrastructure. The test case took place in the two northernmost provinces of I Corps; Quang Tri, adjacent to the demilitarized zone separating North and South Vietnam, and Thua Thien, the location of the pilot marine CAP villages near Phu Bai. This time, 30,000 American and South Vietnamese regulars, including most of the 101st Airborne Division, provided an active buffer to confine enemy main-force units to the remote hinterland. Reconnaissance units extended outward to the Laotian border to detect major enemy concentrations and provide early warning to the regulars. Shielded by these operations, South Vietnamese militia and most especially National Police secured the hamlets and villages along the coast.

Around the same time, South Vietnamese political changes dramatically altered the calculus of the allied pacification push. The Saigon government trumpeted a new land reform policy that when enacted in 1970 actually redistributed farmland to two thirds of the tenant farmer families in South Vietnam. The United States introduced strains of so-called miracle rice that greatly increased yields. The reopening of canals and roads allowed villagers to move their products to market. The net result brought unprecedented prosperity. Simultaneously, the South Vietnamese government expanded the local security forces, including the Popular Forces and the People's Self-Defense Force.

In January 1969 General Abrams told his commanders that pacification was the "gut issue." He said that "if we are successful in bashing down the VC and the government can raise its head up, the villages and hamlets can maintain their RF/PF [militia] units and keep a few policemen around and people are not being assassinated all the time, then the government will mean something."[7] Indeed, the period 1969 to 1972 witnessed steady progress in pacification.

What made the new approach, called the Area Security Concept, special was its focus on one objective: population security. Also unique to this concept was the way it maintained its focus by dividing the two trial provinces in I Corps into geographic regions (border, unpopulated hinterland, contested villages, secure villages), assigned appropriately tailored forces to each region, and maintained coordination between the forces. By early 1969, every statistical indicator showed significant improvement in rural security. By year's end, the campaign was successfully separating the main-force units from the populated areas. South Vietnamese militia and police, along with marine CAPs, had established a permanent presence in more than 90 percent of the populated areas. For the first time, the enemy could not routinely slip between allied outposts. Captured documents revealed that the enemy was having great difficulty maintaining morale. Both American and South Vietnamese leaders had signed on for the Area Security Concept. In 1970 they applied it to the entire I Corps. Unable to recruit sufficient replacements from the local population, the Communists increasingly had to commit regulars from North Vietnam against the allied pacification efforts. This was enormously costly, in part became urban North Vietnamese youth were no more at home in rural South Vietnam than were urban South Vietnamese or Americans. Consequently, the Communists were reduced to assassination and terrorism to maintain any hold over the people.

Triumph of the Old Guard
The success in I Corps hinted at what might have been. But entrenched U.S. Army interests resisted. One typical general reacted to proposed changes in tactics and strategy with the comment, "I'll be damned if I

permit the United States Army, its institutions, its doctrine, and its traditions, to be destroyed just to win this lousy war."[8] Indeed, although
Abrams had intended the "one-war plan" to apply countrywide, he was
unable to convince his subordinates.

Back during the early bloom of the marine CAP program, the supervising colonel considered a "good night" to be one in which "not a round
was fired in one of our 114 CAP villages."[9] But such peacefulness did not
please promotion-conscious line combat officers. Quite simply, battalion
commanders did not view their six-month tour in Vietnam as an opportunity to win the hearts and minds of the people. General Julian Ewell, a
celebrated World War II paratroop veteran, commanded the army's Ninth
Infantry Division. Ewell described the conventional attitude: "I had two
rules. One is that you would try to get a very close meshing of pacification . . . and military operations. The other rule is that military operations
would be given first priority in every case."[10]

Like all professional military officers since the dawn of time, American
officers in Vietnam were keenly aware of where lay the fast path to promotion. In Vietnam, the path ran atop a statistic called "body count."
Goaded by ambitious senior generals, subordinates understood they had
to produce results, measured in enemy deaths, or face career-ending poor
evaluations. During 1969, the consequences included meaningless
slaughters such as the notorious "Hamburger Hill" as well as the production of inflated statistics with individual army brigades reporting astro-
nomical kill figures.

Under Ewell's thrusting leadership, during the first half of 1969 the
Ninth Infantry Division achieved the year's highest kill ratios and body
counts. Ewell relentlessly pressured his brigade commanders to obtain
kills and they in turn hectored their juniors. It worked, after a fashion. The
Ninth Infantry operated in the heavily populated Mekong Delta region.
One of its brigades achieved the unsurpassed prize of 1,000 kills in three
straight months, with an average ratio of 158 enemy killed for each American. Here was an attrition figure that could warm any general's heart.
When deconstructed, the numbers revealed highly suggestive anomalies.
Many of the kills came at night, and a large percentage came from the
muzzles of helicopter gunships. When tabulating enemy killed, American
soldiers followed the dictum "If it's dead, it's VC." However, for every fifteen people killed, soldiers found only one weapon. When addressing this
discrepancy, the division's after action report explained that many Viet

Cong operated without weapons. How many civilians were killed is un-knowable, but, as a divisional officer expressed it, "We really blew a lot of civilians away."[11] What is certain is that during the time the Ninth Division wreaked such carnage, by the army's own measures population security did not improve. Regardless, Ewell received promotion to corps command and later contributed to the crafting of the Army's new counterinsurgency doctrine.

After the war, Abrams, best remembered among today's warriors as the namesake of the army's main battle tank, the Abrams M-1, received con-siderable credit for redirecting the army and devising a new counterinsur-gency strategy. Not so, according to Robert Komer, who was present when Abrams replaced Westmoreland: "There was no change in strategy what-soever."[12] Although Komer underestimates Abrams's influence, a large set of factual data shows how hard it was to change a conventional army into a counterinsurgency force. For example, during 1969, artillery support alone cost over five times as much as the cost of supporting the South Vietnamese Territorial Forces who provided physical security for villagers. Overall, about 30 percent of American funding went directly to paying for ground combat operations with another 19 percent paying for the logisti-cal tail that supported these operations. Only 2 percent supported the Na-tional Police and militia.

WANING PUBLIC SUPPORT for the war influenced tremendously the po-litical decision to transfer the burden to the unsteady hands of the South Vietnamese. Toward this goal, in 1969 President Richard M. Nixon an-nounced the new policy of "Vietnamization" and American combat sol-diers began returning home. The marines had been first ashore in Vietnam as the vanguard of the American ground intervention. As the last marines left I Corps in May 1971, there were many signs indicating that the mission had been accomplished. Most metrics pointed positive: a func-tioning and expanding economy, much greater village security, the absence of large-scale North Vietnamese attacks, the comprehensive weakening of both the main-force Viet Cong and their village level infrastructure. Yet some things remained to darken this rosy glow. Statistics from the Hamlet Evaluation Survey showed that almost half of the rural villagers in I Corps lived within one kilometer of a recent terrorist incident. Nationwide, Com-munist terrorists inflicted an average of 26,000 civilian casualties in both

1969 and 1970. While rural people no longer actively supported the Viet Cong, neither did they support the South Vietnamese government. The decline in Viet Cong support was not matched by an increase in progovernment attitudes. The villagers had been through too many changes of control to become confident that this latest shift was permanent. And of course it was not.

The Dirty War

The new pacification strategy that began in the summer of 1968 included the American-inspired Phoenix Program. The launch of the Phoenix Program represented belated recognition of the crucial role of the Viet Cong infrastructure. If the war was to be won, the enemy's ability to recruit, receive intelligence and food, spread propaganda, and terrorize had to be thwarted. The Phoenix Program was the first comprehensive effort to identify the estimated 70,000 people who belonged to the village-level Viet Cong infrastructure. Toward this goal it sought to coordinate all American and South Vietnamese intelligence in order to eliminate Viet Cong operatives by targeted killings and arrests. The U.S. role was supposed to be strictly advisory. This role proved extremely frustrating, leaving American intelligence officers chafing at their inability to get the Vietnamese to perform according to American notions.

The program was controversial from the start, hampered by ineffectual Vietnamese leadership and police corruption. It was all well and good for American management specialists to prepare flow charts showing lines of authority and areas of responsibility, but these efforts ignored the reality that in addition to acting as a national defense force, the Vietnamese military and police served as "a political cabal whose first priorities were to perpetuate the system and to protect the safety, livelihood, and future prospects of those who controlled it."[13] Consequently, the military and police assigned low-level personnel, misfits, and discards to the Phoenix Program. Official indifference and corruption caused Phoenix advisers to estimate that only 30 percent of the suspects arrested in 1969 actually served jail terms.

In keeping with time-honored practice, Vietnamese officials responded to American pressure to achieve results by telling the Americans what they wanted to hear. When a raw but earnest American intelligence officer asked his more experienced sergeant what was wrong, the sergeant replied that the Vietnamese "just go through the motions to please the Americans, sir."[14] But, driven by a mandate to achieve results, the Phoenix Program did produce. While statistics remain controversial, between 1968 and 1971 the Phoenix Program received credit for capturing, convincing to desert, or killing more than 74,000 enemy. What then and thereafter was unclear is how many of the killed were actually enemy operatives. What is certain is that the program generated extraordinary negative press. The antiwar press convinced many that it was merely a cover for an assassination bureau. At the time an American official ruefully observed, "I sometimes think we would have gotten better publicity for molesting children."[15]

At the end of the day, regardless of how effective the Phoenix Program was at killing, killing was not enough. Phoenix created holes in the Communist infrastructure. It needed to operate in conjunction with policies that planted something in the holes.

The Contest for Hau Nghia

Hau Nghia Province, just west of Saigon, was widely regarded as having the best anti–Viet Cong infrastructure program anywhere in South Vietnam. But even here, the Saigon government was unable to capitalize on Communist weakness to develop support for itself. Consequently, everyone, from the people manning the bureaucracy to the militia guarding the village wire, was an outsider. An American adviser described the fundamental reason South Vietnamese government pacification efforts faltered in Hau Nghia: "The people who grew up in Hau Nghia didn't want anything to do with the Government of Vietnam. So all of the officials and the RD [Revolutionary Development] Cadres were from the outside. Nobody in their right mind wanted anything to do with Hau Nghia. Officials were sent there as punishment."[16]

A Phoenix intelligence officer wrote about how a Viet Cong defector enabled him to almost destroy a village's Viet Cong infrastructure. But, in spite of considerable effort to protect the defector, the Viet Cong struck back and assassinated him. Henceforth there was "an unmistakable chill in the people's attitude toward me." The people had trusted the Americans and the government security forces and they had failed. In this way, "a single cell of determined guerrillas had made a mockery of the government's efforts to provide security for the people."[17]

In 1971 the long contest for Hau Nghia Province seemed to have ended with the eradication of the enemy. The Saigon government regarded the province as secure. Run by dedicated and intelligent American officers with enormous assists from Viet Cong and North Vietnamese defectors, the Phoenix Program in Hau Nghia Province almost crippled the Communist infrastructure. But the Communists had prepared for this moment beginning back in the late 1950s when they had started their operations by focusing on building village-level support. The Communist cadres were well schooled in the ebb and flow of protracted revolutionary warfare. A dedicated handful stayed with their tasks, undercover, hidden, but still deeply embedded within the fabric of Hau Nghia village life. In some villages only two or three survived, but they were just enough to instill fear. Even when Hau Nghia was judged most secure, not a single government official in the province would risk sleeping outside the barbed wire. During 1971, assassination teams killed a government official or Communist turncoat every few days in Hau Nghia.

Meanwhile, in remote strongholds in the hinterland and particularly in sanctuaries just over the Cambodian border, North Vietnamese regulars rested and refitted, confident in the knowledge that because of Nixon's Vietnamization policy, time was on their side. Most rural villagers, and many South Vietnamese officials and soldiers, shared their view that the hard-won security would not persist after the Americans departed. They rightly suspected that whatever success pacification had achieved rested on the firm might of superior American military force. So as the American tide went out, government control of rural villages collapsed like a castle built of sand. And the Communist cadres returned to rebuild their shadow governments and prepare for the next offensive.

In addition, the ever-adaptive Communists changed tactics. By 1972 an estimated two thirds of Hau Nghia's Communist infrastructure were disguised as loyal citizens. To uncover them required patient police detective techniques. To thwart such work, North Vietnamese regular formations from sanctuaries just over the Cambodian border raided into Hau Nghia to "bolster revolutionary morale." As a Phoenix officer recalled, "As long as we were up to our ears in sapper attacks and the like, it was difficult to find the time to root out the village political cadre and guerrillas."[18]

Looking back, the years 1969 to 1971 could be seen as the high-water mark for the pacification of rural Vietnam, a time when "the Americans and their South Vietnamese allies came as close as they would ever come to winning the war for the countryside."[19] Indeed, by 1971 Hau Nghia was relatively quiet. But it was not secure. Government supporters continued to live under the cloud of terror. North Vietnamese attacked at will from their cross-border sanctuaries. Consequently, the night still belonged to the Communists and, as the province's senior American adviser recalled, "that's all the enemy needed."[20]

NINETEEN

Lessons from a Lost War

The Finger of Blame

As THE LAST AMERICAN ADVISERS DEPARTED Vietnam in 1972, CORDS officials were cautiously optimistic. By their measures pacification had made steady progress for the past three years. Many provinces appeared free of violence while enjoying unprecedented economic prosperity. The Viet Cong seemed to have abandoned former strongholds and were re-duced to forcible recruitment to replenish losses. In the minds of CORDS officials, the fact that the enemy was using conventional military opera-tions featuring North Vietnamese regular divisions proved the success of the counterinsurgency against the guerrillas. In 1972, the Communist Easter Offensive, a conventional ground invasion, collapsed beneath American aerial bombardment. This too seemed to vindicate the wisdom of the allied pacification campaign. When the 1975 invasion secured vic-tory for the Communists, a photo of a Russian-built tank battering down the gate of the Presidential Palace in downtown Saigon reinforced the no-tion that South Vietnam had fallen to a conventional military invasion. This notion, which overlooked the Viet Cong flag flying atop the tank's tur-ret and ignored the fact that the Viet Cong provided more than half of the invasion's administrative and service personnel and also performed key combat functions, eclipsed most discussion about the American coun-terinsurgency record.[1] Furthermore, by then the blame game was already well under way, with most fingers pointing to the top.

Westmoreland emerged from the war a lightning rod of criticism for his unimaginative, orthodox tactics and strategy. In fact, he had been a model soldier, employing the doctrine taught by his nation's foremost military schools and observing the limitations imposed by his commander in chief. It was not purely his fault that his nation mistakenly supposed that insurgents could be defeated by conventional forces employing conventional tactics according to a strategic doctrine devised to defeat the Russians on the plains of Europe. Perhaps a military mind of the foremost class would have perceived that nothing in the historical record supported this belief, but America's founding traditions work against the emergence of a military genius. It could be observed in Westmoreland's defense that President Johnson expected decisive results within a time span tolerable to the American public. Consequently Westmoreland perceived that he did not have time for pacification. In his mind decisive results could be obtained only through large-scale battle. This thinking was completely in accord with the U.S. bureaucratic bias. In spite of President Kennedy's call for a new approach to combat Communist revolutionary warfare, both the civilian and military components of the government remained wedded to conventional approaches. The marines notably tried to adjust their methods but they were the exception.

Neither senior American military nor political leadership had ever understood the Communist protracted-war strategy. North Vietnamese general Vo Nguyen Giap explained the challenge: "The enemy will be caught in a dilemma: he has to drag out the war in order to win and does not possess, on the other hand, the psychological and political means to fight a long drawn out war."[2] When planning its counterinsurgency strategy, American leaders failed to understand the insurgent strategy with its emphasis on the seamless interplay between political and psychological factors and military actions. The Vietnamese Communist generals had a clearer comprehension of one of the Western world's most famous strategic dictums, Clausewitz's statement "War is a mere continuation of policy by other means."[3] The National Liberation Front viewed their armed forces as tools to gain political goals. American generals saw their armed forces as tools to destroy the enemy military forces. Moreover, in the words of a senior Viet Cong official, the Americans "seriously exaggerated their own ability to inflict damage relative to their opponents' elasticity and durability."[4]

American intervention resulted from a strategic analysis shared by three presidential administrations that likened Vietnam to the first in a row of dominos. If the Communists successfully toppled the first, the rest would inevitably fall. When North Vietnam finally conquered South

Vietnam in 1975, the domino theory received its acid test. Instead of triggering a chain reaction of collapse, the fall of the first domino caused the others to turn inward on themselves. Vietnamese fought Cambodians, who defended themselves with Chinese help. China attacked Vietnam. The glue that had bonded Communist solidarity, Western occupation, dissolved after the United States departed. There was unspeakable suffering in the killing fields of Cambodia and in the "reeducation camps" of the former South Vietnam, but Communist expansion through Southeast Asia did not occur. The domino theory proved a fallacy.

This strategic blunder cost the lives of 58,193 Americans. Precise Vietnamese losses are unknowable. South Vietnamese military fatalities were probably close to a quarter of a million. According to a 1995 North Vietnamese government announcement, Communist military losses between 1954, the end of the First Indochina War, and 1975, the end of the Second Indochina War, totaled 1.1 million dead. Two million North Vietnamese and 2 million South Vietnamese civilians perished during this period.

The Question of What Might Have Been

After the war Robert Komer observed, "The greatest problem with pacification was that it wasn't tried seriously until too late."[5] The inability of the Marine Corps and the U.S. Army to agree about an appropriate pacification strategy did impair the counterinsurgency fight. The relationship was so strained that in 1967, after two years of war, the marines felt it necessary to issue a formal "Clarification of Terms" simply in order to define what pacification meant. It was no wonder that South Vietnamese officials, who were supposed to be the lead actors in the pacification fight, remained confused about how to proceed.

A catalogue of program names readily indicates the erratic course of pacification in Vietnam: Reconstruction, Civic Action, Land Development Centers, Agglomeration Camps, Agrovilles, Strategic Hamlets, New Life Hamlets, Hoc Tap (Cooperation), Chien Thang (Victory), Rural Construction, Rural Reconstruction, Revolutionary Development. Until the implementation of CORDS in 1967, pacification in Vietnam was a confusion of agencies, programs, and strategies that were underfunded, uncoordinated, and often in competition. Thereafter pacification became a highly bureaucratized program groaning under the weight of management assessment tools. The resultant focus on program management had the unforeseen consequence of losing touch with South Vietnam's real social, political, and military problems.

While American pacification efforts focused on improved efficiency, reorganization, and the application of more resources, American-sponsored civic action and civil affairs efforts were highly biased toward engineering projects such as opening roads and waterways and building service infrastructure. By emphasizing management and engineering solutions, the Americans were doing what they did well. However, because underdevelopment was not the foundation of the insurgents' strength, development was not a relevant response.

The two most promising approaches to pacification were the Special Forces' Civilian Irregular Defense Group and the Marine Corps' Combined Action Platoon. The CIDG program developed effective militia who could defend their homes and find enemy forces better than conventional American forces. The focus on the big-unit war sucked in the CIDGs to the detriment of their original purpose of providing local security and intelligence. Yet, just as had been the case in Malaya or in all other counterinsurgencies, intelligence was the key. The departing commander of the Fifth Special Forces reflected in June 1966 that "the single greatest U.S. shortcoming in Vietnam is our lack of timely, accurate intelligence. Soldiers' complaints about their repeated 'walks in the woods' without contact give evidence of this problem."[6] American leaders never had the patience to develop their own intelligence networks and dismantle the Viet Cong infrastructure. Instead, they flung even their Special Forces and their loyal CIDG units into the effort to find and destroy the enemy's big units. Between 1965 and 1968 the CIDGs operated more like mobile mercenaries than local defense teams. They were good at it, but it was an unwise use of their potential.

As with the CIDG forces, so with the marines; in Westmoreland's mind, elite American soldiers were being wasted in passive village security missions and he could not stand it. At the time and during the subsequent, ongoing refights of the war, the marines' CAP approach to counterinsurgency offered an appealing alternative to what actually transpired. As Robert Thompson declared at the time, the CAPs were "quite the best idea I have seen in Vietnam."[7] It is useful to reflect that by the summer of 1969, the program total peaked at 114 CAPs, just under the goal of 120 originally envisioned as a starting point back in the heady days of 1966. In other words, after years of effort, the CAP program was stuck near the number from where the "ink blot" spread of pacification was supposed to begin. By then, as Komer noted, it was too late.

The CAP approach was based on the clear-eyed analysis that defeating an insurgency required patience and a long-term commitment. In 1965 the Johnson administration was unwilling to accept such a commitment. It made no effort to persuade the American public that a protracted effort was required. So the question of whether the American public would have tolerated an ongoing expenditure of blood and treasure associated with an open-ended commitment to Vietnam is unknowable. What is certain is that if faced with the marine approach nationwide, the inventive foe would have altered his tactics and strategy.

The largest segment of the South Vietnamese population, the rural peasantry, simply never supported the South Vietnamese government. Since the arrival of the Japanese in 1941, villagers had seen outsiders representing different governments and political views come and go. They perceived the American-supported South Vietnamese government to be a continuation of rule by an alien elite little different from the French colonial administration. They considered it aloof, corrupt, inefficient, and totally lacking in legitimacy, a viewpoint widely shared by those Americans who lived among the villagers. At best, in places where enough American or South Vietnamese soldiers occupied the ground, the rural people acquiesced to Saigon's rule. Genuine, deeply held support was rare. Within the time span that American politicians gave themselves to win the war, no amount of American sacrifice would alter this fact.

THE UNITED STATES and its Vietnamese allies defined security as freedom from enemy attack. Both South Vietnamese and American generals complained that they lacked the manpower to protect rural areas. American manpower was unavailable for this mission because of the focus on the big-unit war. Robert Komer claimed, "While many initiatives, experiments and even programs were undertaken at one time or another, none was on a scale or in a manner to have sufficient impact and all were overshadowed by the big-unit war."[8] According to MACV strategy, the relentless pursuit of enemy main-force units would provide a shield behind which the South Vietnamese government would pacify the villages. In 1969 a marine officer challenged this concept: "The rationale that ceaseless U.S. operations in the hills could keep the enemy from the people was an operational denial of the fact that in large measure the war was a revolution which started in the hamlets and that therefore the Viet Cong were already among the people when we went to the hills."[9]

Indeed, back in 1967 a district adviser serving in I Corps complained that the security situation was terrible. An army colonel replied he did not see it that way: his division was in the hills killing the enemy at a fantastic rate. The adviser replied, "Colonel, that's your war, not mine." That night a Viet Cong sapper team infiltrated district headquarters and killed the adviser. Months later, his replacement reported that the situation had not improved; the Viet Cong still dominated the villages, bitterly adding that the same American "division was still out in the hills bringing them security."[10]

In the postwar debate, veterans and military analysts alike spilled a great deal of ink about what had gone wrong. Some, like Marine Corps commandant General Leonard Chapman, were quite willing to dismiss bluntly the entire war as an aberration: "We got defeated and thrown out, the best thing we can do is forget it."[11] Most attention focused on the war's best-known features: the conduct of the air war, the efficacy of large-scale search-and-destroy operations, and the wisdom of a strategy of gradual escalation. When specialists examined the actual design and conduct of pacification programs, interservice rivalry—the historic tension between the army and the Marine Corps—tended to produce more heat then light.

Advocates of the so-called enclave strategy argue to this day that the marines' Combined Action Program provided a winning model. Critics maintain that as long as North Vietnam was able to send reinforcements, any pacification program could not succeed. Still others said that absent real political reform, the South Vietnamese government was never going to enlist enough popular support to defeat the Viet Cong military-political infrastructure.

One conclusion is unavoidable: in Vietnam the insurgents employed a deft blend of propaganda and terror to control enough of the population to maintain the fight. Regardless of a variety of American assistance programs and promises from the South Vietnamese government, most civilians never felt secure from Communist reprisal. Before U.S. combat troops arrived, villagers experienced a variety of poorly conceived and poorly executed pacification programs. After 1965, they saw American and South Vietnamese forces routinely occupy and then abandon their villages. They learned to believe Viet Cong propaganda teams who delivered the not so veiled threat that the government and American forces would soon leave but "we will be here forever."[12]

Vietnam was a failed counterinsurgency with terrible consequences for the vanquished. During the war, the U.S. military had numerous opportunities to conduct the war in a different way, to build and utilize classic components of successful counterinsurgency campaigns. Instead, it always chose to expend most of its resources on the big-unit war, the war of attrition that it thought it understood and could win. What might have happened had it instead focused on the "Other War" and committed to securing the population against Communist control and terror? Certainly the human and financial costs would have been much lower and presumably the erosion of American popular support for the war would have been much slower. But regardless of American strategy and tactics, there remains the question of whether the South Vietnamese government and the army could have overcome its internal rivalries, elitist attitudes toward their own people, and chronic corruption to achieve meaningful popular support.

Memories of the Vietnam War's horrors fade, replaced by images of more recent conflicts. Even with the advantage of more than forty years of hindsight, the lessons of Vietnam remain contentious. The counterinsurgency strategy finally adopted after the 1968 Tet Offensive arguably points the way toward a strategy superior to that employed earlier in the war. However, such a "winning strategy" would have required a sustained effort lasting an unknowable amount of time and entailed a steady loss of blood and treasure. Given that the foe was willing and able to sacrifice its own youth—recall the words of a North Vietnamese officer who acknowledged the terrible losses suffered during Tet: "We had hundreds of thousands killed in this war. We would have sacrificed one or two million more if necessary"—it is hard to conceive that the war could have been won at an acceptable price.[13]

Reflections on a War Without End

*In A.D. 6 Roman proconsul Quintilius Varus led a brutal but
successful campaign into Germany to suppress tribal rebellion. Three
years later he tried to repeat this campaign. This time tribal
warriors ambushed and destroyed the Roman legions. Before his
death, Varus was heard to lament in reference to his previous
victory, "Not like yesterday."*[1]

The Challenge

THE CONTEMPORARY FACE OF WAR is undergoing a startling transformation. On September 11, 2001, nineteen terrorists hijacked four commercial jets, deliberately crashed them into three iconic buildings, killed 3,000 people, and triggered invasion, occupation, and an ongoing counterinsurgency campaign in Afghanistan. Seven years later, on November 27, 2008, ten men inflicted a three-day reign of terror in Mumbai, bringing India's business capital to a standstill. This book's point of departure was a metaphor used by the former director of the Central Intelligence Agency, James Woolsey, that likened the conflict against insurgents to trying to survive in a jungle full of poisonous snakes. Today those snakes show the capacity to emerge from their hideouts to strike worldwide with lethal fury.

From Roman times to the present day, history records an explosive increase in the destructive power available to combatants. Technological advances shape this irregular, but always upward, path of lethality. Insurgents—people who rebel violently against established governmental rule—wield weapons possessing vastly more firepower than ever before. The first time American soldiers entered combat in Asia occurred in the Philippines. By 1901, the peak of the guerrilla war, Filipino guerrillas were lucky if they had a bolt-action rifle. Many carried only machetes. Sixty-four years passed before American soldiers again entered a guerrilla war in Asia. In Vietnam, the Viet Cong's weapon of choice became the AK-47, a Russian-designed, rugged automatic rifle that turned a single man into the firepower equivalent of a World War II light machine gunner.

Now the AK-47 is everywhere. Mozambique honors its iconic status as an implement of national liberation by displaying it on its national flag. For the purchase price, as little as $100 from a Bulgarian factory, a drug lord's bodyguard in Colombia, a Taliban fighter in Afghanistan, or a twelve-year-old child soldier in Africa becomes a formidable foe. And it is only one part of the arsenal available to today's insurgents. A foreign correspondent described an arms bazaar in Mogadishu, Somalia, in 1991: "Behind the stalls were stacked artillery rounds and mortars of all sizes like a selection of candy. There were oily boxes of screw-in detonators, banks of rocket-propelled grenades and launchers—some still packed in their factory grease—and long, slender missiles for big spenders. There was enough firepower to repel an invasion."[2] Two years later, militiamen followed the training they had received from Al Qaeda advisers and shot down a U.S. Army Black Hawk helicopter with a rocket-propelled grenade, killing three Americans. They later ambushed Task Force Ranger, killing another nineteen Americans and wounding eighty-four more. The image of a fallen American soldier being dragged through the streets of Mogadishu by jubilant militiamen altered the American appetite for intervention, thereby inflicting a major political defeat leading to the United States' and United Nations' exit from Somalia.

In Iraq, small-arms fire ranked third as the killer of American soldiers and marines. Roadside bombs were number one, and here too we see technology's contribution to dramatically enhanced lethality. An Iraqi civilian setting an Iranian-manufactured improvised explosive device with an explosively formed penetrator deployed a weapon that surpassed the destructive capacity of a mine laid by a combat engineer in any previous war. As stupendous as they are, advances in weapons technology do not provide today's insurgents with their most important tool. The Mumbai terrorists wielded AK-47s, but they coordinated their operations using cell phones and BlackBerry devices, and the horrified world followed the ensuing mayhem via the Internet and satellite television.

Modern telecommunications transmits the images and sounds of conflict from anywhere on the globe regardless of how remote. In times past, commanders understood the value of controlling perceptions of combat. Napoleon's field headquarters included a mobile printing press to allow him first crack at shaping how his own army, the enemy, civilian populations, diplomats, and rulers perceived a battle's outcome. T. E. Lawrence, known to history as Lawrence of Arabia, observed that the printing press was a modern commander's greatest weapon. In their time, printed descriptions were a powerful tool. But as the bolt-action rifle gave way to the AK-47, so print gave way to photographs and then moving imagery. With the advent of satellite communications, insurgents can rely upon a single violent event becoming known if not seen by every concerned actor within a short time span. In military terms, modern communications are a force multiplier, enabling a handful of insurgents to spread terror like never before.

David Kilcullen, an insurgency expert whose advice has influenced General David Petraeus, one of the American architects of the Iraq counterinsurgency strategy, has said, "The globalized information environment makes counterinsurgency even more difficult now."[3] Kilcullen illustrates this with the example of two insurgencies confronted by the Indonesian government. In West Java during the 1950s and 1960s, the Indonesian government defeated a separatist Muslim insurgency that was bigger than the Communist insurgency in Malaya. In 1975, a Christian separatist insurgency began on East Timor. The Indonesian government again intervened and used the same approach: forced population concentration, conscription of the local population into a militia, heavy coercion applied to civilians to persuade them to back the government. The conflict continued through the late 1990s. By that time a Timorese international propaganda campaign had generated enough media coverage to prompt condemnation of Indonesian methods and bring in the United Nations' involvement. East Timor became independent in 2002.

Counterinsurgency methods that had worked in obscurity in West Java were unacceptable when exposed to international scrutiny. Looking back, it is easy to see that practices commonly employed in the two successful counterinsurgencies described in this book, ranging from the concentration zones in the Philippines to Operation Starvation, the British food denial program in Malaya, would have brought worldwide scrutiny in today's globalized media.

In contemporary conflicts, including Iraq and Afghanistan, American forces have followed the common pattern of history by heavily focusing on killing terrorists and insurgents. The Americans have brought an impressive technological prowess to this aspect of the fight. However, Al Qaeda's resilience is predicated not on its current numerical strength but rather on its capacity to continue to recruit and inspire future fighters, supporters, and sympathizers; in other words, its resilience hinges on its success in the information fight. Again it must be emphasized that modern insurgents understand the importance of the media and manipulate it with great skill. Meanwhile, the United States continues to struggle in its efforts to explain to the world why a global war on terror is necessary. Moreover, U.S. attempts to justify the way it conducts this war have too often been inept. If, as has been asserted, the war on terror is at heart an information war, it is hard to see that the United States is winning.

One hallmark of successful counterinsurgencies is a willingness to learn and adapt on both the individual and institutional levels. Here the future looks brighter. After the successful invasion of Iraq and subsequent capture of Saddam Hussein, President George W. Bush's administration was very slow to recognize accurately what the United States confronted. By the beginning of 2007, it appeared that Iraq was lost to the insurgents. Insurgent suicide bombers had triggered a deadly cycle of escalating sectarian violence for which the American occupation forces seemed to have no answer. Many of the problems in Iraq were familiar to students of counterinsurgency: unsecured borders that allowed the insurgents a free flow of men and supplies; a suspicious civilian population who resented the presence of foreign forces; a lack of security that prevented any except the bravest from providing the Americans with useful intelligence; an American public growing ever more discouraged.

Finally, staring defeat in the face, Bush made the politically unpopular decision to send more combat soldiers to Iraq, the so-called Surge, to confront the insurgents. The employment of those troops was informed by an essential institutional adaptation. In December 2006 the Department of Defense published Field Manual 3-24, *Counterinsurgency*. It was a collaborative effort between the U.S. Army and the Marine Corps involving

many of the nation's brightest military minds. The result was a short distillation of the lessons of history that yielded a set of "principles and im-
peratives" to fight and win a counterinsurgency and a guide for the way
forward. It began with a statement that with hindsight may seem obvious
but at the time injected into the strategic discussion a much-needed call
for change: "You cannot fight former Saddamists and Islamic extremists
the same way you would have fought the Viet Cong."[4]

It takes exceptional officers to overcome the institutional bias of military
cultures. In 1840, at a time when France was embroiled in its fifteen-year-
long war against Algerian insurgents, a new commander arrived on the
scene. Marshal Thomas Bugeaud, the man who would eventually win the
war, said upon first meeting his officers, "Gentlemen, you have much to
forget." Lieutenant General David Petraeus had been closely involved in
the production of Field Manual 3-24. Assigned at the beginning of 2007 as
the commanding general in Iraq, Petraeus and his chief subordinates
proved willing to change and adapt. They committed their forces to a counterinsurgency campaign featuring new practices, including sending American troops to live among the Iraqi people for whom they were trying to
provide security. Given the difficult circumstances—a stressful and dangerous physical environment, a mysterious cultural environment rife with
sectarian and tribal conflict—the American soldiers performed their duties
with surpassing courage and skill.

However, any amount of intelligent doctrine or good leadership probably would not have ultimately mattered had not a fundamental change occurred among the Iraqis. Quite simply, the Al Qaeda leadership in Iraq
overplayed their hand. The indiscriminate terror of foreign fighters—
young Muslim zealots recruited from the entire span of the Muslim world,
from Saudi Arabia to Chechnya to North Africa—and their stern demand
that Iraqis live under a hard, fundamentalist version of Islam turned an
important element of Iraqi society against the insurgents. This was the so-
called Sunni Awakening, a movement that began among the Sunnis of An-
bar Province, a population that heretofore had been the sympathetic base of
the insurgency, and steadily spread elsewhere. In congressional testimony
on September 10, 2007, Petraeus observed that tribal leaders were beginning to reject Al Qaeda. He called this trend one of the most significant developments in Iraq in the past eight months.

By any measure—reduction in the number of terror acts, substantial decline in civilian and military casualties—the Surge accomplished its goals. In recognition of nineteen months of progress in Iraq, Secretary of Defense Robert Gates promoted Petraeus. Of course, the "Endless War" was not over. Gates emphasized the importance of Petraeus's posting to head the Central Command and explained that Islamic extremism within the Central Command, an area that encompassed the Middle East, South Asia, and Africa, still posed a special challenge "characterized by asymmetric warfare," a conflict among professional national militaries and insurgents and other guerrilla fighters.[5]

As a new administration prepared to enter office in 2009, President-elect Barack Obama promised to reduce the American presence in Iraq and intensify the fight against the insurgents in Afghanistan. What this portends is unknowable. The American presence on the street corners of restive Baghdad slums dramatically tamped down sectarian violence, but would not American soldiers operating in the slums of Chicago or Detroit also reduce criminal gang violence? And when they left would security endure? As a result of the Surge, daily life in many Iraqi urban neighborhoods features comprehensive disruption with security provided by concrete barriers that divide Shiite from Sunni. Entry to one's own neighborhood is through a fortified gate guarded by armed men, formerly Americans, as of early 2009 Iraqis backed by American soldiers, but in the near future Iraqis alone.

Meanwhile the insurgents in Afghanistan have risen from defeat to control large areas of the countryside. The American-backed president, Hamid Karzai, is derisively known as the "mayor of Kabul" because his rule does not extend beyond gun range of his foreign benefactors who provide security in his capital. A glance at the map of Afghanistan shows that the "secure" areas match the areas held by Soviet forces during their failed attempt to dominate a country whose most cherished history is a tale of opposition to foreign occupation. And then there are the familiar problems of counterinsurgency: unsecured borders; insurgent sanctuaries off-limits to the counterinsurgent force; a bewildering array of family and tribal relationships that trump an outsider's understanding of the Afghan power structure; intelligence so uncertain that in spite of years of effort Osama bin Laden's hideout somewhere along the Afghan border cannot be found. History informs us that foreign powers try to control Afghanistan at their peril. Yet apparently this is to be the task of the American military.

In sum, the luster of a new century of change has become tarnished by terrorism and war. How well the fight will go against those who resist America's notion of world order remains an open question.

A Vicious Circle

Security

Insurgents blend into a population that includes active supporters— especially when the population views the counterinsurgents as foreign oc- cupiers propping up an ineffectual or corrupt government—and neutrals who are held in thrall by insurgent terror. The historical record of coun- terinsurgency plays out as a vicious circle in which insurgents create an environment where the people are insecure. Under the threat of terror, the people offer no intelligence to the government forces. Absent intelligence, military operations are unsuccessful, perpetuating poor security. To break this circle, a nation embarking on a counterinsurgency fought in a foreign land has to advance along multiple, interconnected paths. Progress along each path requires special qualities, including language skills and cultural awareness that are outside traditional military talents. A first destination is the provision of physical security for the people.

On the eve of his campaign against the Filipino insurgents in Batan- gas Province, General J. Franklin Bell described the paramount impor- tance of security:

> The people became so terrorized they did not dare to help us. Anyone suspected of sympathy or friendship for Americans was promptly assas- sinated. We could get no information and could accomplish nothing. There was no organized insurrection, but those who possessed the guns were living in the towns by day and raiding the countryside by night. The necessity for garrisoning every town, in order to give protection to those peaceably inclined, soon became apparent. The troops were obtained and the towns garrisoned. When the people saw we were able to protect them they began to help us, and through persistent efforts in detecting, arresting and confining the scheming, murdering, unscrupulous lead- ers and ladrones among the people, and through running down and cap- turing the arms, the province became very tranquil and peace reigned supreme. This was not accomplished, however, without having to do many disagreeable things.[6]

Sixty-seven years later, a high-ranking American civilian official serving in Vietnam, John Paul Vann, came to some similar conclusions. Vann noted that six years of failure proved very little about specific programs because no program would work until the first basic requirement of security was achieved. "This does not mean that the job of pacification is hopeless. It merely means we have to recognize the overriding requirement for security. Whether security is 10 percent of the total problem to be resolved or 90 percent, it is, inescapably, the first 10 percent or the first 90 percent."[7]

The American experience in Iraq confirms this truth.

Intelligence and the Question of Torture

To provide physical security, the counterinsurgents need good intelligence. The battle for timely intelligence is a battle that must be won if a counterinsurgency is to succeed. Given that insurgents are hiding among the civilian population, civilians are an invaluable intelligence source. Throughout history insurgents deliberately blur the line separating combatant from civilian. They stage incidents to provoke retaliation that harms civilians. The security forces endure casualties under the apathetic gaze of local civilians and grow bitter. They know that some civilians had foreknowledge of the peril and they are tempted to extract that knowledge by whatever means necessary.

When William Howard Taft testified before a Senate committee on the topic of torture in the Philippines, a senator asked him, "When a war is conducted by a superior race against those whom they consider inferior in the scale of civilization, is it not the experience of the world that the superior race will almost involuntarily practice inhuman conduct?"

Taft replied, "There is much greater danger in such a case than in dealing with whites. There is no doubt about that."[8]

Well-documented instances of abuse, including the routine use of torture, have been attributed to the security forces in two of the four case studies offered in this book, namely, the Americans in the Philippines and the French in Algeria. The French master torturer, General Paul Aussaresses, defended torture in these words: "Once a country demands that its army fight an enemy who is using terror to compel an indifferent population to join its ranks and provoke a repression that will in turn outrage international public opinion, it becomes impossible for that army to avoid using extreme measures."[9] The ongoing war against terror has again brought the disturbing subject of torture to the forefront of public debate.

Advocates of harsh interrogation methods, including what most people would call torture, justify the policy by using the "ticking bomb" analogy: a time bomb is hidden somewhere ticking toward a detonation that will kill countless innocents. To prevent a catastrophe, torture is not only justified but morally imperative.

Aussaresses defends his conduct on precisely this basis: by torturing suspects he could foil a planned bombing and thereby prevent casualties to the innocent. During the Battle of Algiers, the paratroop leader Colonel Roger Trinquier asked the divisional chaplain to sanction torture. The chaplain obliged and told the soldiers, "Between two evils: making a bandit, caught in the act—and who actually deserves to die—suffer temporarily, and [letting the innocent die] . . . it is necessary to chose [sic] without hesitation the lesser [evil]: an interrogation without sadism yet efficacious."[10]

Today's debate posits an even graver situation: authorities capture a person suspected of planting a nuclear or biological time bomb. Should such an extraordinary hypothetical serve as the basis for national policy? It should not. Surely a line can be drawn separating the catastrophic (a potential nuclear detonation in New York City) from the vile (a truck bomb at a mosque in the Middle East).

Torture sometimes provides useful tactical intelligence that can foil a suicide bomber or reveal the location of a roadside bomb. However, as victims of torture observe, a person under extreme physical duress will say whatever is required to escape the agony. The intelligence service thereby obtains an overwhelming volume of information, most of it false. It is not an efficient method to obtain intelligence. But the practice of torture is not done in a moral vacuum; it is not amoral. Civilized society condemns it. A country that endorses it suffers not only because it debases its moral standing but also because it is ultimately counterproductive. As the ugly American experience with Iraq's Abu Ghraib prison demonstrated, abuse and torture drive innocent victims into the enemy camp. Moreover, it provides insurgents with a powerful tool to convince the wavering to support them. "Successful" torture may uncover one plot, but it creates scores of new plotters who eventually extract a price higher than would have been paid.

In his book *Defeating Communist Insurgency*, Robert Thompson eloquently argued that torture not only was "morally wrong" but created more practical problems than it solved: "A government which does not act in accordance with the law forfeits the right to be called a government and cannot then expect its people to obey the law."[11] By abandoning the high moral ground associated with a lawfully constructed government, a counterinsurgency power descends toward the level of the terrorist. In a civil war, such a descent means neither side can claim legitimacy, thereby leaving the people without a strong reason to favor the government over the insurgents. Furthermore, when a government fails to act in accordance with its own laws it cannot expect its people to obey the law.

That is not to say that a government cannot enact very tough laws to meet an emergency. But this has to be done by regular legal processes. In the United States, the June 12, 2008, Supreme Court decision regarding the legal rights of detainees at Guantanamo is a highly encouraging affirmation of this position.

Insurgencies rely on guerrilla action and terrorism. That creates an enormous temptation for government forces to respond by unlawful acts, to use the excuse that the other side is not playing by the same rules, to assert that legal processes are too cumbersome and ill-suited to contend with such affronts as terror. A French intellectual addressed this during the height of the Algerian War: "If really we are capable of a moral reflex which our adversary has not, this is the best justification for our cause, and even for our victory."[12]

Understanding Culture

The famous phrase coined by British general Gerald Templer and adopted by Americans for the Vietnam War, "winning the hearts and minds of the people," can serve as a useful component of a counterinsurgency strategy because it focuses on the role of the civilian population. By itself, it is an inadequate and flawed formulation. Neither in Vietnam nor anywhere else is there one "people." Instead, all societies are made up of individuals and groups who form relationships based on status, economics, and power.

Foreigners often accuse Americans of cultural arrogance, an accusation that astonishes most Americans, who are quite certain that they possess no such thing. They would probably concur with William Howard Taft, who said that his experience with Filipinos convinced him that they are "moved by similar considerations to those which move other men." Taft did add the niggling caveat that "it is possible that crimes, ambush, assassination, are more frequent there than in other countries," but the thrust of his comments was clear and remains widely shared: namely, that there are universal cultural norms.[13]

However valid this view—and it is important to note that other cultures firmly believe in universal norms, only they are not the same ones endorsed by Western society—it leads to the position that what others want must be similar to what we want. This outlook frames the mind-set of those who go overseas to combat the nation's enemies. It ill-prepares them for what they actually confront. A war correspondent, Albert Robinson, who traveled extensively in the contested provinces in the Philippines during the Filipino insurrection concluded that the people plainly hated the Americans. He attributed the hatred to irreconcilable cultural differences and concluded, "We may mean well, but they don't understand our ways. Neither do we understand theirs. When patience and forbearance would be immensely effective, the American methods hurry and irritate the people."[14]

As the insurgency continued, Robinson revised his view, warning that the greatest obstacle to success in the Philippines was misguided American interference: "We assert a glorious American liberty and insist that all shall live by American standards."[15] Trouble arose, in Robinson's mind, from American inflexibility that "makes no allowance for people whom it does not know and for conditions it does not understand."[16]

In contrast to Americans in the Philippines and Vietnam, the French *képis bleus* of the Special Administrative Section (SAS) possessed considerable knowledge of North African culture. By war's end, SAS officers as well as many in the regular army had come to realize that knowledge about an Algerian village's history and how that history had formed village attitudes was not a matter of mere academic interest. Rather it was a necessary prerequisite for an effective pacification program. It is noteworthy that the capture of Saddam Hussein resulted from painstaking social analysis of tribal connections performed by an American special intelligence group.

However, it is discouraging to observe that only in late 2007, six years into the Afghan war, did the U.S. military come to the conclusion that its troops did not sufficiently understand how to battle the Taliban insurgency. The U.S. Army captain charged with creating a new "Afghanistan

Counterinsurgency Academy" told his American students that the important battles are 80 percent political and 20 percent military. To engage in the political contest, the students had to learn about local culture and history in order to think like the Taliban.[17] If the United States is to engage effectively in the "Long War," it should not take six years to arrive at the starting point.

Language

Back in 1940 the Marine Corps' *Small Wars Manual* had emphasized the importance of cultural knowledge and most especially language skills, noting that "political methods and motives which govern the actions of foreign people and their political parties . . . are practically beyond the understanding of persons who do not speak their language."[18] Sadly, this key insight has had little influence on policy.

In the 1950s, when American advisers began training the South Vietnamese army, fewer than a dozen men in the Military Assistance Advisory Group spoke Vietnamese. The U.S. Army did not have a Vietnamese-language school. Little had changed by 1965 when the marines landed. Even those serving in Combined Action Platoons seldom acquired anything beyond a few words picked up while working in the villages. More than forty years later the challenge of overcoming a lack of language skills and ignorance of a foreign culture returned to hamper a new generation of counterinsurgency warriors. A March 2007 article in the *Marine Corps Gazette* paraphrased comments from the codirector of the navy's Center on Terrorism and Irregular Warfare: "The general lack of cultural preparation for the Iraq campaign, including an insufficient number of people with language skills to understand even the basic information, is one of the causes of failure to effectively combat this insurgency."[19]

Given the circumstances preceding the 2003 U.S. invasion of Iraq—the United States had fought this same foe in 1990 and been on armed watch against Saddam Hussein ever since; the 2000 U.S. Census reported almost 1.2 million citizens of Arab descent—this negligence is astonishing.

Reform and the Political Arena

The realization that victory over an insurgency must begin by providing people with physical security has gained wide acceptance. As with every other aspect of counterinsurgency, the "security first and foremost" imperative is not as simple as it seems. Perceptions of security differ. Year after year around 42,000 Americans die in vehicle accidents. The country's nearly 200 million drivers shrug off the fact that for almost all of them it is by far the most dangerous activity they routinely perform. In contrast, serial sniper attacks that killed ten people over a three-week period in October 2002 in the Washington, D.C., area so terrorized the region's inhabitants that hundreds of thousands made substantial alterations in their life routines. Iraqis experienced a drumbeat of terror orders of magnitude worse. They proved sensitive to and appreciative of improvements in security. But they expect and will undoubtedly demand more. Weeks after a battle with insurgents had destroyed a market in Baghdad's Sadr City, an Iraqi merchant returned to deliver a truckload of potatoes. Free-flowing raw sewage ran through the market. Clouds of flies swarmed around heaps of uncollected garbage. At home, frequent electricity outages left him sweltering in 110-degree heat. While acknowledging the improvements in security, he observed, "This is no way to live."[20]

The comments of French and British counterinsurgency specialists affirm the idea that there must be progress along multiple paths that go beyond the mere provision of security. General Jacques Allard summarized lessons learned from the counterinsurgency in Algeria: "Destruction will achieve nothing if we don't go beyond it. If the population were left to itself, the rebel organization would soon emerge again. After having destroyed, we must construct."[21]

Robert Thompson observed, "Security by itself is not enough to make the peasant willing to choose to support the government."[22] Successful pacification may begin with security but thereafter the government must deliver services to the people in order to prove itself worthy. The twin challenges of security and reform are the major challenges a counterinsurgency power confronts. No matter how skillfully or massively applied, military might alone will not solve a conflict's underlying political causes.

Yet these are the easier tasks compared to tackling the root causes of the insurgency. That effort requires redistributing political and economic power. Fundamental, endemic problems exist that will require much time to fix and there is no certainty that the imposed solutions will either work while the counterinsurgency power is present or endure after it leaves. These facts should give pause to political and military leaders who advocate intervening to thwart an insurgency.

Commitment

Like some contemporary American planners in Iraq, the Philippine Commission under William Howard Taft believed that the institution of good government would win the support of most Filipinos. Taft understood it would take time—he guessed fifty or a hundred years—for the Filipinos to develop Anglo-Saxon political principles. The process had to start by educating the children. In the meantime, since the United States could rely only on a very small nucleus of educated Filipinos, the Americans needed to supervise closely all levels of government. He observed that, "lacking the American initiative, lacking the American knowledge of how to carry on a government, any government there must be a complete failure."[23]

The postwar Senate inquiry into the conduct of the Philippine War also considered prospects for the future. Many senators were bothered by an apparent open-ended commitment of American soldiers and gold to the Philippines. During his testimony, General MacArthur addressed this concern. He said that although the Filipinos had made great strides, they still held "rudimentary republican ideas and aspirations." With American tutelage they could continue on the path to progress. He then warned, "American withdrawal from the islands, therefore, would, in my opinion, result in permanent failure of republicanism in the East, and the devastation of the archipelago by internecine and fratricidal war, which would continue indefinitely until suppressed by some external force."[24]

Whether in 1898 or 2009 Americans are not a patient people when it comes to foreign entanglements. After helping guide the United States to victory in World War II, George C. Marshall made reference to the protracted struggle that pitted Britain and its American colonists against the French and observed that the American public would not tolerate another Seven Years' War. Westmoreland's chief intelligence officer in Vietnam agreed. He believed that foremost among America's weaknesses in waging war in Vietnam was a weakness inherent to democracies: the "incapacity to sustain a long, unfocused, inconclusive, and bloody war far from home, for unidentified or ill-defined national objectives."[25]

In conventional war there are many obvious metrics to measure progress, such as enemy territory captured or enemy soldiers killed. Not so in a counterinsurgency, and this particularly wears on patience. Even professional military men often completely fail to perceive actual trends. American generals in the Philippines twice claimed the war all but over only to have a fresh outbreak of violence rock the public's confidence. After a 1960 inspection tour in Algeria, a French general warned, "I want to caution generals and commanders of sectors against exaggerated optimism, which leads them to pretend that pacification has been achieved." Claims that "peace has returned" were invariably only "superficially true."[26]

The general pointed to continued enemy activity in an area where two very capable officers had skillfully conducted two operational approaches that were polar opposites. The tough Indochina veteran Colonel Marcel Bigeard had "pacified" his zone by emphasizing unfettered military and police action. In contrast, in a nearby zone another colonel had relied upon political and psychological methods that emphasized building friendly relations with the local people and increasing the authority of native leaders. Both approaches significantly tamped down violence. Both allowed the claim that pacification was achieved. Yet both seemed to run up against a ceiling beyond which they could not ascend. Hidden somewhere beyond reach was an insurgent hard core capable of acts of terror in order to deny, if not reverse, apparent progress.

At the end of the day, military counterinsurgency is a holding operation, designed not to gain a specific, war-winning objective (since by definition there is no such objective) but rather to gain time to institute the reforms necessary to undermine the insurgents. Algerian-born correspondent Michael Clark had considerable firsthand experience witnessing the French struggle in Algeria. Clark cogently observed, "It has been said that even if the F.L.N. suffers grievous reverses, terrorist agitation can never be stamped out. I do not agree. In any conflict of this sort, uncertainty as to the final outcome gives the terrorist the margin of complicity he needs for protection. But if it becomes manifest that defeat, not victory, awaits the masters whom the terrorists serves, that protective margin will vanish; the terrorist, isolated, can then be destroyed."[27]

A MODERN ANALYST, Colonel John Nagl, describes victory in this manner: "The way you win a counterinsurgency campaign is that you don't— you help the host nation defeat the insurgency."[28] If that is so, then American leaders have to assess accurately the host nation's capacities before intervening.

This was not done in Vietnam. Instead of asking if anything could be done, American political leaders made the fundamental mistake of asking what should be done. In the future the decision to offer assistance against an insurgency should follow a careful examination of whether the United States has the leverage to move the host nation in the direction the United States thinks it should move. It may well be that America's nominal ally, the host nation that actually has to win the fight, finds necessary reforms unacceptable because its leaders know they will lose power if they accept reform.

Opposition to foreigners is a powerful recruiting tool for almost all insurgencies. This fact must also be addressed by today's strategists who argue that victory in the "Long War" currently requires or will require the presence of American forces in Afghanistan and Iraq, through the arc of instability, and even in Central and South America. The ability of Americans to defeat an insurgency and the costs associated with this effort have to be weighed against the fact that the American presence provides some of the fuel that feeds the insurgency.

The lessons of history and the case studies in this book do not necessarily refute the belief that an insurgency cannot be defeated by an outside, foreign force. A strategic doctrine can be built that provides a path to victory. Some, perhaps much, of what is propounded in the U.S. military's current counterinsurgency doctrine presents useful signposts for that path.

What is absolutely certain is that any victory achieved by American warriors and their allies will require a long-term commitment of blood and treasure. Given this fact, certain conclusions follow. An American president in his role as commander in chief must decide if an insurgency truly poses a mortal threat to the nation. This should be the litmus test for American involvement against foreign insurgencies. Then the commander in chief has to convince the American people that his assessment is correct. Having done this, he—and almost certainly his successors—must continue over the ensuing painful years to make the case why the war is necessary. Otherwise public support for keeping American troops in harm's way will dissolve. Otherwise a president is trifling with the blood of America's warriors as well as the lives of foreign civilians who inevitably will become part of the collateral damage of war.

On this subject the historical record is perfectly clear: a successful counterinsurgency requires a long-term commitment. How long is unknowable. It is the dreaded open-ended commitment that politicians fear to make, but it is the only way.

Words written in the year 44 B.C. by the great Roman statesman and philosopher Marcus Tullius Cicero provide an enduring guide for the way forward: "An army abroad is of little use unless there is wise counsel at home."[29]

Acknowledgments

Jungle of Snakes emerged from a protracted series of discussions among myself, Peter Ginna of Bloomsbury Press, and my agent, Jeff Gerecke. Peter wanted to know about relevant military history that would inform a reader about America's ongoing counterinsurgency operations in Afghanistan and Iraq. My research produced a very broad list of possible topics. Then Jeff acted as invaluable referee, employing his keen knowledge of history to help weigh and assess. The three-person process of refining and distillation yielded this book. My first set of thanks goes out to Peter and Jeff for their efforts and ultimate confidence.

After a book's concept is defined, the writer embarks on a period of research; this is always a mixture of thrilling discovery and face-reddening frustration. In spite of technological advances that allow access to information in ways that seemed unimaginable just two or three books ago, at the end of the day any author's research still depends upon the contributions of dedicated librarians and archivists. I am profoundly appreciative of the help received at the University of Virginia, Charlottesville, Virginia; and at the Virginia Military Institute, Washington and Lee University, and Rockbridge Regional Library, all in my hometown of Lexington, Virginia.

The U.S. Army Military History Institute, Carlisle, Pennsylvania, now located in a fine new building, remains a fabulous resource. Their collection of letters and diaries provided insight into the minds of a generation of American warriors who confronted challenges more than 100 years ago that would be utterly familiar to today's soldiers and marines.

I had the privilege to discover the exceedingly helpful resources provided by the Marine Corps University in Quantico, Virginia. The marine archivists and historians, particularly Danny Crawford and Fred Allison, could not have been more helpful as they shared their printed and oral history files. The marine library provided open-handed access to many arcane tomes devoted to counterinsurgency. It was particularly poignant that while I was at Quantico, young marines just back from Iraq were also present. Heading home to the mountains that evening, I drove through the Chancellorsville and Wilderness battlefields and experienced another somber reminder of the consequences of committing the nation's military to war.

After research coalesces into some semblance of a coherent manuscript, editors sharpen their pens and set to work. I was fortunate to benefit from outstanding editors. As she has done for more than thirty years, my soul mate and wife, Roberta, again provided professional editing. Her encouragement, combined with a sometimes stern reminder, "Try using English, please," will probably be remembered to my grave. The book also benefitted enormously from Peter Ginna's insightful editorial critiques. Mike O'Connor and Sue Warga skillfully oversaw the always difficult task of copyediting. Meanwhile, from production headquarters, Pete Beatty cheerfully kept the project moving ahead.

Again, thank you all.

James R. Arnold
Lexington, Virginia, 2009

Notes

Introduction

1. "Testimony of R. James Woolsey, U.S. House of Representatives Committee on National Security, February 12, 1998," Strategic Intelligence Homepage, http://www.loyola.edu/dept/politics/intel/19980212woolsey.html (May 2008).
2. Editorial on the Philippine Insurrection, *New York Times*, January 2, 1901.
3. "Guardians at the Gate," *Time*, January 7, 1966, 10, http://www.time.com/time/magazine/article/0,9171,834900-10,00.html (May 2008).
4. George Packer, "Knowing the Enemy: Can Social Scientists Redefine the 'War on Terror'?" *New Yorker*, December 18, 2006, 61.

Chapter 1: An American Victory Yields a Guerilla War

1. McKinley to Otis, December 21, 1898, in U.S. Army Adjutant-General's Office, *Correspondence Relating to the War with Spain* (Washington, D.C.: U.S. Army Center of Military History, 1993), 2:859.
2. John R. M. Taylor, *The Philippine Insurrection Against the United States* (Pasay City, Philippines: Eugenio Lopez Foundation, 1971–73), 2:277.
3. Emilio Aguinaldo, "Proclamation to the Philippine People," February 5, 1899, in Daniel B. Schirmer and Stephen Rosskamm Shalom, eds., *The Philippines Reader: A History of Colonialism, Neocolonialism, Dictatorship, and Resistance* (Boston: South End Press, 1987), 20–21.
4. Albert G. Robinson, *The Philippines: The War and the People; A Record of Personal Observations and Experiences* (New York: McClure, Phillips & Co., 1901), 354.
5. Brian McAllister Linn, *The Philippine War: 1899–1902* (Lawrence: University Press of Kansas, 2000), 27.
6. J. F. Bell to AG, 2nd Div, 8th Army Corps, January 21, 1900, in U. S. War Department, *Annual Reports of the War Department: Report of the*

Lieutenant-General Commanding the Army, vol. 1, part 8 (Washington, D.C.: Government Printing Office, 1900), 331.

7. Leon Wolff, *Little Brown Brother: How the United States Purchased and Pacified the Philippines* (Oxford, UK: Oxford University Press, 1991), 289.

8. Forrest C. Pogue, *George C. Marshall: Education of a General, 1880–1939* (New York: Viking Press, 1963), 52–53.

9. William McKinley, Third Annual Message to Congress, December 5, 1899, The American Presidency Project, http://www.presidency.ucsb.edu/ws/index.php?pid=29540.

10. Robinson, *The Philippines*, 376.

11. "Orders to the Detachments," November 16, 1899, in Taylor, *Philippine Insurrection*, 5:142–43.

12. Taylor, *Philippine Insurrection*, 2:345.

13. "To the Chiefs of Guerrillas," November 15, 1900, in Taylor, *Philippine Insurrection*, 5:113.

14. Brian McAllister Linn, *The U.S. Army and Counterinsurgency in the Philippine War, 1899–1902* (Chapel Hill: University of North Carolina Press, 1989), 125.

15. Ibid., 37.

Chapter 2: Chastising the *Insurrectos*

1. Edwin Segerstrom to mother and sister, March 20, 1899, in Frank Harper, ed., *Just Outside of Manila: Letters from Members of the First Colorado Regiment in the Spanish-American and Philippine-American Wars* (Denver: Colorado Historical Society, 1992), 72.

2. John R. M. Taylor, *The Philippine Insurrection Against the United States* (Pasay City, Philippines: Eugenio Lopez Foundation, 1971–73), 2:304–5.

3. *Affairs in the Philippine Islands, Hearings Before the Committee on the Philippines of the United States Senate*, 57th Congress, 1st Session, Senate Doc. 331 (Washington, D.C.: Government Printing Office, 1902), part 2, 1928.

4. William Thaddeus Sexton, *Soldiers in the Philippines* (Washington, D.C.: The Infantry Journal, 1944), 212.

5. MacArthur to Adjutant-General, September 19, 1900, in U.S. Army Adjutant-General's Office, *Correspondence Relating to the War with Spain*, (Washington, D.C.: U.S. Army Center of Military History, 1993), 2:1211. My count is based on the names of killed and wounded provided in MacArthur's telegram. Note that Brian Linn states that casualties were twenty-one killed and twenty-three wounded in his *The U.S. Army and Counterinsurgency*, 138.

6. U.S. War Department, *Annual Reports of the War Department: Report of the Lieutenant-General Commanding the Army* (Washington, D.C.: Government Printing Office, 1900), part 5, 60.

7. John Jordan to mother, January 10, 1900, John Jordan Papers, U.S. Army Military History Institute, Carlisle, Pennsylvania.

8. Albert G. Robinson, *The Philippines: The War and the People; A Record of Personal Observations and Experiences* (New York: McClure, Phillips & Co., 1901), 379.

9. Ibid., 384–85.

10. "To the Military Central and Zone Commanders of National Militia of the Township of Ligao," August 24, 1900, in Taylor, *Philippine Insurrection*, 5:228.

11. Glenn Anthony May, *Battle for Batangas: A Philippine Province at War* (New Haven, CT: Yale University Press, 1991), 161.

12. General Order 202, June 27, 1900, in Taylor, *Philippine Insurrection*, 5:104.

13. Caílles to Estilla, August 6, 1900, in Taylor, Philippine Insurrection, 5:227.

14. See telegram from Associated Press reporter Martin in U.S. Army Adjutant-Generals Office, *Correspondence Relating to the War with Spain*, 2:1220.

15. Henry F. Pringle, *The Life and Times of William Howard Taft* (New York: Farrar & Rinehart, 1939), 1:160–61.

16. Ibid., 1:170.

17. For Taft's comments on this, see his testimony in *Affairs in the Philippine Islands, Hearings Before the Committee on the Philippines of the United States Senate*, 57th Congress, 1st Session, Senate Doc. 331 (Washington, D.C.: Government Printing Office, 1902), part 1, 64.

18. Robinson, *The Philippines*, 355.

19. Stuart Creighton Miller, *"Benevolent Assimilation": The American Conquest of the Philippines, 1899–1903* (New Haven, CT: Yale University Press, 1982), 167, 296–97.

20. Robinson, *The Philippines*, 384.

Chapter 3: The War Is Won Again

1. John Morgan Gates, *"Schoolbooks and Krags": The United States Army in the Philippines, 1898–1902* (Westport, CT: Greenwood Press, 1973), 169.

2. "Report of Maj. Gen. Lloyd Wheaton," in U.S. War Department, *Annual Reports of the War Department: Report of the Lieutenant-General Commanding the Army and Department Commanders*, 57th Congress, 2nd Session, House Document No. 2 (Washington, D.C.: Government Printing Office, 1902), 9:231.

3. *Affairs in the Philippine Islands, Hearings Before the Committee on the Philippines of the United States Senate*, 57th Congress, 1st Session, Senate Doc. 331 (Washington, D.C.: Government Printing Office, 1902), part 2, 1942. MacArthur tried to wiggle away from this conclusion when questioned by Senator Culberson.

4. "Investigation into the Methods Adopted by the Insurgents for Organizing and Maintaining a Guerrilla Force," in U.S. War Department, *Annual Reports of the War Department: Report of the Lieutenant-General Commanding the Army*, vol. 1 (Washington, D.C.: Government Printing Office, 1900), part 5, 257–64.

5. Ibid., 262.

6. Ibid., 263.

7. Gates, *"Schoolbooks and Krags,"* 173.

8. Batson to wife, November 9, 1900, box 3, Matthew Batson Papers, U.S. Army Military History Institute, Carlisle, Pennsylvania.

9. Batson to wife, October 29, 1899, box 3, Matthew Batson Papers.

10. U.S. War Department, *Annual Reports of the War Department*, vol. 1 (Washington, D.C.: Government Printing Office, 1901), part 4, 90.

11. U.S. War Department, *Annual Reports of the War Department*, vol. 1 (Washington, D.C.: Government Printing Office, 1901), part 4, 93. MacArthur's chief of staff, Thomas H. Barry, penned the actual words.

12. The full proclamation is reprinted in U.S. War Department, *Annual Reports of the War Department*, vol. 1 (Washington, D.C.: Government Printing Office, 1901), part 4, 91–92.

13. Glenn Anthony May, *Battle for Batangas: A Philippine Province at War* (New Haven, CT: Yale University Press, 1991), 229.

14. Stuart Creighton Miller, *"Benevolent Assimilation": The American Conquest of the Philippines, 1899–1903* (New Haven, CT: Yale Univ. Press, 1982), 163.

15. Editorial, *New York Times*, January 2, 1901.

16. Miller, *"Benevolent Assimilation,"* 153.

17. See article 3 of Aguinaldo's proclamation of January 17, 1901, in John R. M. Taylor, *The Philippine Insurrection Against the United States* (Pasay City, Philippines: Eugenio Lopez Foundation, 1971–73), 5:137.

18. Batson to wife, November 17, 1899, box 3, Matthew Batson Papers.

19. "The Flight and Wanderings of Emilio Aguinaldo, from His Abandonment of Bayambang Until His Capture in Palanan," diary entry of February 7, 1900 in Taylor, *Philippine Insurrection*, 5:38.

20. Ibid., 5:27.

21. February 10, 1900, in ibid., 5:28.

22. March 29, 1900, in ibid., 5:54.

23. Emilio Aguinaldo, *A Second Look at America* (New York: Robert Speller & Sons, 1957), 126.

24. Douglas MacArthur, *Reminiscences: General of the Army Douglas MacArthur* (New York: McGraw-Hill Book Company, 1964), 26.

Chapter 4: The Policy of Destruction

1. Brian McAllister Linn, *The Philippine War: 1899–1902* (Lawrence: University Press of Kansas, 2000), 217.

2. Henry F. Pringle, *The Life and Times of William Howard Taft* (New York: Farrar & Rinehart, 1939), 1:212.

3. Chaffee's telegraphic report of the attack is in Chaffee to Adjutant-General, May 5, 1902, in U.S. Army Adjutant-General's Office, *Correspondence Relating to the War with Spain* (Washington, D.C.: U.S. Army Center of Military History, 1993), 2:1295–6.

4. Pringle, *Life and Times*, 1:212.

5. See Chaffee to Adjutant-General, May 5, 1902, in U.S. Army Adjudant-General's Office, *Correspondence Relating to the War with Spain*, 2:1336.

6. "To all station commanders," December 24, 1901, in U.S. War Department, *Annual Reports of the War Department: Report of the Lieutenant-General Commanding the Army and Department Commanders*, vol. 9, 57th Congress, 2nd Session, House Document No. 2 (Washington, D.C.: Government Printing Office, 1902), 208.

7. See Corbin to Chaffee, April 16, 1902, in U.S. Army Adjudant-General's Office, *Correspondence Relating to the War with Spain*, 2:1328.

8. Bell also held the rank of major of volunteers in 1898.

9. Albert G. Robinson, *The Philippines: The War and the People; A Record of Personal Observations and Experiences* (New York: McClure, Phillips & Co., 1901), 361.

10. Robert D. Ramsey III, *A Masterpiece of Counterguerrilla Warfare: B. G. J. Franklin Bell in the Philippines, 1901–1902* (Fort Leavenworth, KS: Combat Studies Institute Press, 2007), 3.

11. William Henry Scott, *Ilocano Responses to American Aggression 1900–1901* (Quezon City, Philippines: New Day Publishers, 1986), 143.

12. Glenn Anthony May, *Battle for Batangas: A Philippine Province at War* (New Haven, CT: Yale University Press, 1991), 247.

13. U.S. War Department, *Annual Reports of the War Department: Report of the Lieutenant-General Commanding the Army and Department Commanders*, 57th Congress, 1st Session, House Document No. 2 (Washington, D.C.: Government Printing Office, 1902), part 8, 389.

14. Telegraphic Circular No. 3, Batangas, December 9, 1901, James Franklin Bell Papers, U.S. Army Military History Institute, Carlisle, Pennsylvania.

15. "To all station commanders," Batangas, December 15, 1901, in *Affairs in the Philippine Islands, Hearings Before the Committee on the Philippines of the United States Senate*, 57th Congress, 1st Session, Senate Doc. 331 (Washington, D.C.: Government Printing Office, 1902), part 2, 1614.

16. Andrew J. Birtle, *U.S. Army Counterinsurgency and Contingency Operations Doctrine 1860–1941* (Washington, D.C.: Center of Military History, 1998), 131.

17. Stuart Creighton Miller, *"Benevolent Assimilation": The American Conquest of the Philippines, 1899–1903* (New Haven, CT: Yale University Press, 1982), 209.

18. U.S. War Department, *Annual Reports of the War Department: Report of the Lieutenant-General Commanding the Army and Department Commanders*, vol. 9, 57th Congress, 2nd Session, House Document No. 2 (Washington, D.C.: Government Printing Office, 1902), 233.

19. "To all station commanders," Batangas, December 9, 1901, in *Affairs in the Philippine Islands*, part 2, 1607, 1609.

20. Confidential Telegraphic Circular No. 18, Batangas, December 23, 1901, James Franklin Bell Papers.

21. Telegraphic Circular No. 19, Batangas, December 24, 1901, James Franklin Bell Papers.

22. Telegraphic Circular No. 22, Batangas, December 24, 1901, James Franklin Bell Papers.

23. "Bell to Wheaton," December 27, 1901, in *Affairs in the Philippine Islands*, part 2, 1690–92.

24. Telegraphic Circular No. 12, Batangas, December 21, 1901, James Franklin Bell Papers.

25. May, *Battle for Batangas*, 254.

26. Miguel Malvar, "The Reasons for My Change of Attitude," April 16, 1902, in John R. M. Taylor, *The Philippine Insurrection Against the United States* (Pasay City, Philippines: Eugenio Lopez Foundation, 1971–73), 5:358.

27. Reynaldo C. Ileto, "The Philippine-American War: Friendship and Forgetting," in Angel Velasco Shaw and Luis H. Francia, eds., *Vestiges of War: The Philippine-American War and the Aftermath of an Imperial Dream 1899–1999* (New York: New York University Press, 2002), 17.

28. Ibid., 18.

29. Ibid.

Chapter 5: Why the Americans Won

1. U.S. War Department, *Annual Reports of the War Department: Report of the Lieutenant-General Commanding the Army and Department Commanders*, vol. 9, 57th Congress, 2nd Session, House Document No. 2 (Washington, D.C.: Government Printing Office, 1902), 284–85.

2. Brian McAllister Linn, *The Philippine War: 1899–1902* (Lawrence: University Press of Kansas, 2000), 304.

3. Telegraphic Circular No. 32, January 26, 1902, James Franklin Bell Papers, U.S. Army Military History Institute, Carlisle, Pennsylvania.

4. General Orders No. 66, "To the Army of the United States," July 4, 1902, in U.S. Army Adjutant-General's Office, *Correspondence Relating to the War with Spain*, (Washington, D.C.: U.S. Army Center of Military History, 1993), 2:1352–53.

5. James H. Blount, *The American Occupation of the Philippines, 1898–1912* (New York: G. P. Putnam's Sons, 1913), 393.

6. Corbin to Chaffee, April 16, 1902, in U.S. Army Adjudant-General's Office, *Correspondence Relating to the War with Spain*, 2:1328.

7. Linn, *The Philippine War*, 223.

8. Glenn Anthony May, *Battle for Batangas: A Philippine Province at War* (New Haven, CT: Yale University Press, 1991), 147.

9. Leon Wolff, *Little Brown Brother: How the United States Purchased and Pacified the Philippines* (Oxford, UK: Oxford University Press, 1991), 305.

10. *Affairs in the Philippine Islands, Hearings Before the Committee on the Philippines of the United States Senate*, 57th Congress, 1st Session, Senate Doc. 331 (Washington, D.C.: Government Printing Office, 1902), part 2, 1927.

11. Linn, *The Philippine War*, 221.

12. Glenn A. May, "Filipino Resistance to American Occupation: Batangas, 1899–1902," *Pacific Historical Review* 52, 4 (November 1983): 553.

13. Stuart Creighton Miller, *"Benevolent Assimilation": The American Conquest of the Philippines, 1899–1903* (New Haven, CT: Yale University Press, 1982), 260.

14. Glenn A. May, "Why the United States Won the Philippine-American War, 1899–1902," *Pacific Historical Review* 52, 4 (November 1983): 367.

15. *Affairs in the Philippine Islands*, part 1, 667.

16. Ibid., part 1, 411–12.

17. Among other activities, Abu Sayyaf reportedly provided Ramzi Youssef, who planned the 1993 World Trade Center bombing, and Khalid Sheikh Mohammed with sanctuary on Jolo.

18. Albert G. Robinson, *The Philippines: The War and the People; A Record of Personal Observations and Experiences* (New York: McClure, Phillips & Co., 1901), 404–5.

19. E. J. McClernand, "Our Philippine Problem," *Journal of the Military Service Institution of the United States* 29, 114 (November 1901): 327–29.

Chapter 6: Terror on All Saints' Day

1. Michael K. Clark, *Algeria in Turmoil: A History of the Rebellion* (New York: Frederick A. Praeger, 1959), 121.

2. Alistair Horne, *A Savage War of Peace: Algeria, 1954–1962* (Middlesex, England: Penguin Books, 1985), 27.
3. Clark, *Algeria in Turmoil,* 119.
4. Horne, *A Savage War,* 98–99.
5. Ibid., 545.
6. Ibid., 107.
7. Ibid., 110.
8. Ibid., 174.
9. Jacques Soustelle, *L'espérance trahie, 1958–1961* (Paris: Editions de l'Alma, 1962), 91.

Chapter 7: Terror Without Limits

1. Michael K. Clark, *Algeria in Turmoil: A History of the Rebellion* (New York: Frederick A. Praeger, 1959), 131.
2. University of San Francisco, "Algerian War Reading," http://www.usfca .edu/fac_staff/webberm/algeria.
3. Alistair Horne, *A Savage War of Peace: Algeria, 1954–1962* (Middlesex, England: Penguin Books, 1985), 123.
4. Gil Merom, *How Democracies Lose Small Wars: State, Society, and the Failures of France in Algeria, Israel in Lebanon, and the United States in Vietnam* (Cambridge, UK: Cambridge University Press, 2003), 101.
5. Horne, *A Savage War,* 160.
6. David Galula, *Pacification in Algeria: 1956–1958* (Santa Monica, CA: RAND Corporation, 2006), 23.
7. Martin S. Alexander and J. F. V. Keiger, eds., *France and the Algerian War 1954–62: Strategy, Operations and Diplomacy* (London: Frank Cass, 2002), 5.
8. Peter Paret, *French Revolutionary Warfare from Indochina to Algeria: The Analysis of a Political and Military Doctrine* (New York: Frederick A. Praeger, 1964), 50.
9. Paret provides the numbers for 1959: 1,287 officers, 661 NCOs, 2,921 civilian specialists. See ibid., 50.
10. Ibid., 30.
11. Ibid., 8.
12. Ibid., 30.
13. Frédéric Guelton, "The French Army 'Centre for Training and Preparation in Counter-Guerrilla Warfare' (CIPCG) at Arzew," in Alexander and Keiger, *France and the Algerian War,* 42.
14. Ibid., 49.

Chapter 8: The Question of Morality

1. David Galula, *Pacification in Algeria: 1956–1958* (Santa Monica, CA: RAND Corporation, 2006), 70.
2. Ibid., 176.
3. Ibid., 218.
4. Charles de Gaulle, *Charles de Gaulle, Memoirs of Hope: Renewal and Endeavor,* trans. Terence Kilmartin (New York: Simon & Schuster, 1971), 15.
5. Alexander Zervoudakis, "A Case of Successful Pacification: The 584th Battalion du Train at Bordj de l'Agha (1956–57)," in Martin S. Alexander and J. F. V. Keiger, eds., *France and the Algerian War 1954–62: Strategy, Operations and Diplomacy* (London: Frank Cass, 2002), 56.
6. Paul Aussaresses, *The Battle of the Casbah: Terrorism and Counter-Terrorism in Algeria 1955–1957* (New York: Enigma Books, 2005), 77.
7. Ibid., 93.
8. Ibid., 119.
9. John Talbott, *The War Without a Name: France in Algeria, 1954–1962* (New York: Alfred A. Knopf, 1980), 91.
10. Among the first to make this incendiary allegation was the journalist Claude Bourdet, who denounced what he called "your Algerian Gestapo" in *France-Observateur.*
11. University of San Francisco, "Algerian War Reading," http://www.usfca .edu/fac_staff/webberm/algeria.

Chapter 9: The Enclosed Hunting Preserve

1. John Talbott, *The War Without a Name: France in Algeria, 1954–1962* (New York: Alfred A. Knopf, 1980), 184.
2. Gil Merom, *How Democracies Lose Small Wars: State, Society, and the Failures of France in Algeria, Israel in Lebanon, and the United States in Vietnam* (Cambridge, UK: Cambridge University Press, 2003), 86.
3. Michael K. Clark, *Algeria in Turmoil: A History of the Rebellion* (New York: Frederick A. Praeger, 1959), 371.
4. Ibid., 404.
5. Charles de Gaulle, *Charles de Gaulle, Memoirs of Hope: Renewal and Endeavor,* trans. Terence Kilmartin (New York: Simon & Schuster, 1971), 15.
6. De Gaulle used this phrase at an October 23, 1958, press conference that is remembered because he offered "the peace of the brave."
7. Alistair Horne, *A Savage War of Peace: Algeria, 1954–1962* (Middlesex, England: Penguin Books, 1985), 333.
8. Jules Roy, *The War in Algeria,* trans. Richard Howard (New York: Grove Press, 1961), 86.
9. Horne, *A Savage War,* 338.

Chapter 10: The Sense of Betrayal

1. Some estimates claim two million Algerians were relocated.
2. Peter Paret, *French Revolutionary Warfare from Indochina to Algeria: The Analysis of a Political and Military Doctrine* (New York: Frederick A. Praeger, 1964), 44.
3. Jules Roy, *The War in Algeria*, trans. Richard Howard (New York: Grove Press, 1961), 66–67.
4. Charles de Gaulle, *Charles de Gaulle, Memoirs of Hope: Renewal and Endeavor*, trans. Terence Kilmartin (New York: Simon & Schuster, 1971), 73–74. Of course de Gaulle writes about this conclusion with the virtue of hindsight.
5. Alistair Horne, *A Savage War of Peace: Algeria, 1954–1962* (Middlesex, England: Penguin Books, 1985), 348.
6. Dorothy Pickles, *Algeria and France: From Colonialism to Cooperation* (New York: Frederick A. Praeger, 1963), 85.
7. The statistics are broken down by category at University of San Francisco, "Algerian War Reading," http://www.usfca.edu/fac_staff/webberm/algeria.htm.
8. David Galula, *Pacification in Algeria: 1956–1958* (Santa Monica, CA: RAND Corporation, 2006), 18.
9. Paul Aussaresses, *The Battle of the Casbah: Terrorism and Counter-Terrorism in Algeria, 1955–1957* (New York: Enigma Books, 2005), 127.
10. Horne, *A Savage War,* 546.

Chapter 11: Crisis in Malaya

1. Richard L. Clutterbuck, *The Long Long War: Counterinsurgency in Malaya and Vietnam* (New York: Frederick A. Praeger, 1966), 3.
2. Noel Barber, *The War of the Running Dogs: The Malayan Emergency, 1948–1960* (New York: Weybright and Talley, 1971), 21.
3. Ibid., 22.
4. Ibid., 45–46.

Chapter 12: Personality and Vision

1. Once the government declared the Emergency, reinforcements flowed in. Various authors provide strengths of ten to thirteen battalions. My total derives from Anthony Short, *The Communist Insurrection in Malaya, 1948–1960* (New York: Crane, Russak & Co., 1975), 113.
2. Ibid., 136–37.
3. Arthur Campbell, *Jungle Green* (Boston: Little, Brown and Co., 1953), 94.
4. John A. Nagl, *Counterinsurgency Lessons from Malaya and Vietnam: Learning to Eat Soup with a Knife* (Westport, CT: Praeger, 2002), 69.

5. Noel Barber, *The War of the Running Dogs: The Malayan Emergency, 1948–1960* (New York: Weybright and Talley, 1971), 62.

6. Short, *Communist Insurrection*, 98.

7. Ibid., 235–36.

8. Ibid., 173.

9. Richard Stubbs, *Hearts and Minds in Guerrilla Warfare: The Malayan Emergency, 1948–1960* (Oxford, UK: Oxford University Press, 1989), 102.

10. Short, *Communist Insurrection*, 229–30.

11. Ibid., 240.

12. Ibid., 292.

13. Ibid., 297.

Chapter 13: A Modern Cromwell

1. Noel Barber, *The War of the Running Dogs: The Malayan Emergency, 1948–1960* (New York: Weybright and Talley, 1971), 140.

2. John A. Nagl, *Counterinsurgency Lessons from Malaya and Vietnam: Learning to Eat Soup with a Knife* (Westport, CT: Praeger, 2002), 76.

3. Anthony Short, *The Communist Insurrection in Malaya, 1948–1960* (New York: Crane, Russak & Co., 1975), 326.

4. Fifteen years later he dismissed the term as popular cant, calling it "that nauseating phrase I think I invented."

5. Barber, *War of the Running Dogs*, 151.

6. Short, *Communist Insurrection*, 340.

7. Barber, *War of the Running Dogs*, 205.

8. Ibid., 158.

9. Short, *Communist Insurrection*, 343.

10. Nagl, *Counterinsurgency Lessons*, 98.

11. Arthur Campbell, *Jungle Green* (Boston: Little, Brown and Co., 1953), 14.

12. John Chynoweth, *Hunting Terrorists in the Jungle* (Stroud, UK: Tempus Publishing Limited, 2005), 134.

13. Campbell, *Jungle Green*, 26.

14. Richard Miers, *Shoot to Kill* (London: Faber and Faber, 1959), 160.

15. Short, *Communist Insurrection* 483.

Chapter 14: Victory in Malaya

1. Noel Barber, *The War of the Running Dogs: The Malayan Emergency, 1948–1960* (New York: Weybright and Talley, 1971), 152.

2. Anthony Short, *The Communist Insurrection in Malaya, 1948–1960* (New York: Crane, Russak & Co., 1975, 364.

3. John Chynoweth, *Hunting Terrorists in the Jungle* (Stroud, UK: Tempus Publishing Limited, 2005), 83.

4. Ibid., 49.
5. "Personality Profile: Gerard Templer," http://www.mindef.gov.sg/imindef/ publications/pointer/journals/2003/v29n4/personality_profile.html.
6. Sir Robert Thompson, ed., *War in Peace: Conventional and Guerrilla Warfare Since 1945* (New York: Harmony Books, 1982), 83.
7. Richard Stubbs, *Hearts and Minds in Guerrilla Warfare: The Malayan Emergency, 1948–1960* (Oxford, UK: Oxford University Press, 1989), 259.
8. The title of Richard L. Clutterbuck's book, *The Long Long War: Counterinsurgency in Malaya and Vietnam* (New York: Frederick A. Praeger, 1966).
9. Richard Miers, *Shoot to Kill* (London: Faber and Faber, 1959), 200.
10. Stubbs, *Hearts and Minds*, 3.
11. Clutterbuck, *The Long Long War*, 122.

Chapter 15: In Search of a New Enemy

1. Gérard Chaliand, *The Art of War in World History* (Berkeley: University of California Press, 1994), 593.
2. Kidder to Department of State, March 3, 1955, in *Foreign Relations of the United States 1955–1957, Vol. I: Vietnam* (Washington, D.C.: Government Printing Office, 1985), 105.
3. Ronald H. Spector, *Advice and Support: The Early Years of the U.S. Army in Vietnam, 1941–1960* (New York: Free Press, 1985), 312.
4. John F. Kennedy, "Remarks at West Point to the Graduating Class of the U.S. Military Academy, June 6th, 1962," http://www.presidency.ucsb.edu/ ws/index.php?pid=8695.
5. Dennis Warner, "Fighting the Viet Cong," *Army* 12, 2 (September 1961): 20.
6. Roger Hilsman, *To Move a Nation: The Politics of Foreign Policy in the Administration of John F. Kennedy* (Garden City, NY: Doubleday, 1967), 426.
7. Harry Maurer, *Strange Ground: An Oral History of Americans in Vietnam, 1945–1975* (New York: Avon Books, 1989), 110.
8. Francis J. Kelly, *U.S. Army Special Forces, 1961–1971* (Washington, D.C.: Department of the Army, 1973), 7.

Chapter 16: Pacification, Marine Corps Style

1. William C. Westmoreland, *A Soldier Reports* (Garden City, NY: Doubleday, 1976), 98.
2. Ronald Schaffer, "The 1940 *Small Wars Manual* and the Lessons of History," *Military Affairs*, April 1972, 46.
3. Among many connections, one marine battalion commander who served in Vietnam was Major Littleton W. T. Waller, the grandson of the officer who commanded the marines on Samar during the Philippine Insurrection.

4. Larry E. Cable, *Conflict of Myths: The Development of American Counterinsurgency Doctrine and the Vietnam War* (New York: New York University Press, 1986), 162.

5. See Field Manual FM 8-2, U. S. Marine Corps, *Operations Against Guerrilla Forces* (Washington, D.C.: Government Printing Office, 1962), 75.

6. Lewis Walt, *Strange War, Strange Strategy* (New York: Funk and Wagnalls, 1970), 18.

7. Jack Shulimson and Charles M. Johnson, *U.S. Marines in Vietnam: The Landing and the Buildup 1965* (Washington, D.C.: U.S. Marine Corps, 1978), 39.

8. Stuart A. Herrington, *Silence Was a Weapon: The Vietnam War in the Villages* (Novato, CA: Presidio Press, 1982), 29.

9. Victor H. Krulak, *First to Fight: An Inside View of the U.S. Marine Corps* (Annapolis, MD: Naval Institute Press, 1984), 185.

10. Lt. Paul Ek Interview #46, January 24, 1966, Subject Files, Reference Branch, History Division, United States Marine Corps.

11. Ibid.

12. Ibid.

13. Ibid.

Chapter 17: Progress and Setback

1. Al Hemingway, *Our War Was Different: Marine Combined Action Platoons in Vietnam* (Annapolis, MD: Naval Institute Press, 1994), 28.

2. Edward F. Palm, "Tiger Papa Three: A Memoir of the Combined Action Program," *Marine Corps Gazette*, February 1988, 69.

3. Bruce C. Allnutt, *Marine Combined Action Capabilities: The Vietnam Experience* (McLean, VA: Human Sciences Research Inc., 1969), 28.

4. Robert A. Klyman, "The Combined Action Program: A Missed Opportunity," (thesis draft, University of Michigan History Department, December 21, 1985), 41.

5. Ibid., 21.

6. Palm, "Tiger Papa Three," 37.

7. Ibid., 70.

8. Gary L. Telfer, *U.S. Marines in Vietnam: Fighting the North Vietnamese, 1967* (Washington, D.C.: U.S. Marine Corps, 1984), 190.

9. Ibid., 190.

10. William R. Corson, "Marine Combined Action Program in Vietnam," 1, Subject Files, Reference Branch, History Division, United States Marine Corps.

11. Lyndon B. Johnson, *Public Papers of the Presidents of the United States: Lyndon B. Johnson 1966* (Washington, D.C.: Government Printing Office, 1967), 4.

12. Lady Bird Johnson, *A White House Diary* (New York: Holt, Rinehart and Winston, 1970), 360.

13. James R. Arnold, *Presidents Under Fire: Commanders in Chief in Victory and Defeat* (New York: Orion Books, 1994), 269.

14. Charles Kaiser, *1968 in America: Music, Politics, Chaos, Counterculture, and the Shaping of a Generation* (New York: Weidenfeld & Nicolson, 1988), 124.

15. Captain Peter D. Haines, Interview #2534, March 9, 1968, Subject Files, Reference Branch, History Division, United States Marine Corps.

16. Ibid.

17. Klyman, "The Combined Action Program," 34.

18. Ibid.

19. Cpl. William Corcoran, Interview #2079, December 14, 1967, Subject Files, Reference Branch, History Division, United States Marine Corps.

20. Andrew F. Krepinevich, Jr., *The Army and Vietnam* (Baltimore: Johns Hopkins University Press, 1986), 175.

21. United States Marine Corps, *Small Wars Manual, United States Marine Corps 1940* (Washington, D.C.: Government Printing Office, 1940), 1–17.

22. Victor H. Krulak, *First to Fight: An Inside View of the U.S. Marine Corps* (Annapolis, MD: Naval Institute Press, 1984), 185.

Chapter 18: The Army's Other War

1. William C. Westmoreland, *A Soldier Reports* (Garden City, NY: Doubleday, 1976), 69.

2. Jack Shulimson, *U.S. Marines in Vietnam: An Expanding War, 1966* (Washington, D.C.: U.S. Marine Corps, 1982), 233.

3. Andrew F. Krepinevich, Jr., *The Army and Vietnam* (Baltimore: Johns Hopkins University Press, 1986), 197.

4. Richard A. Hunt, *Pacification: The American Struggle for Vietnam's Hearts and Minds* (Boulder, CO: Westview Press, 1995), 141.

5. James W. Trullinger, *Village at War: An Account of Revolution in Vietnam* (New York: Longman, 1980), 124.

6. Nhu Tang Truong, *Journal of a Viet Cong* (London: Jonathan Cape, 1986), 192.

7. Hunt, *Pacification*, 193.

8. Brian M. Jenkins, *The Unchangeable War* (Santa Monica, CA: RAND Corporation, 1970), 11.

9. Colonel William R. Corson, Interview #6338, Subject Files, Reference Branch, History Division, United States Marine Corps.

10. Krepinevich, *The Army and Vietnam*, 222.

11. Ibid., 205.

12. W. Scott Thompson and Donaldson D. Frizzell, *The Lessons of Vietnam* (New York: Crane, Russak & Co., 1977), 79.

13. Douglas S. Blaufarb, *The Counter-Insurgency Era: U.S. Doctrine and Performance, 1950 to Present* (New York: Free Press, 1977), 245.

14. Stuart A. Herrington, *Silence Was a Weapon: The Vietnam War in the Villages* (Novato, CA: Presidio Press, 1982), 11.

15. Hunt, *Pacification*, 236.

16. Eric M. Bergerud, *The Dynamics of Defeat: The Vietnam War in Hau Nghia Province* (Boulder, CO: Westview Press, 1991), 232.

17. Herrington, *Silence Was a Weapon*, 65.

18. Ibid., 98.

19. Ronald H. Spector, *After Tet: The Bloodiest Year in Vietnam* (New York: Free Press, 1993), 290.

20. Bergerud, *Dynamics of Defeat*, 306.

Chapter 19: Lessons from a Lost War

1. For a full discussion see John M. Gates, "People's War in Vietnam," *Journal of Military History* 54 (July 1990): 325–44. Pages 338–41 specifically examine Viet Cong participation in the invasion.

2. Sir Robert Thompson, ed., *War in Peace: Conventional and Guerrilla Warfare Since 1945* (New York: Harmony Books, 1981), 190.

3. Carl von Clausewitz, *On War* (Harmondsworth, UK: Penguin Books, 1982), 119.

4. Nhu Tang Truong, *Journal of a Viet Cong* (London: Jonathan Cape, 1986), 183.

5. John A. Nagl, *Counterinsurgency Lessons from Malaya and Vietnam: Learning to Eat Soup with a Knife* (Westport, CT: Praeger, 2002), 166.

6. Francis J. Kelly, *U.S. Army Special Forces, 1961–1971* (Washington, D.C.: Department of the Army, 1973), 87.

7. Andrew F. Krepinevich, Jr., *The Army and Vietnam* (Baltimore: Johns Hopkins University Press, 1986), 174.

8. W. Scott Thompson and Donaldson D. Frizzell, *The Lessons of Vietnam* (New York: Crane, Russak & Co., 1977), 213.

9. F. J. West, Jr., "Area-Security" (Monograph, Santa Monica, CA: RAND Corporation, 1969), 4.

10. Ibid., 1–2.

11. Michael A. Hennessy, *Strategy in Vietnam: The Marines and Revolutionary Warfare in I Corps, 1965–1972* (Westport, CT: Praeger, 1997), 181.

12. Krepinevich, *The Army and Vietnam*, 216.

13. James R. Arnold, *Presidents Under Fire: Commanders in Chief in Victory and Defeat* (New York: Orion Books, 1994), 272.

Conclusion: Reflections on a War Without End

1. In the past decade the actual site of this ambush has been discovered and explored by archaeologists, thus providing dramatic detail.

2. Scott Peterson, *Me Against My Brother: At War in Somalia, Sudan, and Rwanda* (London: Routledge, 2000), 20.

3. George Packer, "Knowing the Enemy: Can Social Scientists Redefine the 'War on Terror'?" *New Yorker*, December 18, 2006, 61.

4. U.S. Army Headquarters, *FM3-24: Counterinsurgency* (Washington, D.C.: Headquarters, Department of the Army, 2006), vii, 2.

5. Yochi J. Dreazen, "Petraeus Promoted, to Leave Iraq," *Wall Street Journal*, April 24, 2008, A3.

6. Brigadier General J. Franklin Bell's address to his officers, December 1, 1901, Batangas Province, Philippine Islands, in Robert D. Ramsey III, *A Masterpiece of Counterguerrilla Warfare: B. G. J. Franklin Bell in the Philippines, 1901–1902* (Fort Leavenworth, KS: Combat Studies Institute Press, 2007), 36.

7. Jeffrey Race, *War Comes to Long An* (Berkeley: University of California Press, 1972), 263.

8. *Affairs in the Philippine Islands, Hearings Before the Committee on the Philippines of the United States Senate,* 57th Congress, 1st Session, Senate Doc. 331 (Washington, D.C.: Government Printing Office, 1902), part 1, 77.

9. Paul Aussaresses, *The Battle of the Casbah: Terrorism and Counter-Terrorism in Algeria, 1955–1957* (New York: Enigma Books, 2005), xxi.

10. Gil Merom, *How Democracies Lose Small Wars: State, Society, and the Failures of France in Algeria, Israel in Lebanon, and the United States in Vietnam* (Cambridge, UK: Cambridge University Press, 2003), 127.

11. Sir Robert Thompson, *Defeating Communist Insurgency: The Lessons of Malaya and Vietnam* (New York: Praeger Publishers, 1966), 52–54.

12. Alistair Horne, *A Savage War of Peace: Algeria 1954–1962* (Middlesex, England: Penguin Books, 1985), 205.

13. *Affairs in the Philippine Islands, Hearings Before the Committee on the Philippines of the United States Senate,* 57th Congress, 1st Session, Senate Doc. 331 (Washington, D.C.: Government Printing Office, 1902), part 1, 65.

14. Albert G. Robinson, *The Philippines: The War and the People; A Record of Personal Observations and Experiences* (New York: McClure, Phillips & Co., 1901), 379.

15. Ibid., 405.

16. Ibid.

17. Michael M. Phillips, "In Counterinsurgency Class, Soldiers Think Like Taliban," *Wall Street Journal*, November 30, 2007.

18. U. S. Marine Corps, *Small Wars Manual, United States Marine Corps 1940* (Washington, D.C.: Government Printing Office, 1940), 26.

19. Richard M. Cavagnol, "Lessons from Vietnam: Essential Training of Marine Advisors and Combined Action Platoon Personnel," *Marine Corps Gazette*, March 2007, 17.

20. Gina Chon, "Iraq Prime Minister Gets Boost with Ebb in Violence," *Wall Street Journal*, June 13, 2008.

21. Peter Paret, *French Revolutionary Warfare from Indochina to Algeria: The Analysis of a Political and Military Doctrine* (New York: Frederick A. Praeger, 1964), 31.

22. Thompson, *Defeating Communist Insurgency*, 143.

23. *Affairs in the Philippine Islands, Hearings Before the Committee on the Philippines of the United States Senate,* 57th Congress, 1st Session, Senate Doc. 331 (Washington, D.C.: Government Printing Office, 1902), part 1, 61.

24. "Statement of Maj. Gen. Arthur MacArthur," *Affairs in the Philippine Islands, Hearings Before the Committee on the Philippines of the United States Senate,* 57th Congress, 1st Session, Senate Doc. 331 (Washington, D.C.: Government Printing Office, 1902), part 2, 1918.

25. Phillip B. Davidson, *Vietnam at War* (Novato, CA: Presidio, 1988), 798.

26. Paret, *French Revolutionary Warfare*, 94.

27. Michael K. Clark, *Algeria in Turmoil: A History of the Rebellion* (New York: Frederick A. Praeger, 1959), 319.

28. See Yochi J. Dreazen, "Training: Mission Unaccomplished U.S. Army Still Struggles with How to School Iraqi Security Forces," *Wall Street Journal*, February 29, 2008.

29. Marcus Tullius Cicero, *De Officiis*, trans. Walter Miller (Cambridge, MA: Harvard University Press, 1913), 76. The quotation, from book I, chapter 22, is variously translated but the meaning is clear.

Bibliography

Affairs in the Philippine Islands. Hearings Before the Committee on the Philippines of the United States Senate. 3 vols. 57th Congress, 1st Session, Senate Doc. 331. Washington, D.C.: Government Printing Office, 1902.

Aguinaldo, Emilio. *A Second Look at America.* New York: Robert Speller & Sons, 1957.

———. "Proclamation to the Philippine People, February 5, 1899." In *The Philippines Reader: A History of Colonialism, Neocolonialism, Dictatorship, and Resistance.* Ed. Daniel B. Schirmer and Stephen Rosskamm Shalom, pp. 20–21. Boston: South End Press, 1987.

Alexander, Bevin. *The Future of Warfare.* New York: W. W. Norton & Co., 1995.

Alexander, Martin S., and J. F. V. Keiger, eds. *France and the Algerian War, 1954–62: Strategy, Operations and Diplomacy.* London: Frank Cass, 2002.

Allnutt, Bruce C. "Marine Combined Action Capabilities: The Vietnam Experience." McLean, VA: Human Sciences Research Inc., December 1969.

Army-Air Force Center for Low Intensity Conflict. "Joint Low-Intensity Conflict Project Final Report. Vol. 1: Analytical Review of Low-Intensity Conflict." Langley, VA, August 1, 1986.

Arnold, James R. *The First Domino: Eisenhower, the Military, and American's Intervention in Vietnam.* New York: William Morrow and Co., 1991.

———. *Presidents Under Fire: Commanders in Chief in Victory and Defeat.* New York: Orion Books, 1994.

Aussaresses, Paul. *The Battle of the Casbah: Terrorism and Counter-Terrorism in Algeria, 1955–1957.* New York: Enigma Books, 2005.

Barber, Noel. *The War of the Running Dogs: The Malayan Emergency, 1948–1960.* New York: Weybright and Talley, 1971.

Bergerud, Eric M. *The Dynamics of Defeat: The Vietnam War in Hau Nghia Province.* Boulder, CO: Westview Press, 1991.

Birtle, Andrew J. *U.S. Army Counterinsurgency and Contingency Operations Doctrine, 1860–1941.* Washington, D.C.: Center of Military History, 1998.

Blaufarb, Douglas S. *The Counter-Insurgency Era: U.S. Doctrine and Performance, 1950 to Present.* New York: Free Press, 1977.

Blount, James H. *The American Occupation of the Philippines, 1898–1912.* New York: G. P. Putnam's Sons, 1913.

Boot, Max. *The Savage Wars of Peace.* New York: Basic Books, 2002.

Bradford, James C., ed. *Crucible of Empire: The Spanish-American War and Its Aftermath.* Annapolis: Naval Institute Press, 1993.

Braestrup, Peter. *Big Story: How the American Press and Television Reported and Interpreted the Crisis of Tet 1968 in Vietnam and Washington.* Boulder, CO: Westview Press, 1977.

Brands, H. W. *Bound to Empire: The United States and the Philippines.* Oxford, UK: Oxford University Press, 1992.

Cable, Larry E. *Conflict of Myths: The Development of American Counterinsurgency Doctrine and the Vietnam War.* New York: New York University Press, 1986.

Campbell, Arthur. *Jungle Green.* Boston: Little, Brown and Co., 1953.

Cassidy, Robert M. *Counterinsurgency and the Global War on Terror.* Westport, CT: Praeger Security International, 2006.

Cavagnol, Richard M. "Lessons from Vietnam: Essential Training of Marine Advisors and Combined Action Platoon Personnel." *Marine Corps Gazette,* March 2007, 16–19.

Chaliand, Gérard. *The Art of War in World History.* Berkeley: University of California Press, 1994.

Chynoweth, John. *Hunting Terrorists in the Jungle.* Stroud, UK: Tempus Publishing Ltd., 2005.

Cicero, Marcus Tullius. *De Officiis.* Trans. Walter Miller. Cambridge, MA: Harvard University Press, 1913.

Clark, Michael K. *Algeria in Turmoil: A History of the Rebellion.* New York: Frederick A. Praeger, 1959.

Clarke, Jeffrey J. *Advice and Support: The Final Years. The U.S. Army in Vietnam.* Washington, D.C.: Center of Military History, 1988.

Clausewitz, Carl von. *On War.* Harmondsworth, England: Penguin Books, 1982.

Clutterbuck, Richard L. *The Long Long War: Counterinsurgency in Malaya and Vietnam.* New York: Frederick A. Praeger, 1966.

Colby, William. *Lost Victory: A Firsthand Account of America's Sixteen-Year Involvement in Vietnam.* Chicago: Contemporary Books, 1989.

Cordesman, Anthony H. *The Iraq War: Strategy, Tactics, and Military Lessons.* Washington, D.C.: Center for Strategic and International Studies, 2003.

Cosmas, Graham A. *MACV: The Joint Command in the Years of Escalation, 1962–1967*. Washington, D.C.: Center of Military History, 2006.

Damm, Raymond C., Jr. "The Combined Action Program: A Tool for the Future." *Marine Corps Gazette*, October 1998, 49–53.

Davidson, Phillip B. *Vietnam at War*. Novato, CA: Presidio, 1988.

de Gaulle, Charles. *Charles de Gaulle: Memoirs of Hope: Renewal and Endeavor*. Trans. Terence Kilmartin. New York: Simon & Schuster, 1971.

Dreazen, Yochi J. "Training Mission Unaccomplished: U.S. Army Still Struggles with How to School Iraqi Security Forces." *Wall Street Journal*, February 29, 2008.

Evans, Ernest. *War Without Splendor: The U.S. Military and Low-Level Conflict*. Westport, CT: Greenwood Press, 1987.

Fall, Bernard. *The Two Viet-Nams*. New York: Frederick A. Praeger, 1967.

Fishel, John T., and Max G. Manwaring. *Uncomfortable Wars Revisited*. Norman: University of Oklahoma Press, 2006.

Galula, David. *Pacification in Algeria: 1956–1958*. Santa Monica, CA: RAND Corporation, 2006.

Gates, John M. "People's War in Vietnam." *Journal of Military History* 54 (July 1990): 325–44.

———. *"Schoolbooks and Krags": The United States Army in the Philippines, 1898–1902*. Westport, CT: Greenwood Press, 1973.

Gordon, Michael R., and Bernard E. Trainor. *Cobra II: The Inside Story of the Invasion and Occupation of Iraq*. New York: Pantheon Books, 2006.

Griswold, Eliza. "Waging Peace in the Philippines." *Smithsonian* 37:9 (December 2006): 82–92.

"Guardians at the Gate." *Time*, January 7, 1966, 1–12. http://www.time.com/time/magazine/article/0,9171,834900-10,00.html

Harper, Frank, ed. *Just Outside of Manila: Letters from Members of the First Colorado Regiment in the Spanish-American and Philippine-American Wars*. Denver: Colorado Historical Society, 1992.

Hemingway, Al. *Our War Was Different: Marine Combined Action Platoons in Vietnam*. Annapolis, MD: Naval Institute Press, 1994.

Hennessy, Michael A. *Strategy in Vietnam: The Marines and Revolutionary Warfare in I Corps, 1965–1972*. Westport, CT: Praeger, 1997.

Herrington, Stuart A. *Silence Was a Weapon: The Vietnam War in the Villages*. Novato, CA: Presidio Press, 1982.

Hilsman, Roger. *To Move a Nation: The Politics of Foreign Policy in the Administration of John F. Kennedy*. Garden City, NY: Doubleday, 1967.

Horne, Alistair. *A Savage War of Peace: Algeria, 1954–1962*. Middlesex, England: Penguin Books, 1985.

Hunt, Richard A. *Pacification: The American Struggle for Vietnam's Hearts and Minds.* Boulder, CO: Westview Press, 1995.

Jenkins, Brian M. *The Unchangeable War.* Santa Monica, CA: RAND Corporation, 1970.

Joes, Anthony James. *America and Guerrilla Warfare.* Lexington: University Press of Kentucky, 2000.

———. *Guerrilla Warfare.* Westport CT: Greenwood Press, 1996.

———. *Resisting Rebellion: The History and Politics of Counterinsurgency.* Lexington: University Press of Kentucky, 2004.

Johnson, Lady Bird. *A White House Diary.* New York: Holt, Rinehart and Winston, 1970.

Kaiser, Charles. *1968 in America: Music, Politics, Chaos, Counterculture, and the Shaping of a Generation.* New York: Weidenfeld & Nicolson, 1988.

Kelly, Francis J. *U.S. Army Special Forces, 1961–1971.* Washington, D.C.: Department of the Army, 1973.

Kennedy, John F. "Remarks at West Point to the Graduating Class of the U.S. Military Academy, June 6th, 1962." http://www.presidency.ucsb.edu/ws/index.php?pid=8695.

Klyman, Robert A. "The Combined Action Program: A Missed Opportunity." Thesis draft, University of Michigan History Department, December 21, 1985.

Krepinevich, Andrew F., Jr. *The Army and Vietnam.* Baltimore: Johns Hopkins University Press, 1986.

Krulak, Victor H. *First to Fight: An Inside View of the U.S. Marine Corps.* Annapolis, MD: Naval Institute Press, 1984.

Lacouture, Jean. *De Gaulle: The Ruler, 1945–1970.* Trans. Alan Sheridan. New York: W.W. Norton & Co., 1992.

Laqueur, Walter. *Guerrilla: A Historical and Critical Study.* Boston: Little, Brown & Co., 1976.

———. *The Guerrilla Reader.* Philadelphia: Temple University Press, 1977.

Lewy, Guenter. *America in Vietnam.* New York: Oxford University Press, 1978.

Liddell Hart, Basil Henry. *Strategy.* New York: Frederick A. Praeger, 1967.

Linn, Brian McAllister. "Foreshadowing the War in Iraq: The U.S. War in the Philippines, 1899–1902." In *Warriors and Scholars: A Modern War Reader,* ed. Peter B. Lane and Ronald E. Marcello, pp. 254–73. Denton: University of North Texas Press, 2005.

———. *The Philippine War: 1899–1902.* Lawrence: University Press of Kansas, 2000.

———. *The U.S. Army and Counterinsurgency in the Philippine War, 1899–1902.* Chapel Hill: University of North Carolina Press, 1989.

———. "We Will Go Heavily Armed: The Marines' Small War on Samar,

1901–1902." In *Crucibles: Selected Readings in U.S. Marine Corps History*, ed. Robert S. Burrell, pp. 67–82. Bel Air, MD: Academy Press, 2004.

Long, Austin. *On "Other War": Lessons from Five Decades of RAND Counterinsurgency Research*. Arlington, VA: RAND Corporation, 2006.

MacArthur, Douglas. *Reminiscences: General of the Army Douglas MacArthur*. New York: McGraw-Hill Book Company, 1964.

Mackay, Donald. *The Malayan Emergency, 1948–60: The Domino That Stood*. London: Brassey's Ltd., 1997.

Mackey, Robert R. *The Uncivil War: Irregular Warfare in the Upper South, 1861–1865*. Norman: University of Oklahoma Press, 2004.

Mao Tse-tung. "On Guerrilla Warfare." http://www.marxists.org/reference/archive/mao/works/1937/guerrilla-warfare.

Maurer, Harry. *Strange Ground: An Oral History of Americans in Vietnam, 1945–1975*. New York: Avon Books, 1989.

May, Glenn Anthony. *Battle for Batangas: A Philippine Province at War*. New Haven, CT: Yale University Press, 1991.

———. "Filipino Resistance to American Occupation: Batangas, 1899–1902." *Pacific Historical Review* 48, 4 (November 1979): 531–56.

———. "Why the United States Won the Philippine-American War, 1899–1902." *Pacific Historical Review* 52, 4 (November 1983): 353–77.

McClernand, E. J. "Our Philippine Problem." *Journal of the Military Service Institution of the United States* 29, 114 (November 1901): 327–32.

Merom, Gil. *How Democracies Lose Small Wars: State, Society, and the Failures of France in Algeria, Israel in Lebanon, and the United States in Vietnam*. Cambridge, UK: Cambridge University Press, 2003.

Miers, Richard. *Shoot to Kill*. London: Faber and Faber, 1959.

Miller, Harry. *A Short History of Malaysia*. New York: Frederick A. Praeger, 1966.

Miller, Stuart Creighton. *"Benevolent Assimilation": The American Conquest of the Philippines, 1899–1903*. New Haven, CT: Yale University Press, 1982.

Mockaitis, Thomas R. *The Iraq War: Learning from the Past, Adapting to the Present, and Planning for the Future*. Carlisle, PA: Strategic Studies Institute, 2007.

Nagl, John A. *Counterinsurgency Lessons from Malaya and Vietnam: Learning to Eat Soup with a Knife*. Westport, CT: Praeger, 2002.

O'Ballance, Edgar. *Malaya: The Communist Insurgent War, 1948–60*. London: Faber and Faber, 1966.

O'Neill, Bard. *Insurgency and Terrorism*. Dulles, VA: Potomac Books, 2005.

Owen, Norman G. "Winding Down the War in Albay, 1900–1903." *Pacific Historical Review* 48, 4 (November 1979): 557–89.

Packer, George. "Knowing the Enemy: Can Social Scientists Redefine the 'War on Terror'?" *New Yorker*, December 18, 2006, 61–69.

Palm, Major Edward F. "Tiger Papa Three: A Memoir of the Combined Action Program." *Marine Corps Gazette*, January 1988, 34–43; February 1988, 66–76.

Paret, Peter. *French Revolutionary Warfare from Indochina to Algeria: The Analysis of a Political and Military Doctrine*. New York: Frederick A. Praeger, 1964.

Peoples, Curtis. "The Use of the British Village Resettlement Model in Malaya and Vietnam." www.tamilnation.org/armed_conflict/thompson.htm.

Peterson, Michael E. *The Combined Action Platoons: The U.S. Marines' Other War in Vietnam*. New York: Praeger, 1989.

Pfaltzgraff, Robert L., Jr., ed. *Ethnic Conflict and Regional Instability: Implications for U.S. Policy and Army Roles and Missions*. Carlisle, PA: U.S. Army War College, 1994.

Phillips, Michael M. "In Counterinsurgency Class, Soldiers Think Like Taliban." *Wall Street Journal*, November 30, 2007.

Pickles, Dorothy. *Algeria and France: From Colonialism to Cooperation*. New York: Frederick A. Praeger, 1963.

Pogue, Forrest C. *George C. Marshall: Education of a General, 1880–1939*. New York: Viking Press, 1963.

Polk, William R. *Violent Politics: A History of Insurgency, Terrorism and Guerrilla War, from the American Revolution to Iraq*. New York: Harper, 2007.

Pringle, Henry F. *The Life and Times of William Howard Taft*. 2 vols. New York: Farrar & Rinehart, 1939.

Public Papers of the Presidents of the United States: Lyndon B. Johnson, 1966. Washington, D.C.: Government Printing Office, 1967.

Race, Jeffrey. *War Comes to Long An*. Berkeley: University of California Press, 1972.

Ramsey, Robert D., III. *A Masterpiece of Counterguerrilla Warfare: B. G. J. Franklin Bell in the Philippines, 1901–1902*. Fort Leavenworth, KS: Combat Studies Institute Press, 2007.

Robinson, Albert G. *The Philippines: The War and the People; A Record of Personal Observations and Experiences*. New York: McClure, Phillips & Co., 1901.

Roy, Jules. *The War in Algeria*. Trans. Richard Howard. New York: Grove Press, 1961.

Sarkesian, Sam C. *Unconventional Conflicts in a New Security Era: Lessons from Malaya and Vietnam*. Westport, CT: Greenwood Press, 1993.

Schaffer, Ronald. "The 1940 Small Wars Manual and the 'Lessons of History.'" *Military Affairs*, April 1972, 46–51.

Schwartz, T. P. "The Combined Action Program: A Different Perspective." *Marine Corps Gazette* 83, 2 (February 1999): 63–72.

Scott, William Henry. *Ilocano Responses to American Aggression, 1900–1901*. Quezon City, Philippines: New Day Publishers, 1986.

Sexton, William Thaddeus. *Soldiers in the Philippines*. Washington D.C.: The Infantry Journal, 1944.

Shafer, D. Michael. *Deadly Paradigms: The Failure of U.S. Counterinsurgency Policy*. Princeton, NJ: Princeton University Press, 1988.

Shaw, Angel Velasco and Luis H. Francia, eds. *Vestiges of War: The Philippine-American War and the Aftermath of an Imperial Dream, 1899–1999*. New York: New York University Press, 2002.

Shennan, Margaret. *Out in the Midday Sun: The British in Malaya, 1880–1960*. London: John Murray, 2000.

Short, Anthony. *The Communist Insurrection in Malaya, 1948–1960*. New York: Crane, Russak & Co., 1975.

Shulimson, Jack. *U.S. Marines in Vietnam: An Expanding War, 1966*. Washington, D.C.: U.S. Marine Corps, 1982.

Shulimson, Jack, and Charles M. Johnson. *U.S. Marines in Vietnam: The Landing and the Buildup, 1965*. Washington, D.C.: U.S. Marine Corps, 1978.

Shultz, Richard H., Jr., and Andrea J. Dew. *Insurgents, Terrorists, and Militias: The Warriors of Contemporary Combat*. New York: Columbia University Press, 2006.

Silbey, David J. *A War of Frontier and Empire*. New York: Hill and Wang, 2007.

Skuta, Philip C. "Introduction to 2/7 CAP Platoon Actions in Iraq: The CAP Philosophy Shows Signs of Success in Iraq." *Marine Corps Gazette*, April 2005, 35.

Soustelle, Jacques. *L'espérance trahie, 1958–1961*. Paris: Editions de l'Alma, 1962.

Spector, Ronald H. *Advice and Support: The Early Years of the U.S. Army in Vietnam, 1941–1960*. New York: Free Press, 1985.

———. *After Tet: The Bloodiest Year in Vietnam*. New York: Free Press, 1993.

———. "U.S. Strategy in the Vietnam War." *International Security* 11, 4 (Spring 1987): 130–34.

Stubbs, Richard. *Hearts and Minds in Guerrilla Warfare: The Malayan Emergency, 1948–1960*. Oxford, UK: Oxford University Press, 1989.

Sturtevant, David R. *Popular Uprisings in the Philippines, 1840–1940*. Ithaca: Cornell University Press, 1976.

Talbott, John. *The War Without a Name: France in Algeria, 1954–1962*. New York: Alfred A. Knopf, 1980.

Taylor, John R. M. *The Philippine Insurrection Against the United States*. 5 vols. Pasay City, Philippines: Eugenio Lopez Foundation, 1971–73.

Telfer, Gary L. *U.S. Marines in Vietnam: Fighting the North Vietnamese, 1967*. Washington, D.C.: U.S. Marine Corps, 1984.

Thompson, Sir Robert. *Defeating Communist Insurgency: The Lessons of Malaya and Vietnam*. New York: Praeger Publishers, 1966.

——, ed. *War in Peace: Conventional and Guerrilla Warfare Since 1945*. New York: Harmony Books, 1982.

Thompson, W. Scott, and Donaldson D. Frizzell. *The Lessons of Vietnam*. New York: Crane, Russak & Co., 1977.

Trullinger, James W. *Village at War: An Account of Revolution in Vietnam*. New York: Longman, 1980.

Truong, Nhu Tang. *Journal of a Vietcong*. London: Jonathan Cape, 1986.

University of San Francisco. "Algerian War Reading." http://www.usfca.edu/fac_staff/webberm/algeria.

U.S. Army Adjutant-General's Office. *Correspondence Relating to the War with Spain*. 2 vols. Washington, D.C.: U.S. Army Center of Military History, 1993 (facsimile of original publication, Washington, D.C.: Government Printing Office, 1902).

U.S. Army Headquarters. *FM3-24: Counterinsurgency*. Washington, D.C.: Department of the Army, 2006.

U.S. Department of State. *Foreign Relations of the United States, 1955–1957*, vol. 1, *Vietnam*. Washington, D.C.: Government Printing Office, 1985.

U.S. Marine Corps. *Operations Against Guerrilla Forces*. Washington, D.C.: Government Printing Office, 1962.

——. *Small Wars Manual, United States Marine Corps 1940*. Washington, D.C.: Government Printing Office, 1940.

U.S. War Department. *Annual Reports of the War Department: Report of the Lieutenant-General Commanding the Army*. Washington, D.C.: Government Printing Office, 1900.

——. *Annual Reports of the War Department*. Washington, D.C.: Government Printing Office, 1901.

——. *Annual Reports of the War Department: Report of the Lieutenant-General Commanding the Army and Department Commanders*. Vol. 9, 57th Congress, 1st and 2nd Session, House Document No. 2. Washington, D.C.: Government Printing Office, 1902

Walt, Lewis. *Strange War, Strange Strategy*. New York: Award Books, 1970.

Warner, Dennis. "Fighting the Viet Cong." *Army* 12, 2 (September 1961): 20.

West, Francis J., Jr. "Area-Security." Monograph, Santa Monica, CA: RAND Corporation, 1969.

——. *The Village*. Madison: Univ. of Wisconsin Press, 1972.

Westmoreland, William C. *A Soldier Reports*. Garden City, NY: Doubleday, 1976.

Wolff, Leon. *Little Brown Brother: How the United States Purchased and Pacified the Philippines*. Oxford, UK: Oxford University Press, 1991.

Yates, Lawrence A. "A Feather in their Cap?" In *Crucibles: Selected Readings in U.S. Marine Corps History*, ed. Robert S. Burrell, pp. 277–87. Bel Air, MD: Academy Press, 2004.

Archival Sources

Matthew Batson Papers. U.S. Army Military History Institute, Carlisle, Pennsylvania.

James Franklin Bell Papers. U.S. Army Military History Institute, Carlisle, Pennsylvania.

Hugh E. Clapp Letters. U.S. Army Military History Institute, Carlisle, Pennsylvania.

John Jordan Papers. U.S. Army Military History Institute, Carlisle, Pennsylvania.

Subject Files, Reference Branch, History Division, United States Marine Corps:

    Cpl. Richard R Clark, Interview #2926, June 10, 1968

    Cpl. William R Corcoran, Interview #2079, December 14, 1967

    Colonel William R. Corson, Interview #6338, n.d.

    Lt. Col. William R. Corson, "Marine Combined Action Program in Vietnam," unpublished manuscript circulated Marine Corps headquarters circa summer/fall 1967

    Lt. Paul Ek, Interview #46, January 24, 1966

    Cpl. Thomas Foler, Interview #2926, June 10, 1968

    Captain Peter D. Haines, Interview #2534, March 9, 1968

    Captain Raymond E. McMacon (Army), Interview #2533, March 9, 1968

    Sgt. Jerry D. Reposa Interview, Interview #2926, June 10, 1968

    Cpl. Dennis J. Schultz, Interview #2080, December 6, 1967

    Cpl. John D. Webster, Interview #2080, December 6, 1967

Index

A NOTE ON THE AUTHOR

James R. Arnold is the author of more than twenty books, including *The First Domino: Eisenhower, the Military, and America's Intervention in Vietnam*; *Presidents Under Fire: Commanders in Chief in Victory and Defeat*; *Jeff Davis's Own: Cavalry, Comanches, and the Battle for the Texas Frontier*; and *Crisis in the Snows: Russia Confronts Napoleon, the Eylau Campaign 1806–1807*. He lives on a farm near Lexington, Virginia.